VIRGINIA CITY

FEATHER RIVER

YUBA RIVER
GRASS VALLEY

MARYSVILLE

RIVER

N E V A D A

PLACERVILLE

N E V A D A

SUTTER'S FORT
SACRAMENTO

RIVER

SACRAMENTO

M O U N T A I N S

ANTIOCH
SAN JOAQUIN
STOCKTON

COSTA
GANOS

ABLO

RIVER

LIVERMORE

SAN JOAQUIN

MT. HAMILTON

GILROY
PACHECO PASS

SAN JUAN BAUTISTA

ROUTE

James Hazen Hyde

New York

March 10ᵀᴴ 1941

GOLDEN GATE COUNTRY

BOOKS BY GERTRUDE ATHERTON

Historical Novels

THE CONQUEROR
REZÁNOV
THE IMMORTAL MARRIAGE
THE JEALOUS GODS
DIDO
GOLDEN PEACOCK

The San Francisco Series

A DAUGHTER OF THE VINE (The Eighteen Sixties)
SLEEPING FIRES (The Sixties)
THE CALIFORNIANS (The Eighties)
AMERICAN WIVES AND ENGLISH HUSBANDS (The Eighties)
A WHIRL ASUNDER (The Nineties)
ANCESTORS (Twentieth Century)
SISTERS-IN-LAW (Twentieth Century)
THE AVALANCHE (Twentieth Century)
THE HORN OF LIFE (The Nineteen Twenties)
THE HOUSE OF LEE (The Nineteen Thirties)

In Other Parts of the World

TOWER OF IVORY (Munich and England)
JULIA FRANCE AND HER TIMES (B.W.I. and England)
PERCH OF THE DEVIL (Montana)
THE WHITE MORNING (World War I)
RULERS OF KINGS (Austria, Hungary, and the Adirondacks)
BLACK OXEN (New York)
THE CRYSTAL CUP (New York)
THE TRAVELLING THIRDS (Spain)
MRS. BALFAME (New York)
THE GORGEOUS ISLE (Nevis, B.W.I.)
SENATOR NORTH (Washington, D. C.)
PATIENCE SPARHAWK AND HER TIMES (California and New York)
THE ARISTOCRATS (Adirondacks)
THE DOOMSWOMAN (Old California)
THE SOPHISTICATES

Short Stories

THE SPLENDID IDLE FORTIES (Old California)
THE BELL IN THE FOG
THE FOGHORN

Autobiography

ADVENTURES OF A NOVELIST

History

CALIFORNIA! AN INTIMATE HISTORY
A FEW OF HAMILTON'S LETTERS

Miscellaneous

THE LIVING PRESENT
CAN WOMEN BE GENTLEMEN?
GOLDEN GATE COUNTRY

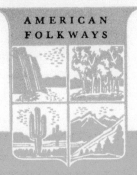

AMERICAN FOLKWAYS

EDITED BY ERSKINE CALDWELL

GOLDEN GATE COUNTRY

by

GERTRUDE ATHERTON

DUELL, SLOAN & PEARCE • NEW YORK

To

George Sheldon Russell

Acknowledgments

Hildegarde Hawthorne:
Romantic Cities of California—D. Appleton-Century Co.

Julian Dana:
Sutter of California—Press of the Pioneers, New York

Joseph Henry Jackson:
Anybody's Gold—D. Appleton-Century Co.

George D. Lyman:
John Marsh, Pioneer—Charles Scribner's Sons

Edward F. Treadwell:
The Cattle King (Henry Miller)—The Macmillan Co.

"Quarterly" of the Society of California Pioneers

"The Pony Express Courier"

Gertrude Atherton:
California, An Intimate History—Liveright Corp.
Rezánov—Lippincott-Stokes
The Splendid Idle Forties—Lippincott-Stokes

And many thanks to Mrs. Helen Putnam Van Sicklen, editor of the Pioneer "Quarterly"; Miss Dorothy H. Huggins, corresponding secretary of the California Historical Society; Mr. H. H. Hamlin, editor of "The Pony Express Courier," and Mrs. Therese José, assistant editor; Mrs. Mary Octavia Carmody of the San Francisco Mechanics' Library; Mrs. Eleanor Ashby Bancroft of the Bancroft Library, University of California; General McKinstry; Mrs. Willis Polk; Mrs. Macondray Moore; Miss Fanny Friedlander; and Francisca Vallejo McGettigen, grand-daughter of "The Lord of the North."

Contents

PART ONE

1. Old California

IN 1775, Rivera y Moncada, Commandante Militar of Monterey and San Diego, galloped across a great valley, floundered through sand dunes, and, drawing rein on the edge of a cliff, cast a scornful glance over a large expanse of inland water that had been recorded on the maps as San Francisco Bay. He decided that this was no site for Presidio or Mission and might as well be left to the Indians paddling their canoes or sweating in their temascals, like the infernally lazy and stupid brutes they were. He whirled about and, leaving his retinue to follow at a more leisurely pace, galloped back to Monterey. His report to the City of Mexico, capital of New Spain, was to the effect that the bay was of no strategic importance, the region unfit for civilized Spaniards to dwell in, and, unlike the beautiful and fertile south, entirely without a future.

But Father Junipera Serra, president of the California Missions, was obdurate and undismayed. It was his fervent wish to establish a Mission near that bay hallowed by the name of the patron saint of California. Bucareli, Viceroy of New Spain, who loved and revered Serra above all men, sent Lieutenant Ayala of the Royal Navy to navigate the Bay of San Francisco. Ayala, although but moderately impressed, did his duty thoroughly and even named two of the islands: Alcatraz and Nuestra Señora de los Angeles.

So it came about that the city of San Francisco, as yet undreamed of, underwent its birth pangs in 1776, that date revered throughout the United States of America.

3

On the gentle slope of the sand hills close to the Golden Gate (then known as The Straits) a large square was laid out, and quickly surrounded by a high wall with embrasures for cannon. Within were buildings of adobe roofed with tules: a chapel, barracks, dwellings of one story with a corridor (veranda) before each, the longest for the Commandante Militar. Later all were whitewashed, and the tules replaced with bright red tiles.

In due course, officers in undress uniform of black and scarlet, peaked straw hats with cords of gold or silver, deer-skin boots gaily embroidered, and immense silver spurs, were cavorting about the square on thoroughbred horses exciting the admiration of bright eyes behind gratings. When they were tired of showing off, they amused themselves with cock fights, gambling, and horse racing. And every night there was a dance in the sala of the Commandante. The girls wore white or flowered silks, with Castilian roses in their hair, and danced El Son, La Jota, or the stately contradanza—severely chaperoned by a dado of large brown matrons.

The Mission of Saint Francis d'Assisi, three miles inland, rose at a more leisurely pace. A small church, beautifully proportioned, a long line of rooms with the usual corridor, it stood in the shadow of the San Bruno Hills facing a great valley of some twenty-six miles of sand, rock, thickets of live oak and stunted pines. Down on the western shore of the Bay where it turned to the south, there was a confused mass of hills and narrow ravines.

Behind the Mission was the rancheria, a group of small huts accommodating some six hundred Indians; a grist mill and a large building where the women weaved, spun, and made garments and chocolate. The ranchos owned by the Mission were further down the peninsula, but there were fertile spots in the valley where the Indians planted fruit trees and small crops. They worked under protest, those Indians of Old California, for, with the exception of a very few tribes, they deserved the imprecations of Rivera; they were lazy, sullen, subhuman—and hideous. But the good padres had been sent by the Viceroy of New Spain not only to save the souls of the heathens but to do their part in converting land as well as savages to the glory of God and King. Moreover, they were expected to make the Missions self-supporting; there was a limit to the Pious Fund. Therefore the good padres drove the Indians to work with a whistling reata, and put the recalcitrant into stocks.

2

The renowned Captain Anza had chosen the sites for Presidio and Mission, the latter close to a lagoon which, it being the last day of Lent, he christened Laguna de los Dolores. Then, having done his duty, he returned to Monterey, and Lieutenant Moraga, accompanied by the Padres Palou and Cambon, several hundred colonists, two hundred and sixty cattle (the church equipment and heavy stores went by the barque *San Carlos*), left Monterey for the new settlement in the north. Moraga and the priests rode, the others tramped the forty leagues and arrived, a weary caravan of men, women, and children, at the end of ten days. The small company Anza had left behind had already induced the Indians with presents and threats to haul wood and make bricks of adobe, and the padres were well pleased.

But the colonists were not. They vowed that the region was a barren waste, no better than the deserts they had crossed from Sonora to California.

Moraga shrugged, told them they were riffraff, failures in their own Department of New Spain, and that any part of California was too good for them, but finally conducted them down the peninsula to found the pueblo of San José near the Mission Santa Clara.

3

The aristocracy of Old California—*gente de razón*—was composed of the families of officers who had brought their wives from the City of Mexico. In the valleys near the coast, large grants of land had been their compensation for exile, and, although they put Indians to work on their fertile ranchos with overseers as stern as the padres, they were obliged to live at the Presidios. The names of these haughty patricians have come down to us: Vallejo, De la Guerra, Carillo, Castro, Oreña, Ortega, Estudillo, Alvarado, Pico, Pena, Orios, Gonzales, Requena, Ximeno, Del Valle, Martinez, Pacheco, Estrada, Peralta, Bandini, Avila, Sanchez, and Argüello. Many of their descendants are with us still.

As time went on, the older men retired from the service and lived in drowsy comfort on their ranchos. Their large low houses, each surrounding a patio, were built of adobe with bright red tiles on the roofs, and they had many Indian servants to minister to every want. Every Spanish woman was a good cook, and the Indians were taught the succulent dishes of Spain and Mexico, and had their ears boxed or dodged a green-hide reata if they did not learn quickly enough.

The sons of these Dons either entered the army or became gay caballeros, giving some attention to the rancho but spending most of their time in the expanding pueblos of Los Angeles and Santa Barbara, or in Monterey, the capital of Alta (Upper) California, where they gambled the ruffled shirts off their backs, sang the liquid songs of Spain at the gratings of fair señoritas, rode furiously about the country in quest of nothing in particular, danced in the sala of the Commandante until the maidens were herded off to bed, and, unless engaged in one of the wars with hostile tribes, when they fought as gallantly as any soldier, were happy in the belief that life was made for pleasure and California was Arcadia.

The caballero, like the peacock, was more elaborate in costume than his future mate. His long hair was curled and tied back with a ribbon. He wore silks of gay color with ruffles of lace at wrist and neck, high botas of embroidered deerskin, sombrero laden with gold and silver eagles. His saddle was as magnificent as himself and he sat his horse as lightly as he danced at night. When he condescended to walk, his carriage was erect, graceful, and not without dignity. When the chill of evening followed the often torrid heat of even a winter day, he enveloped himself in a serape, a large square of colored cloth or velvet with a slit for the head.

The señoritas and young matrons wore simple garments of white lawn with elaborate deshalados (drawn work) during the day, white or flowered silk for the dance. The middle-aged and elderly wore calico or linen by day, heavy red or yellow satin for the sala.

Not all of the material for these garments came from the City of Mexico. Enterprising firms in Boston discovered this new trade mart and their skippers brought not only silks and satins, high-heeled slippers, silk stockings, embroidered scarves, shawls, and perfumes, but pots, pans, carpenters' tools, horsehair furniture; all of which were traded for hides and tallow.

But a prospective bridegroom must send to the City of Mexico for the *donas* of the bride: mantillas, black and white, white silk stockings, slippers, fans, lace flounces, Roman sashes, a string of Baja (Lower) California pearls, a necklace of topaz, a rosary of amethyst—and the fine flower of his wedding gift, which if forgotten would cost the bridegroom his bride, six camisas as fine as cobweb, embroidered, deshaladoed, trimmed with precious lace.

Save for the jewels, the *donas*, to a chance visitor from a foreign shore, would have seemed superfluous: for three months before the wedding Indian maids had sat all day long drawing fine threads for delicate undergarments, while the fiancée and her friends embroidered the white evening gowns with a fair semblance of the pink Castilian rose and the red-gold California poppy. The maidens also cut and hemmed long strips of colored silk into rebosas, the only headgear, save the mantilla, known to the women of Old California. The mantilla was for weddings and other ceremonious occasions; the rebosa for daily wear, and was disposed with coquetry and grace.

4

The good padres of Mission Dolores, as it was soon called to avoid confusion with Presidio and Bay, wrote to a number of the rancheros of the south and invited them to build in the "beautiful valley" they had appropriated. They dwelt cannily upon the temperate climate, the cooling fogs, the refreshing winds, the magnificent bay on which they could canoe to the islands (to do them justice, they knew nothing of its treacherous currents), the Presidio where life was gay for the young people. Being men of God and devoted to truth, they admitted that the fogs were sometimes too heavy and persistent, but could not their excellencies return to their ranchos for two or three months during the summer? Was it not well known that a change of climate once a year invigorated mind and body?

Four families responded, weary of the monotonous heat of the south, and the Indians were forced to build spacious mansions surrounding the usual patio. The acre was enclosed by a high wall set with grilles here and there; the gates locked at night, for the *gente de razón* had little faith in the virtue of even converted Indians. They also sent to the pueblo San José for rich garden soil; gardens they must have, Castilian roses above all. The padres blessed each house in turn, and forbore to send a bill for tithes before the end of the year.

California families were large; they were also hospitable. The many sons and daughters brought almost as many friends for visits of six months, and all were warmly welcomed at the Presidio—so far from Monterey, so seldom visited by even a governor on a tour of inspection. They met daily and nightly, either in the new mansions or in the long sala of the Commandante for the dance. There were meriendas (picnics) on the islands of the Bay—all heavily wooded save that barren rock, Alcatraz. When Governor Borica installed the Battery Yerba Buena, down on the western shore of the valley where the Bay turned below a high rocky hill and sent a long arm to the south, the officers of that dismal outpost erected a large shed to serve as a sala, and the officers of the Presidio, the caballeros of the valley, galloped the six miles or more, each with his doña on the saddle before him, one arm lightly encircling her waist. The elders followed in the carreta, a low springless cart drawn by an ox or a mule; the men swearing audibly as they lumbered through sand dunes or jolted over the bases of rocky hills, the women groaning, but with never a thought of evading the proprieties.

And so time drifted along, pleasantly, happily, marred but seldom by a broken heart or inevitable death, and, on the whole, with fewer of the ills to which mortal flesh is heir than anywhere in the world beyond California. The Indians were cowed into submission and the padres rejoiced in the number of converts. On Sundays the families of Presidio and valley came to Mass, the officers in full uniform; the caballeros in their finest silks, ribbons and ruffles; white mantillas draping the dark heads of the señoritas (there was an occasional brown or red head); the matrons, young and old, stately in black. Despite occasional alarms caused by foreign ships bearing inquisitive navigators, and the settlement of

Russians in the frozen north, it looked as if this Arcadian life must last forever, for was not this land of the poppy designed by the Almighty for the sons and daughters of Spain who asked for nothing better than their terrestrial paradise, this side of heaven?

5

Don José Argüello, His Majesty's most honored subject in the Californias, came from Santa Barbara to become Commandante Militar of the San Francisco Presidio. Unlike others of his present rank, he had left the City of Mexico a son of the people, but his natural abilities, his gift of leadership, his outstanding character—he was known affectionately as *El Santo*—were quickly recognized and his career was rapid and brilliant. He married a daughter of the noble house of Moraga, who bore him thirteen children, the eldest of whom, Maria Concepcion Argüello y Moraga, was destined to become the most famous woman in the history of Old California.

"Concha" Argüello was born in the Presidio of San Francisco and baptized in the Mission Dolores on February 26, 1791. Don José was alternately Commandante of Santa Barbara and San Francisco, and she was educated in the schools established by the wise Borica. As there was none in the northern settlement, she spent eight months of the year, unless her father was stationed in Santa Barbara, in the house of the governor in Monterey. Don José, more liberal in his ideas than the haughty dons, was proud of his bright little daughter and, although he was frequently reminded that mere rudiments were quite enough for future wives and mothers, he was determined that she should have as good an education as any boy.

In this he was upheld by Governor Borica, who, as the girl grew older, lent her biographies, histories, and books of travel. There were no novels in his extensive library, and if

Concha knew more of the great world than any California girl—or woman—of her time, she learned nothing of the relations of the sexes beyond what she might see with her own observing eyes. Men were ardent but respectful; girls were innocent and chaste; it was their destiny to marry after a year or two of coquetting with handsome caballeros, dancing, sighing happily behind gratings as sweet or strident voices mingled with the twanging of guitars. Babies were left under a rosebush by the Blessed Virgin; sometimes they arrived every year—and once lovely señoritas grew fat and brown, finally withered like old leaves in late autumn and prepared their souls for a better world, where, no doubt, they privately hoped babies were not.

But not for Concha Argüello! She vowed it! Some day a gallant officer from the City of Mexico would visit this far-off corner of New Spain, marry her, take her not only to Madrid but to the capitals of France, Italy, Greece.

Spanish girls mature early. When Concha was fifteen, her school days were over and she attended her first ball, given in the large hall of the San Francisco barracks in honor of a great man—old, alas!—from the capital of New Spain. She was hailed as the most beautiful and bewitching girl in California—*La Favorita,* that title so coveted by all lovely maidens —and her fame traveled to San Diego, Los Angeles, Santa Barbara, and to the capital, Monterey, where she visited whenever the opportunity offered.

It is possible that she was the most beautiful girl in a land noted for its beautiful women (when young), but even had nature been less generous she would have known how to make the caballeros believe she surpassed them all, for she was ambitious in little things as in great. Not only was she abundantly dowered with the coquetry of her years and race, and as happy and exalted with her first triumphs as any ordinary girl, but pride alone would have commanded her to be first in all things. The other girls envied her, but her disposition was sweet and friendly and they loved her. After all, there were plenty of caballeros and she could marry only one. Those she wearied of and treated with scorn were glad enough to find consolation in the responsive eyes and quivering lips of maidens more appreciative of their charms.

But the caballeros sighed as they gazed at La Favorita even from afar. That tall and willowy grace—*Madre de Dios,* but the willows that drooped over lakes and rivers were less graceful—those great flashing black eyes with their phenomenal lashes, that white skin, an inheritance from her Castilian ancestors, that full curved sweet mouth and delicate Roman profile, that long white throat, those long white flexible hands and tiny arched feet—not for them! Not for them!

Concha was a good child and pious. Those eyelashes—oh, assuredly unparalleled in all New Spain—had led her to confess to Father Abella that she feared her vanity in them would imperil her soul. Would not such a decline from grace offend Almighty God? For her soul's sake (sighing deeply) should it not be her duty to deprive them of half their length? The wise padre repressed a smile and replied sternly: "Did not the good Lord give you those eyelashes—the better, no doubt, to protect your eyes from the fierce rays of the sun? Where is your humility that you presume to question his purpose?" And Concha sighed no more, and, sad to relate, flirted those eyelashes more wickedly than ever.

But she sighed for other things and grew more and more weary of her shallow caballeros, with the monotonous round of pleasure in the "terrestrial paradise." Even books did not suffice, although every packet boat from the City of Mexico brought her more. She longed for something momentous to happen, even more to visit the great world of Europe with its infinite variety; its magnificent galleries of pictures, of which she had seen a few reproductions; the sublime architecture of historic cities; its courts; its colorful peasants. Why could not some grandee from Madrid come to this remote province of His Catholic Majesty, fling himself at her feet as other men had done, take her away?

Such was Maria Concepcion Argüello y Moraga, La Favorita, when the curtain rose on the immortal romance of Old California.

It is beyond the scope of this book to tell in detail the story of that romance. I have set it forth at length in my novel, *Rezánov.* But in bare outline here it is.

In the month of April, 1806, Nicolai Petrovich de Rezánov, Privy Councilor and High Chamberlain to Alexander I, Tsar of all the Russias, and chief partner in the great Golikov-Shelikov fur company of Russian America, sailed through the Golden Gate. He came on no romantic errand; the men in his employ at Sitka were suffering from scurvy, and it was his purpose to trade the cargo he had brought for an abundance of farinaceous foods and fruits.

Although suffering from malnutrition himself, he was a strikingly handsome man of imposing stature; he had charm as well and all the graces of a man of the great world.

He fell in love with Concha. She fell in love with him. The match was violently opposed by parents, padres, and Governor; Rezánov had been brought up in another faith and was therefore a heretic, unfit to wed a girl of the one and only Church. But Concha bedeviled them all until they finally consented to the marriage—provided Rezánov would go in person to Rome and obtain the consent of the Holy Father, thence to Madrid and win the blessing of the King of Spain.

That journey would take two years—at least. But there was no alternative. Rezánov sailed with his cargo of corn, grain, vegetables, and dried fruit.

Siberia must be crossed on horseback. Rezánov, his great strength depleted by malnutrition and malaria, died in the little town of Krasnoiarsk. He lies there under an altar-shaped tombstone.

The navigator, Otto von Kotzbue, brought the confirmation of his death to California in 1816. Concha had long since renounced hope and assumed the habit of the Third Order of Franciscans. She devoted her life to the poor and to teaching the children of her friends until Bishop Alemany arrived from Mexico and founded a convent in Monterey. She was the first woman in California to take the veil. The convent was later removed to Benicia, and she lies there today in the last resting-place of the Dominican nuns, the most desolate cemetery in all California.

2. *Russia Comes to California*
(*and a Legend of Fort Ross*)

CALIFORNIA had not known the last of the Russians. When Rezánov passed through Sitka, he told Baránov of the immense number of otters he had seen along the coast north of his goal, and as soon as the news of his death arrived, Baránov wrote of this possible source of revenue to St. Petersburg. Russia instructed her ambassador in Madrid to negotiate a treaty with Spain giving Russia permission to establish a colony some twenty leagues north of the Presidio of San Francisco "for the sole purpose of hunting the fur-bearing animals and curing their skins." The treaty was signed in 1811, and a hundred Russians and a hundred Kodiak Indians were quickly established on the coast several miles north of Bodega Bay. They remained until they had exhausted the otters, in 1841.

The Californians were indignant and uneasy, but protests to the Viceroy availed not. What could he do? Could a Viceroy dictate to a King? And why worry? What was the loss of a few thousand otters to them, who had never shown the slightest interest in otters, although they abounded about the Bay of San Francisco? No land grant other than a strip of coast had been given the Russians, nor ever would be.

The successive Governors replied that they had cause for both worry and anger. The Russians, in their sealskin canoes, which they called *cayubas,* hunted all over the Bay of San Francisco, avoiding only the Presidio and the Mission Valley, invading both arms of the bay, the coves, creeks, swamps, and marshes. The Viceroy shrugged. Let the Californians be thankful for a friendly neighbor, remember that Russia, instead of behaving as one honorable empire to another, might have sent its great fleet, seized the entire Pacific coast and massacred its inhabitants.

The profits exceeded the highest expectations of the Russians. They slew and cured as many as a thousand otters a month, and the skins they sent to the capital brought from eighty to a hundred dollars apiece. Otter skin coats became the fashion in St. Petersburg and Moscow, in London, even in Paris after the final defeat of Napoleon Bonaparte.

The Russian settlement that came to be known as Fort Ross was beautifully situated on a high cliff. The land, a garden in springtime of gold-red poppies, wild roses, purple and yellow lupins, blue iris, yellow buttercups, and wild pansies, burnt gold and bare in the summer, sloped upward to a mighty forest of redwoods, the tallest and most majestic trees in the world.

The fort was a square enclosure with round bastions, ramparts—on which sentries paced day and night, ever on the lookout for hostile Indians—a Greek chapel furnished with all the pious splendor of the homeland, and spacious log houses for the Governor and his staff. Beyond were a grist mill, a large building for the curing and packing of skins, and the village of the hunters and humbler workers, many of them convicts from Siberia. When these wretches tried to escape and were caught, they were either beheaded on the beach or made to walk the plank from one of the ships.

Baránov also was successful in establishing trade relations with the Californians, and Fort Ross as well as Sitka was abundantly supplied from the great ranchos of the south. As time went on the haughty grandees became convinced of the good faith of the northern barbarians and reconciled themselves to the inevitable—mainly through the diplomatic persuasiveness of the Russians' neighbor, Colonel Mariano Guadalupe Vallejo, "Lord of the North." But that pleasant state of affairs was a later development.

2

The Governors of California were sent from the City of Mexico. When Figueroa arrived he conceived a deep distrust of these settlers in the north, and sent Vallejo, the most brilliant and energetic officer in the service, one who had subdued many tribes of hostile Indians, to keep a sharp eye on the Russians. Vallejo established a fort at the new Mission in Sonoma, a large square surrounded by barracks, several houses, a tower from which he could survey the surrounding country, embrasures for cannon, and the Mission church. He had little fear of the Russians, but the Indians were among the most pestiferous in California. They soon ceased to attack him, however; he was ruthless in reprisal and cannon balls were more effective than bows and arrows. But he also knew how to conciliate, and he eventually made a friend of Solano, an exceptionally intelligent Indian and chief of his tribe, and thereafter had little to complain of save occasional raids on his livestock.

He received three grants of land until his northern ranchos covered more than a hundred thousand acres. How many thousand head of cattle, flocks of sheep, blooded horses roamed those fertile hills and valleys even his vaqueros could hardly have told. Like the padres, he engaged in contraband trade with the Boston skippers; his now docile Indians built an immense granary, and he shipped large quantities of grain to Sitka; he brought Indians from the rancho he had inherited from his father in the south to teach his new minions how to make furniture, shoes, chocolate, carpets, cloth; everything but the luxuries supplied by the Bostonians, and sometimes by Russia.

He had recently married Doña Francisca Benicia Carrillo of San Diego, a handsome girl with the large round eyes of her family, strikingly different from "the eagle-eyed Vallejos." They entertained in their large adobe house, known as Casa Grande, with true California hospitality and, despite the long weary miles, their invitations were eagerly accepted. Often he and Doña Francisca, in magnificent state, visited the capital, and the Montereños outvied one another in entertaining them. During the horse-racing season his own blooded stock carried off the honors, for he had a race track of his own and his horses were in constant training. There were dances every night, bull-bear fights in the plaza, meriendas in the forest on the hills behind Monterey; all the rancheros within a hundred miles came to do him honor.

But the Governors who succeeded Figueroa both feared and disliked the Lord of the North. He was arrogant and imperious, showing no deference whatever to Gobernador Propietarios, for he never forgot that no grandee in Spain itself had a longer descent than he. There were many noble families in California, but his ancestral tree scraped the gilt off the stars. The Governors were too indolent to take action, however, for they not only deferred to his superior abilities, his great reputation as an Indian fighter, but, since he could be the most charming of men, they enjoyed his society. The women voted him the handsomest man in California: he was nearly six feet tall, with broad shoulders, a graceful carriage —however imperious—a slender but powerful figure. His "eagle eyes" were dark brown instead of the prevailing black, his profile commanding, his mouth mobile and beautifully curved. Nature had been too kind to him, the caballeros sometimes thought, but were proud of him withal.

He was no more popular with the padres than with the Governors, for he refused to pay the customary tithes, even to the poor Missions of San Rafael and Solano in the north. As he was the most generous of men otherwise, and as extravagant as all Californians, his parsimony in this respect has always remained a mystery. It may be that he enjoyed defying the power of the padres, who, with their great ranchos, owned too much of California's wealth as it was. He was a good Catholic and went to Mass on Sunday. Let that suffice.

The Russians were among his most congenial friends, for they were educated men with whom he could talk—in French —of books and of the affairs of the great world. He kept their larders full and would accept no recompense, vowing he was glad to get rid of the stuff and asked only the boon of their society in return.

With his rock-like character and the deep wells of sympathy and affection within that haughty shell, he was a pillar of strength for which the Russians gave thanks in their Greek chapel when Fort Ross was visited by an appalling tragedy.

3

When Alexander Rotschev, one of the most brilliant and distinguished men in the court society of St. Petersburg, eloped with the lovely Princess Hélène de Gagarin, the fiancée of a royal prince, there was no recourse but to flee from the wrath of the Tsar; the penalty if captured would be death. They fled on horse and by sled, over the frozen wastes of Siberia, undergoing many hardships, but they were young, hardy, in love; they reached New Archangel (Sitka) in good health and were the welcome guests of their friends, Governor Koupreanov and his wife, born Princess Maksoutov. They had brought money and jewels and quickly exchanged their rags for fine raiment, were married, and took part in the gay life of the colony. News traveled slowly, and the Russian court had long since given them up for dead. When word of the happy ending to their adventure did reach St. Petersburg, the Tsar's wrath had cooled. He revoked the sentence of death, but condemned Rotschev to perpetual exile from Russia and ordered him to Fort Ross.

There was another guest at Castle Baránov, one whom the Rotschevs had met in the capital before her sudden disappearance. Her story was well known. Natalie Ivánov, one of the beauties of the court, had been engaged to Prince Alexis Mikhailov, with whom she was deeply in love. A few days before the wedding was to have taken place, he had been banished to Siberia to spend the rest of his life as a convict; for what offense Natalie never knew—one did not ask questions in Russia. Rumors had drifted back of his escape . . . recapture . . . death . . . escape; rumors that were never confirmed. She had finally traveled to her friends in New Archangel, hoping for definite news of him there; but Koupreanov had heard nothing and knew better than to make inquiries.

She had given up hope when the Rotschevs invited her to go with them to Fort Ross. An adventurous life in the new world, which she conjured up as a land inhabited by painted savages, might banish memories, for a time at least.

The governor's mansion at Fort Ross, always comfortable, became an abode of luxury. Rotschev had brought Persian carpets, tapestries for the walls, handsome furniture, pictures, ornaments, and a large case of books; crystal and silver for the dining room, elegant covers for the beds—all sent by sled from his castle in Russia to Sitka and thence to Fort Ross.

Vallejo and Doña Francisca called in state, accompanied by the entire staff of the Sonoma garrison. The Russians and Californians were mutually enchanted. Vallejo brought over his next house party, whose members returned to San Francisco with such glowing accounts of the graciousness and vivacity of the Princess Hélène—who wore the loveliest clothes imaginable. Aye! Aye!—of the beautiful Countess Natalie, whose silver-gold hair was said to be as long as her tall graceful body, and whose large gray eyes, brilliant at times with laughter, at others were so heavy and sad they were sure she had a tragic and romantic past; of the luxury and even grandeur in which they lived—such furniture and rugs, so different from horsehair and Indian mats!—that other families of Presidio and the valley felt it their duty to pay their respects to these distinguished Russians and offer them the hospitality of California in return.

Vallejo informed the Rotschevs of the honor in store for them and warned them that the visitors would expect to be entertained for a week. The distance from San Francisco to Fort Ross might be only forty leagues as the crow flew, but they must ride down twenty leagues to the southern end of the Bay, turn northward again on the farther side, following its ramifications until they could strike across country and wend their long and weary way to Sonoma, thence to Fort Ross. True, they would change horses and spend their nights at hospitable ranchos, but when they arrived they would want to sleep for twenty-four hours.

The Rotschevs were not daunted, and it was decided that Vallejo and his brother Salvador would put up a number of the party; the rest would be accommodated in the governor's mansion, the houses of the staff officers, and the barracks.

And so traveled officers and caballeros, each with his doña on the saddle before him. The chaperons were young (the elders had flatly refused to martyrize themselves in carretas) and rode with their husbands, followed by carretas laden with fine raiment. And, as nothing could tire a Californian for long, they were all ready to dance on the night after arrival.

Few of the Californians could speak French, but eyes, fans, hands, were as expressive as words, and dancing feet have a language of their own.

On the following day Rotschev took the men out in *cayubas* to watch the otter hunt, and twice thereafter he took them into the forest at night on a more exciting adventure.

In one of the little clearings on the mountain behind the fort was a small Indian farm, the scene of many a bear hunt amiably provided by the Indians, for Rotschev was a generous neighbor. When the party arrived they killed a bullock, and all retired to the dense shade of the redwoods. It was not long before a bear came prowling out of the forest and began upon the meal he had scented from afar. When he was fully engaged, the hunters, still mounted, left cover swinging their lassos. The bear showed fight; he charged, backed, reared on his hind legs, formidable paws sawing the air. But one lasso caught him about the neck, another a hind foot, and he was strangled and strained to death. Another bear appeared, then another and another. All were dispatched, if not with equal celerity, with a skill no bear could withstand for long. Glorious sport!

That was a gay week at Fort Ross. The Russian officers fell in love with the dark-eyed señoritas and were as gallant as the caballeros, whom they thought ridiculous in their gay silks, lace, and ruffles. The Californians returned the compliment by dubbing them—inaudibly, for they were ever models of courtesy, save when excited—big blond boors; but they liked the genial governor and were captivated by their petite handsome hostess, to whom they gave a lesson in Spanish every day after siesta. They were charmed by the other ladies of the little court, and regarded with awe and cool admiration the exquisite, remote, but ever gracious Russian girl whose like they had never seen.

A month later the Rotschevs and Natalie, escorted by Vallejo, paid a visit to San Francisco. They were guests at the house of the Commandante, but entertained night and day by every family in the Presidio and valley; and they had the sensation of dwelling for a time in fairyland. Assuredly this was another world. Could it be true that Russia, war-torn Europe, existed on the same planet?

Nevertheless, they were glad to return to Fort Ross and take a long rest.

4

Frequently, while the Rotschevs were taking their siesta, a California habit they thought well of, Natalie left the fort and walked along the cliffs. It became a melancholy pleasure to indulge in the luxury of grief, the while she tired her restless body. She avoided the forest, for wild beasts lurked there and she had no desire to be eaten alive—although it was possible she would steal out some dark night and throw herself over the cliffs.

It was a day in late autumn. There was a high fog and the air was chilly; she drew her gray mantle more closely about her, but did not lift the hood; the massive coils of her silver-blonde hair kept her head warm.

She walked rapidly, occasionally throwing a glance over her shoulder to make sure she was not followed; she had been annoyed and sometimes vaguely alarmed by the gaping admiration of the miller's son, a mongrel whose hair met his eyebrows. But after she passed the village, she might have been alone in the world.

And then she turned the corner of a boulder and came face to face with Alexis Mikhailov.

For a moment she did not recognize him. He wore the garb of a convict, his grizzled hair was unkempt, his eyes were sunken and bloodshot, his face was haggard, deeply lined, burnt almost black by the sun. Terrified, she stared at this formidable object. Then she gave a cry of mingled horror and rapture, staggered, and was caught in a fierce embrace.

When they were calm enough to talk, he told her that he had frequently watched her when she took her lonely walks, but had meant never to reveal himself—miserable, broken creature that he was; old, ragged, hideous, his spirit broken, a man no longer. But he would never trespass again. He had lived long enough. He bade her go and forget him.

But Natalie, shaken as she was, was able to think coherently and rapidly. Hope beckoned with an imperious hand. She told him she had made a friend of one of the smaller rancheros of the north, a frequent visitor at the fort. He knew her story. He would help them to escape. He was dining with them that night. She would manage to have a word alone with him. She would ask him to have horses at the edge of the forest on the following night. He would not only be proud to do her bidding, but would escort them to his rancho in the south, where they could spend the rest of their lives in happiness and safety. Everyone at the fort, save the sentry on the rampart, was asleep by eleven o'clock. He was to meet her at the mill before midnight.

His tired brain responded slowly, but that faint spark of hope which alone had kept him from putting an end to his wretched existence, suddenly flamed upward. Why not? Why not?

5

Not a sound was to be heard but the roar of the ocean, the soft pacing of the sentry on the wall, the cry of a panther in the forest. Natalie, trembling with excitement, changed her evening gown for a gray traveling frock. Her heavy hair came unbound and her shaking hands refused to readjust the coils. As it fell over her gray mantle it looked so lovely, enveloping her with a silvery mist, that she recalled happier days and decided to let her lover see it so. She could braid it at the mill.

A few minutes before twelve she raised her window and swung herself to the ground. The sentry was on the wall opposite; she could not make her exit by the postern gate. She stole softly around the buildings and reached the gates facing the forest. They were not difficult to unbar and in a moment she stood outside—free! She could not see the forest;

a heavy bank of fog lay against it, resting after its long flight across the sea.

She walked with noiseless tread up the path, then turned and went swiftly toward the mill. Once she thought she heard a step behind her, and paused, her heart beating audibly. But the sound ceased with her own footfalls, and the fog was so dense she could see nothing. She was now beyond the sentry's earshot; she ran fleetly across a field, down a gorge and up the steep knoll where the mill stood. As she reached the top she was taken in Mikhailov's arms.

They entered the mill and he lit a lantern and held it above her head, his eyes dwelling passionately on her beauty. Then he put it down and lifted her hair, letting it flow through his hands; both remembered that he had often told her that he loved her hair almost as much as he loved her.

He bent his head and kissed her, a moment of deep and peaceful happiness for both. But that moment was brief. He felt something tug at the hair his hands had caressed. At the same moment he became aware that the profound silence had been shaken by a loud whirr. He glanced upward. Natalie was standing with her back to one of the band wheels. It had begun to revolve. It increased in speed. He saw a glittering web on its surface. With a cry of horror he jerked her forward. He was too late. The wheel was now spinning with the velocity of midday, the whole silver cloud in its spokes, and Natalie was whirled upward. Her feet hit the rafters; she was whirled around and around, screams of torture torn from her rather than uttered, her body describing a circular right angle to the shaft, the bones breaking as they struck. Then, in swift finality, she was sucked between belt and wheel.

Mikhailov plunged to his death over a cliff. Natalie, in a copper coffin, was buried on a knoll across a gulch beyond the chapel. She sleeps there still, between the sunless forest and the desolate ruins of Fort Ross.

3. *The Lord of the North*

MEANWHILE, California had undergone many changes. In 1821, New Spain, after a successful revolution, called itself Mexico. It embraced the large area known to us as Texas, New Mexico, Utah, Nevada, Arizona, California, and the present nation of Mexico. Iturbide Augustín I proclaimed himself Emperor, but his reign was brief. In 1823, he was compelled to resign and Mexico became a republic.

California had taken no part in the revolution; she was passionately loyal to Spain, and when the royal standard that had waved so long above the Presidios was hauled down, and the Mexican flag run up, there was no celebration and many wept bitterly. And as time went on, indolent as they were, they found more and more cause for uneasiness and resentment.

Luis Argüello was the first governor of Mexican California. He had none of his countrymen's petty jealousy and distrust of foreigners and during his administration a number of visitors were encouraged to remain and farm or engage in business. An old law had not been revoked, but he resumed trade with the Boston skippers, for which the neglected Missions, to say nothing of the ladies, were clamoring.

But Mexico, indifferent as she was to the well-being of California, awoke to the fact that the son of good old José Argüello was an independent man who thought for himself and acted on his own initiative. Governors were supposed to receive their instructions from the City of Mexico and do as they were told. In 1825, José Maria de Echeandia was sent to replace him, with orders to curb the power of the padres and prepare them for secularization of the Missions; they owned too much property and exercised too much power to suit a republic.

Luis became Commandante of the San Francisco Presidio and died there in 1830, at the age of forty-six. He lies under a tall pointed tombstone beside the little church of the old Mission Dolores, whose thousands of fertile acres have shrunk to a cemetery.

2

Vallejo brooded in his northern fortress. California, with its incomparable resources, should be the most prosperous and progressive Department in the Republic, and she was stagnating. Mexico should have sent a thousand of her finest citizens to develop the great interior valleys, as well as the immense estates taken from the missions. But despite the most glowing representations from himself, Alvarado, José Castro and other prominent men, Mexico had sent none. Her only contribution had been a low-class military to man the Presidios, men who resented their exile, hated California, and debauched the women of the Indian tribes.

The Presidios were in a disgraceful condition. All but a few of the Missions were falling to ruin. Vallejo had disapproved of the power and wealth of the padres—before secularization they had reigned over vast ranchos and thirty thousand neophytes, possessed more than four hundred thousand cattle, sixty thousand horses, and twenty thousand sheep, goats, and hogs; thousands of acres were covered with wheat fields, vineyards, orange groves, olive groves, orchards—but after they were reduced to impotence and poverty his sympathy went out to them and he gave abundantly of his own stores to his wretched neighbors in the Missions San Rafael and Solano. He also applauded the indignant padres of the great central and southern Missions, who, after selling what property they could to Americans and other foreigners, up-rooted their vineyards and slaughtered their herds. No more of their fine wines would go to the City of Mexico, and the hides they sold to the skippers.

And where all had been peace, gaiety, harmony—Arcadia!—there were now constant rows between Monterey and Los Angeles. Pio Pico, the most able and ambitious man in the south, maintained that the city dedicated to the angels should be the capital of California, and Monterey screamed defiance. There had been more than one clash of arms.

And the Governors! A few had been worthy; others such tyrannical, incapable, and contemptible creatures that the Californians had run them out, bidding them be thankful to escape with their lives.

Gutierrez had lasted three months; Chico three months; Gutierrez returned and fled at the end of one month.

In 1836, California announced itself a free and sovereign state, and Juan Bautista Alvarado, one of Old California's few able men, became Gobernador Propietario. He appointed Mariano Guadalupe Vallejo General of all the California forces. Pio Pico sulked but knew better than to pit himself against the Lord of the North.

Vallejo, sunning himself in his patio, thought of Alvarado with affection and admiration. The governor was a man of great dignity, resource, energy. Of commanding stature, with black hair and eyes, regular features, his manner courteous but reserved, his authoritative mien, he looked and was a born leader of men.

The Congressional deputation, which heretofore had been called at the pleasure of the Mexican government, Alvarado re-formed as a Constitutional Congress to meet at regular intervals. Also, religious freedom was granted to all; there was now a considerable number of foreigners in the "sovereign state" who had either bought small ranchos from the padres or engaged in business.

Peace reigned for nearly a year. Mexico was engaged with political upheavals in the capital and ignored California.

Once more the little towns, the ranchos, were as gay and carefree as in the days of the Viceroys. The young people danced every night; the caballeros, their doñas on the saddles before them, rode from rancho to rancho; sang the love songs of Old Spain before the gratings of the loveliest señoritas; gambled as recklessly as when the present and the future were one.

In time, Alvarado, knowing that both England and the United States coveted California, whose fame had been spread by explorers, deftly wheeled the Department back to its old status under the protecting eagle of Mexico; giving her to understand that thereafter California would elect her own governor and administer her own affairs to please herself. Mexico yielded.

3

Those foreigners! Vallejo, pacing his corridor, jerked his haughty head and even paused to stamp his arched Spanish foot. There were now one hundred and forty-seven of them in California: rancheros, merchants, traders, school teachers— estimable enough, most of them, but there was also an increasing number of hunters and trappers of a low class, who were frequently in the calaboose.

He liked some of those peaceful invaders: Alfred Robinson, who had married Anita de la Guerra at a wedding so magnificent that all the world read of it in Richard Henry Dana's *Two Years Before the Mast;* William E. P. Hartnell, a fine Englishman; Alexander Forbes, a Scot; Jacob Leese and Victor Prudon, his neighbors in the fort; William A. Richardson, the first American resident of Yerba Buena; Captain John Wilson, who had married Doña Ramona Pacheco— and Thomas O. Larkin, United States Consul, who lived in state at Monterey.

But John Augustus Sutter! Vallejo ground his teeth and muttered round Spanish oaths as he thought of that German-Swiss who had arrived in 1839 with twelve men and three of their wives and brazenly informed Alvarado that he wished to live in California and found a colony! And Alvarado had thought well of him! The Swiss had brought letters of introduction from important men, was important-looking himself—imposing and handsome, Vallejo was willing to admit—and called in state upon the governor. Alvarado, after several conversations, was convinced that here was a man of uncommon ability and serious purpose, who intended to become a citizen of California and would improve conditions in whatever area of the Department he might settle.

The great interior valleys, as yet ignored by the white man of repute, were infested by men of the lowest type, outlaws in their own countries who had wandered over the Sierra Nevada Mountains or up the coast from South America. It was also the haunt of the more savage tribes of Indians. Was Sutter the man to drive out the whites and subdue the Indians? Sutter had convinced the governor that he was. Alvarado had given him an immense grant of land on the Sacramento River and a garrison. Eventually he had made him his "Representative of the Sacramento Frontier."

Caramba!

And there Sutter had built himself a "Fort"—a large square within a high wall of redwood logs with embrasures for cannon; a big house; barracks; stores from which he supplied—at a good price, no doubt—the needs of those American immigrants who were beginning to crawl over the Sierras in wagons that looked like houses on wheels. Flaunting the Mexican flag, he also supplied the traders going up and down the river, for, oh, yes! Sutter had lost no time in becoming a citizen of the Republic. There he reigned with the arrogance of a monarch who had inherited an empire.

Those immigrants, lured by tales of the wonderful climate

and fertility of California, had rented small farms from Sutter, and knew no other law in California than his. To his credit it must be said that he had disposed of the vagabonds who had infested the valley by threatening to turn the cannon on them, and the Indians had also departed or become his servants. He had prospered exceedingly and was already a great name in California.

Caramba!

4

Vallejo's mind swung from Sutter to Thomas O. Larkin, United States Consul, and he smiled with good-natured irony. He liked the American better, but had soon divined his double purpose in coming to California: it was his duty, no less, subtly to convince its more intelligent citizens that they would be far better off under an enlightened and stable government than at the mercy of one that was in a constant state of turmoil and totally indifferent to their welfare.

Larkin was a brilliant talker, in Spanish as in English, and could hold such men as Alvarado, José Castro, and Vallejo spellbound with his recital of the brief but glorious history of the American Republic; of her fine cities, her culture, her many diversions and interests; her final security from aggression—had she not repulsed England, with all that country's wealth and power, a second time? Moreover, her laws were beneficent, democratic, vastly different from those of England who had driven her colonies to rebellion—and, *mes amigos,* England was now established in that large area north of California known as Oregon; only a small weak colony so far, but it would be well for the Californians not to wait too long!

Alvarado, although not wholly convinced, could not hear enough of Washington, who appealed to him as the greatest man in history. Castro, although too intelligent not to see the possibilities, was Spanish to his marrow and unresponsive. "California for the Californians," he would mutter. "Would that we were strong enough to defy Mexico and stand alone."

But Vallejo, resentful at first, was deeply impressed by Larkin's delicate hints that the United States would develop the vast resources of California so criminally neglected by Mexico. The great interior valleys north and south would be populated by industrious and enterprising Americans; engineers would build bridges over the turbulent rivers; trading would be conducted on the grand scale; pueblos would develop into fine cities. California, in due course, would become one of the wealthiest and most important states in the Union.

Finally, when they were alone one day, he told Larkin bluntly to lay his cards on the table. Did the United States intend to take California by force if more subtle methods failed?

Larkin, who knew that he could trust Vallejo, replied with equal frankness that it was not the policy of the United States to "grab." Had she not refused to annex Texas until the large American colony in that vast region had won independence from Mexico by force of its own arms and then voluntarily placed itself under the American flag? But Mexico was a constant source of irritation to the United States and war was inevitable. The United States would not be the one to provoke it, however, for she was careful to "keep herself in the right"; she was merely awaiting some overt act by Mexico that would give her the excuse to send her navy to the Bay of Monterey and an army into California. In fact, certain ships of the American fleet would sail for the Pacific coast when war appeared to be imminent; and when word came of the outbreak of hostilities, the American flag would be run up on the Custom House at Monterey.

Although Spain had had no more loyal subject, Vallejo had only contempt and hatred for Mexico, and all his allegiance had been given to his beloved California. He pondered long and deeply. He had finally come to the conclusion that his distracted country's only hope of salvation lay in annexation to the United States, when that thunderbolt, John Charles Frémont, descended upon California.

5

Frémont, however, made his first appearance as a sucking dove on this visit—he had appeared casually in California twice before. Pio Pico was now governor of the Department— Alvarado having retired with failing health, and Micheltorena, sent by Mexico to succeed him, having been driven out after another of the "wars" between north and south. Larkin took the handsome and dashing young topographical engineer to call on General Castro, Alvarado, and the Alcalde.

Frémont knew how to make a good impression. His manner was frank and straightforward, genial and dignified; above all, he impressed these proud hidalgos as a man of the highest breeding—a factor even more in his favor than his gallant reputation. He informed them that he was engaged in surveying the nearest route from the Atlantic states to the Pacific coast, the object of the survey being geographical and in the interests of science and commerce. His men were resting at Sutter's Fort, and he had come to Monterey to crave the governor's permission to bring them to one of the settlements in order to replenish their ragged outfits as well as to buy new saddles for the horses and lay in the necessary supplies for his topographical expedition.

Permission was given. He sent for his men and established them on a rancho south of San José and remained there until the 22nd of February. The year was 1846.

6

Frémont had arrived in December. The impression made by his fascinating personality and persuasive tongue receded as the weeks passed. Alvarado and Castro grew uneasy. They were not only aware of Frémont's ambitions and ever successful career, but that he was the son-in-law of Senator Benton, a man deep in the confidence of the American Government. Moreover, he had come with a retinue of sixty men, a large number to Californians, whose army rarely exceeded two hundred. Frémont had asserted that these men, with the exceptions of hunters and trappers—so necessary to any hazardous expedition—were all scientists, and unarmed. But, not always prudent, he had let fall upon one convivial occasion that ten thousand colonists were prepared to emigrate to California and Oregon in the spring.

What if that ambitious young gringo had come to consolidate the Americans already in the province and provoke an uprising?

On the outskirts of every community were large sunken tubs where the women of the people washed the linen of the *gente de razón*. These women, known as "The Wash-tub Mail," were the gossips of California, for the couriers riding back and forth between Presidios and pueblos had wives and sweethearts among them, and always paused to relate the cream of the news before proceeding to headquarters. Every household listened avidly to these tidbits.

On a certain day Doña Modeste Castro's maid, while dressing the luxuriant black hair of California's social dictator, whispered that one of El Capitan Frémont's men and a young ranchero had exchanged shots over a woman, and the scandal had traveled as far as San José and shocked the entire pueblo. When Don José came home to the midday meal, he heard the news with satisfaction; here was an excuse to get rid of the unwanted guest and his suspicious band.

Pio Pico was still in the south. Castro need consult no one but himself. He wrote a peremptory letter to Frémont ordering him to leave the Department at once. But Frémont was not a man easily to be disposed of. He replied that such an order was an insult to the United States Government, and he should remain in California until his surveys were completed.

It was too soon for Frémont to give battle, unless forced to defend himself, for news had not yet come of the outbreak of hostilities between the two republics, but he removed his camp to the top of Gavilan Peak. His men hastily erected a log fort and Frémont naughtily unfurled the American flag. Let these Californians make the first move. Attack *him*. Attack the flag of the United States of America. Would it not be the overt act on the part of the enemy that the United States—always technically "in the right"—impatiently awaited?

The *Portsmouth,* in command of Captain Montgomery, was now anchored off Yerba Buena; the *Cyrene* and the *Levant* were in the Bay of Monterey—all on "friendly visits." Commodore Sloat was at Mazatlan awaiting the final word of the outbreak of war.

Frémont enjoyed the view from Gavilan Peak: the green valley; the fields of green and yellow mustard, like miniature trees; the red tiles on the low roofs of San José; at his feet the beautiful Mission of San Juan Bautista, still in good repair, shaded by trees, a priest pacing the corridor telling his beads; the family mansion of General Castro and other red-tiled houses about the plaza; a few miles away the blue Coast Range, rising to irregular heights. He almost fancied he could see the dark forbidding crest of the Sierras far away in the east and bounding the Sacramento and San Joaquin Valleys. Good old Sutter! How glad he would be to hear that

Sloat was in Monterey. He had made the mistake of fighting with Micheltorena and was worrying about his land grants. But he would be safe under the American flag.

Frémont's musings were brief.

On the second day after the raising of the American flag had thrown the entire countryside into a ferment, he saw a regiment of cavalry galloping across the valley. Whatever these Californians called themselves, they were technically Mexicans, and if they fired on the American flag it would be as good as a declaration of war. He called his men, well-drilled sharpshooters, to arms, and awaited the onslaught.

He was doomed to disappointment. The cavalry dashed through the plaza and began the ascent. But in a few moments they halted and appeared to confer.

Castro, infuriated when a swift courier brought the news to Monterey, had determined to drive this impertinent gringo out of California at the point of the bayonet. He had ridden at top speed to San Juan Bautista. But the Gavilan was steep and the horses, despite relays, were tired and refused to gallop. With time to cool off, he began to reflect. He would be playing into this adventurer's hands if he committed an act that might precipitate war. No! The United States must be the aggressor. After a short conference with his aides, who agreed with him, he gave a sharp command, the cavalry wheeled, galloped down the mountain and across the valley.

But California had not heard the last of John Charles Frémont.

7

On the morning of June 14th, Vallejo was awakened by a thunderous knocking on his massive front door. He sprang out of bed, opened the window, and leaned out. The plaza was a seething mass of armed men—Americans!

There were no soldiers in the garrison; all troops were

concentrated in Monterey and Los Angeles, General Castro and Governor Pico being once more engaged in a furious controversy over which should be the capital of California. Moreover, both were expecting to hear news of war at any moment, and Frémont was fomenting trouble between the Californians and the Americans, who, Castro claimed to have discovered, were massing to destroy the properties of those who had so generously and so mistakenly welcomed them. Many had flocked to Frémont's banner for "protection."

Vallejo had anticipated trouble, for Frémont's emissaries had been active in the north, but he demanded haughtily of these intruders what they wanted and how they dared to disturb the sleep of General Mariano Guadalupe Vallejo at such an unseemly hour. Three men began to talk at once. The dawn was breaking and he recognized them as Dr. Semple, William Knight, and Ezekiel Merritt. At the same moment he saw an armed guard escorting his brother Salvador and his neighbors Jacob Leese and Victor Prudon to the corridor of his house.

Knight finally made himself heard. General Castro had issued a proclamation ordering all Americans to swear allegiance to the Mexican flag—become Mexicans, forsooth!—or leave the country at once. The Americans were determined to take matters into their own hands—he carefully avoided any mention of Frémont—and General Vallejo and other Sonomans were to consider themselves prisoners.

Vallejo closed the window, dressed himself in uniform, buckled on his sword, and calmed the fears of Doña Francisca, sitting up in bed wringing her hands. Did not Mariano Guadalupe Vallejo know how to take care of himself? Moreover, the Americans were not a bloodthirsty people; they had their grievances and Castro had pushed them too far. He should have waited until the United States fleet was in the harbor of Monterey. Meanwhile her husband would be sensible and do what they asked.

The fiery Vallejo was no fool.

He opened the front door, smiled amiably, and invited the three men to enter and have a glass of wine; they must have come a long way and the morning was cold.

The Americans, who had expected the Lord of the North, the proudest and most intolerant hidalgo in California, to receive them with curses, drew a long breath of relief and accepted the invitation. This was true California hospitality! They seated themselves about the dining-room table and drank not of wine but of brandy. Semple handed a paper to Vallejo to read and sign. All drank another glass of brandy and yet another.

It was very cold in the plaza and the crowd waxed impatient. They knew Vallejo only by his formidable reputation. Such a man was capable of anything. No doubt he had poisoned their leaders and escaped by an underground route. John Gillespie volunteered to enter and investigate. He was received at the door with the same warm hospitality and invited to join his friends in emptying a bottle, while their genial host finished studying the articles of surrender.

Time passed. A beautiful white fog had rolled in from the coast and enveloped the little army. It blew its respective noses, coughed, swore, spat, stamped its cold feet. Finally William Ide, who aspired to be the leader of the party, strode into the house without ceremony, bellowing and flourishing his pistol. He was a large hairy person, vainglorious but able.

He found Gillespie, Knight, Merritt, Semple, sprawled across the table, dead drunk, Vallejo signing the articles of capitulation. The Lord of the North smiled charmingly, handed the paper to Ide, and asked suavely if Colonel Frémont were enjoying his usual robust health. Ide, inarticulate with wrath, snatched the paper, left the house as abruptly as he had entered, and read the articles to a wildly cheering crowd.

They seized the fort and hauled down the Mexican flag.

But they had neglected to bring the Stars and Stripes with them and a flag they must have. There was an artist among them. The Indian servants had fled, but he rummaged the kitchen and found an empty flour sack, which he cut into the proper oblong pattern. One of the men wore a red flannel shirt; he was persuaded to sacrifice a strip, which was roughly sewn on a white background. Then the artist found a pot of paint, executed a star in the northwest corner of his flag, and finished off his masterpiece with an object intended to resemble a bear but looking more like a large maternal sow. Beneath he painted the pregnant words CALIFORNIA REPUBLIC. It was then delivered to the breeze, now routing the fog, with a mighty, verbal display of American patriotism.

Such was the Bear Flag Revolution.

8

The ladies—who had been hanging out of the windows—were not to be molested. At eleven o'clock the prisoners were ordered to horse, and rode out of the Fort escorted by ten Americans bristling with arms. Vallejo, who had been told they were being taken to Frémont, now encamped in the Sacramento Valley near Sutter's Fort, had no misgivings. Whatever that young devil might be up to, he would take the word of a gentleman—one who desired nothing more than American occupation—and would set him and his companions free on parole.

They slept that night on the Vaco rancho. All were weary and no guard was on duty. A man named Juan Padilla crept into the camp at midnight and found the prisoners asleep on a pile of straw at some distance from the Americans. He whispered to the General that he had come with a strong force to rescue him. But Vallejo refused his aid. There might be a clash of arms and if any of the Americans were killed, dire vengeance would be wreaked on the women at Sonoma.

And Padilla's own men might be sacrificed—for nothing. He knew that Frémont would behave like a gentleman.

Padilla crawled away.

They reached Frémont's camp late on the following afternoon. He received them curtly and stared at Vallejo without offering his hand.

Vallejo realized his mistake, and as the spirit of conciliation was not in him he demanded icily what Frémont wanted of him. Frémont left the tent without deigning to reply and conferred with the Bear Flag Revolutionists. All but Semple were for executing the prisoners at once, but Frémont would accept no such responsibility and they were finally persuaded that imprisonment was the better policy until the American flag was flying over all California. Frémont returned to the tent and informed his temporary guests that he was obliged to defer to the wishes of their captors: they should at once be transferred to Sutter's Fort and be locked up there.

Prudon, Leese, and Salvador were dismayed and remonstrated volubly, but Vallejo merely gave Frémont a look of withering scorn and strode out of the tent.

Escorted by twenty of Frémont's small army, they rode to the Fort. Here is the popular version of their imprisonment:

Sutter received them with distant courtesy, preceded them across the plaza and showed them into a large room unfurnished but for a few benches. There they remained until the following morning when they were transferred to separate rooms. Frémont sent a guard of twelve men. Sutter held no intercourse with them.

And there they remained in close confinement, sometimes ill for want of fresh air and exercise, knowing nothing of what was happening in the world beyond, with no news of their families until August 3rd.

Here is Sutter's version copied from his diary:

"When the prisoners arrived at the Fort I placed them in my best rooms and treated them with every consideration.

I did not approve of these arrests; they seemed to me a futile show of impolitic force. I could see nothing to be gained. . . . They took their meals at my table and walked out with me in the cool of the evening. Their rooms were not guarded night or day, nor did any guard accompany us when we strolled. They were, however, closely watched by the men Frémont had left at the Fort as a military garrison. I deemed it wholly unnecessary to be severe in my treatment of these personages. I appreciated them as gentlemen under stress of misfortune. . . . It was my custom to visit the captives often and talk with them. One day Dr. Townsend warned me privately that if I continued to associate with them on such friendly terms my castle might become my prison. So I visited them no more until the American flag went up over New Helvetia."

Sutter was the kindest, the most humane of men. It was not in his power to defy Frémont, who wanted the Lord of the North out of the way until the war was over; he had enough on his hands with Castro and Pico.

And Vallejo was no liar. Old letters are often illegible and easy to misread, willfully or otherwise.

One fact, however, is on record. Vallejo and Sutter, who had been enemies before, were the best of friends thereafter.

9

On the morning of July 7, 1846, accompanied by the thunder of cannon and exultant cheering, Commodore Sloat ran up the American flag over the Custom House at Monterey, capital of California for nearly a century.

There was no more beautiful spot in California than Monterey. The little town swept like a crescent about the blue sparkling bay. There was a wide central street from which other streets radiated with the utmost irregularity and on all were white red-tiled houses, their gardens heavy with the perfume of Castilian roses. A few straggled up the hill-side on the right. Toward the center was a plaza with a small church—the San Carlos Mission was farther down the coast—the mansions of the Governor, General Castro, Alvarado, and the Alcalde. The perfect curve of the hill that encircled the town like a rampart was sandy and bare on its horns but the greater part was covered with a forest of stately pines and dense green undergrowth.

At the sound of the cannon, men and women ran from their houses and down to the shore. The men were excited but philosophical. Why worry over the inevitable? Don Thomas Larkin—now greeting Commodore Sloat with both hands outstretched—had accomplished his purpose: the Montereños were persuaded that California would live again under the enlightened American rule. Trade would be active, wealth would flow into the country; life would be gay and carefree once more.

Not so the women. They were fiercely patriotic—not to Mexico but to the Spanish tradition. They hated that greedy, grasping, insolent, upstart nation on the Atlantic shore; a nation that not only coveted the great harbor of San Francisco and other fine harbors along the Pacific coast, but would send thousands of her paupers to grow fat on the fertile acres of California. Oh, abomination! Oh, profanation! *Madre de Dios,* would that the women of California were men!

Some of the women wept and wrung their hands. Others of stronger fiber cursed the indolent caballeros and the American flag. One great lady cried aloud that she would give every league of her ranchos and throw her jewels to the pigs if she could but feel a necklace made from the ears of twenty Americans about her neck. (She eventually married an American, her daughter another.) Only Doña Modeste Castro, although her lovely green eyes were flashing, pre-served her dignity. It was a day of bitter mortification, but she had faith in her husband, practiced in the art of war. All the south would rally to his banner, on fire with wrath at this insolent intrusion. Frémont, even with his renegade Americans and small army, would be no match for José Castro. She was glad that Vallejo was still detained at Sutter's Fort; José need share the glory of driving these gringos, like whipped curs, out of California with no one—and be the next Gobernador Propietario!

But alas!

General Kearny arrived with a small army by the overland route and joined forces with Frémont. The Californians fought as they had never fought before and bedeviled the surprised Americans for six months. But neither Castro's courage nor strategy availed. They were pitted against experienced forces hardened by Indian warfare. They were vastly outnumbered, outmaneuvered. On the 13th of January, 1847, they surrendered to Frémont.

Old California was no more.

4. The First of the Cattle Kings

JOHN MARSH was descended from a long line of educated forebears. Born in Danvers, Massachusetts, in 1799, he had all the advantages of birth and breeding. His parents were religious, and so was he as a boy; he was a diligent student and graduated from Phillips Academy, Andover, in 1819, and from Harvard in 1823. He was gay, good-looking, and popular. He had a violent temper which he took little pains to discipline, and it was long before he discovered that cruelty (as well as cupidity) lurked in the roots of his nature. Study, pleasure, ambition absorbed him. It was his desire to take a medical course at Harvard after graduation, but to this his father would not consent; Mr. Marsh expected him to live on the old homestead and cultivate the soil. His mother cherished the hope that he would become a minister of the gospel. But John had no love for the soil and his religion had expired in the long dreary Sundays at Harvard College.

He was determined to be a physician and surgeon, and, as his father refused to spend any more money on his education and he was of a roving disposition, he accepted the position of tutor in the family of Colonel Snelling at Fort St. Anthony in far-away Minnesota. There he lived with the family and was able to save the greater part of his salary. He also founded the first school in the territory, and studied medicine with a Dr. Purcell. He added further to his hoard upon one occasion by carrying some important mail on foot six hundred miles to Prairie du Chien through an almost trackless wilderness. When he received his wage of forty dollars, a large sum in those days, he was so elated that he could not bring himself to part with the few dollars due his Indian guide. His experience with Dr. Purcell had cemented his determination to take the course at Harvard and every dollar was precious.

He had intended to remain only two years at the Fort, but before his time was up two things happened. The governor of the territory, Lewis Cass, was impressed with his abilities and offered him the lucrative post of sub-agent for Indian Affairs at Prairie du Chien; moreover, shortly before, Marsh had fallen passionately in love with a beautiful and intelligent half-breed—Canadian-French, and Sioux—Marguerite Decouteaux. It was the great romance of his life. Marriage was out of the question, nor could he take her to Boston as his mistress. Love conquered, and he accepted the offer. Governor Cass also appointed him Justice of the Peace of Crawford County with headquarters at Prairie du Chien.

With Marguerite's help, he learned the Sioux language and was popular with the tribe; he became an admirable executive and won the enthusiastic approval of his superior and Governor Cass. He was also completely happy with his gentle, lovely, and helpful "bride," who, in due course, presented him with a fair-haired, blue-eyed boy, with no trace of his Indian inheritance, no defect but a webfoot. Marsh had a good salary, he made money in the fur trade, and, although he had few expenses, he loved money for its own sake. Marguerite was received everywhere as his wife according to the frontier custom, and for seven years he was happy and successful.

Then came a chapter of events that drained all the softness out of his nature and left him an unhappy, disillusioned, and embittered man. The agent died and Marsh was disappointed and resentful at not being appointed his successor. Despite the insistence of the governor, a Kentuckian named Street was given the post and there was hostility between the two men from the first. Finally Street complained to the Secretary of War that Marsh, through his friendship with the Sioux, had fomented trouble between the tribes, and Marsh was discharged. He opened a general store which paid him handsomely.

But after seven years of domestic happiness, Marguerite died in her second childbirth. He was so desperately unhappy that his friends advised him to leave Prairie du Chien and seek fortune and distraction elsewhere; but there was an Indian uprising and Marsh was ordered to recruit the Sioux and Menominees and go to the relief of the general in charge of the American force. His bravery, leadership, strategy, and diplomacy won him great praise, and for a time gave him the distraction he needed. When the conflict was over and cholera broke out at Prairie du Chien, he made use of his medical lore and saved many lives.

While he was winning new laurels, however, it was discovered that he had secretly sold guns and ammunition to the Sioux. Immediately a warrant was issued for his arrest. His son was safe with a friend in a neighboring town. He stowed all his ready cash in his belt, packed his medical and favorite books in a carpet bag, and escaped in a canoe down the Mississippi. At St. Louis he joined a party of fur traders bound for the Rocky Mountains, and, after many adventures, reached the town of Independence, known as the outpost of civilization. He left the party and established himself as a general merchant and fur trader. Three years later he received word that the authorities were once more on his trail, and he fled in the night on his horse. This time his destination was California, of which he had heard, no doubt for the first time, during his sojourn in Independence. He would become a rancher and cattle raiser in a country under the flag of Mexico, and be safe for all time from his pursuers.

After many more adventures and hair-breadth escapes, he arrived in Los Angeles in February, 1836.

This was the background of the first of the cattle kings of California. It is an injustice to George D. Lyman's admirable and exciting biography, *John Marsh, Pioneer,* to condense so ruthlessly two hundred pages of it, but we are concerned only with John Marsh's life in California.

2

During a sojourn in Santa Fé, Marsh had acquired some knowledge of the Spanish language, and immediately upon his arrival in Los Angeles he appeared before that august board known as the *Ayuntamiento,* introducing himself as Dr. John Marsh, physician and surgeon, and asking permission to practice. He was by no means charmed with Los Angeles, although it was a pretty little pueblo with red-tiled, white adobe houses set among palm trees, with a plaza and a church. He had hoped to find a large town and it looked like a village to him. But he was almost penniless and a cattle ranch was a dream to be realized in the future. He had no medical degree, but he exhibited his Harvard diploma, a treasure he always carried with him. It was an imposing document and as its characters were in Latin he judged rightly that none of these Mexicans could read it. There was no doctor in Los Angeles, nor had there ever been; an epidemic of smallpox had broken out, and a physician was badly needed. After the proper amount of deliberation and consultation with the priest, who agreed that the sheepskin might as well be a medical certificate as anything else, the *Ayuntamiento* gave the impressive and self-assured young man permission to practice. There was already a number of Americanos in the province and most of them were well-liked; several had married into families of the old Spanish régime. This stranger looked manly and trustworthy.

Marsh established himself in an adobe house on the plaza and his services were in demand from the moment he hung out his sign, "Dr. John Marsh, Physician and Surgeon." Besides the Californians, both Mexican and Spanish, there were about fifty Americans in the pueblo. All found the welcome doctor likeable despite his melancholy reserve, and there was no doubt of his ability; notwithstanding his scant active acquaintance with his profession, he had forgotten nothing of what he had learned with Dr. Purcell, and he reread his medical books.

He was now thirty-three, tall, muscular, and graceful. His face, although not handsome, was impressive with its hard, piercing eyes and strong features. His manners were brusque but he could be affable when it suited his purpose, and the dignified Californians of pure Spanish blood approved his aloofness.

He handled the smallpox epidemic successfully, used his scalpel deftly, and even delivered babies with a skill that appealed to his saturnine humor.

There was little or no currency in the province; the media of exchange were livestock, hides, and tallow. His grateful patients were liberal in payment, and before a year had passed he was almost crowded out of his house by stacks of well-cured hides. He was more than content, however, for he knew their value, and when a Boston trader arrived he sold them for $500 cash.

He bade farewell to his reproachful friends and started on his journey north to look for a ranch. Meanwhile he had become a Mexican citizen and was entitled to be a property holder in the province.

3

Marsh made a leisurely tour through the beautiful country in which he was to spend the rest of his life. The softness had gone out of him; his was not the nature to be ennobled by adversity, and he now had but one purpose in life: to accumulate riches and more riches, to own a great rancho with thousands of cattle, horses, and hogs, to be famous and envied, not for his personal qualities but for his wealth and importance. He now knew the names of many of the great rancheros, who lived a life of ease and plenty, the elders loafing in the sun, the caballeros singing at gratings of lovely señoritas, dancing, gambling, ranging the country on their richly caparisoned horses. He despised them all, he with his stern New England inheritance; but they should receive him in their haciendas, not because he had a sociable instinct left in him but because it was his due. Even that Lord of the North, Don Mariano Guadalupe Vallejo, should welcome him to his Casa Grande in Sonoma, recognizing that the blood of one of the first families of New England was of a deeper blue than any mere Spaniard could boast. But that was for the future, and a side issue at that. Gold should be his compensation for all that he had suffered and lost; gold should be his god. His only regret was that there was so little of it in California—beautiful, tangible gold that he could handle and caress. He gave many a loving pat to the belt that contained his own small store.

At the various pueblos where he rested, more particularly at San José and the capital, Monterey, he talked with many men and learned much of the soil and livestock of the California valleys. With the exception of Vallejo's vast principality, the greatest ranchos were in the south; it was possible, he was told, that the younger rancheros might sell him a few thousand acres if he had the cash to pay for them; more than one would like to visit the City of Mexico.

But Marsh had had enough of the south, and the farther he traveled north the better he liked the moderate temperature, the cooling winds, even the fogs that sailed in from the Pacific like the wraiths of ancient ships.

He heard a great deal of Contra Costa, the valley that bordered the eastern shore of the San Francisco Bay; of the Sacramento and San Joaquin Valleys; and he met a Californian named José Noriega who owned a large tract of land in the latter valley and was willing to sell. The young grandee admitted, however, that he was afraid to live on the place himself, for it was infested by hostile and savage Indians, the worst in the province. Others also warned him to avoid the San Joaquin. But Marsh merely laughed; fear was but a word to him. His character may have deteriorated, but one thing could always be said of John Marsh: he was a man, every inch of him.

He told Noriega he would consider his offer, and after exploring the country further would give him a definite answer.

He arrived in Yerba Buena in March, 1837, nine years before the American occupation. It was a wretched, tumbledown place, but he met there two congenial Americans, Jacob P. Leese and William A. Richardson. The former kept a general store for the benefit of neighboring rancheros and the whalers and Boston skippers who anchored in the Bay for supplies.

Here Marsh remained for several months, the guest of Leese, and helped him in his store. Mayordomos from the northern valleys, from the San Mateo and Santa Clara Valleys down the peninsula, from Contra Costa on the opposite side of the water, liked to linger and gossip. Marsh learned even more than he knew already of the everlasting "wars" between the north and the south, or, speaking more precisely, between Monterey and Los Angeles, each of which claimed to be the capital of California, although the latter was recognized by the City of Mexico as it had been by New Spain. . . . "Ay, señor, how different it was then with the presidios full of gallant men and prancing steeds, its missions so beautiful and flourishing— *Caramba!* what delicious wines the good priests made."

Insecurity had never troubled men's dreams in those days, "Ay yi! And now who could tell what would happen? Was it not known that Britain, France, Russia, coveted this beautiful and fertile land? And Mexico weak and always in a turmoil over one thing or another! Any day the navy of one of those grasping countries might sail into our Bay, its men swarm over the land, and what could even the great General Vallejo do—except fight to the death and be killed?"

This talk made Marsh uneasy. He had had enough of life's insecurities. He wanted to live in California and realize his dream, not only of wealth but of safety. Would it not be taking too great a risk to relinquish his precious gold for land that might be taken from him? Oh, for a stable government— like that of his own United States of America!

He had met Thomas O. Larkin in Monterey and enjoyed several conversations with that subtle and persuasive American Consul.

Gradually Marsh conceived a plan to promote American immigration on a large scale from the eastern and other states and territories into California. Numbers would count.

He had seen Noriega's ranch and desired it. He made up his mind to take all risks, including hostile Indians, closed with Noriega, who had followed him about hopefully, and paid out his $500 for a rancho twelve miles long and nine miles wide.

Then he bade good-by to Mr. Leese, upon whose bounty he had lived for nearly a year, incidentally demanding fifty cents he had once paid for a haul of fish. He got his fifty cents and lost a friend. The story flew about and by no means endeared him to the generous and extravagant Californians. But Marsh wanted no man's love and valued friendship only as it served his ends.

4

The Rancho Los Meganos lay along the eastern side of the Contra Costa range of mountains, whose highest point was Monte Diablo, named in honor of a fiery devil believed by the Indians and the more superstitious Mexicans to inhabit it. Far away on the other side of the great San Joaquin Valley were the towering Sierra Nevada Mountains, dark and somber with their pine forests, their peaks white and dazzling in winter. The ranch was forty miles distant from Yerba Buena and farther still from San José.

Los Meganos was a magnificent tract of land, well watered, flat, its surface, when Marsh took possession of it, a lovely sweep of green grass and yellow mustard.

Opposite Monte Diablo and on the other side of a stream, dwelt the tribe of Indians who, Marsh had been told, were savage and, no doubt, if the truth were known, cannibalistic. But they were suffering from an outbreak of malaria, and their medicine men were unable to cope with it.

The day after Marsh had pitched his tent, he crossed the stream and walked among them fearlessly. Always quick at languages, he had picked up several Indian dialects and managed to make himself understood. He told them, with the ingratiating smile that lit his face at will, that he was a medicine man of wide experience and had come to cure them. They were awed by his manly appearance and daring, and charmed by his smile. Moreover, they were eager to be rid of the pestilence. They permitted him to dose them with quinine. The effect was miraculous and they were his slaves thereafter. They built him a house at the foot of Monte Diablo, sowed fields with grain, brought cuttings from San José and planted orchards and vineyards—and stole a few horses, a bull, and cows from a far-off rancho, which they tethered to the trees before his door at night; with unexpected delicacy forbearing to mention the source of supply. Marsh asked no questions.

He now had his rancho, some seventy thousand acres, one of the finest in the north, but no cattle and no money wherewith to buy them. There was no immediate resource but his medical skill, and this he exploited to the utmost. His Indians spread his fame among other tribes and they carried it to ranchos and pueblos. A doctor in California! A gift from Heaven, no less. He was soon so busy that he had little time to think of anything else.

Not that he ever forgot his objective. He demanded his payments in cattle—which his vaqueros branded with something that looked like an anchor. His fees were high: twenty-five head for a dose of salts, of quinine, a tonic, a poultice, a blood-letting; fifty for ushering an infant into the light; a hundred for an amputation. When obliged to travel a long distance, he charged four or five hundred.

General Sutter sent him patients from his fort in the Sacramento Valley. He was summoned to San José, to Merced, to Monterey, and to Sonoma where he was the guest of Vallejo, whom he doctored so successfully that the General, in his usual lordly manner, presented him with a thousand head of cattle, which his own vaqueros drove down to Los Meganos fifty miles away.

It was a life spent on horseback, but Marsh was rarely conscious of fatigue. No matter how long the journey, twenty miles, fifty miles, sometimes a hundred—never mind. His herds increased with his fame. He could always get a change of horses at the ranchos he passed, as well as breakfast, dinner, or supper. To offer payment would have been an insult. Far be it from him to violate the traditions of this hospitable land.

But for hospitality, save as it suited his convenience, he cared nothing. He repulsed the overtures of the neighboring rancheros, replying brusquely, to all but Vallejo, that he had no time for dawdling. All desire to be entertained by grandees had expired. What leisure he had he preferred to spend alone. He read and re-read the books he had brought with him and others lent him by Vallejo, who had a fine library. He wanted no other companions.

He was by no means popular. Many of his patients hated

him for his extortions, but that caused him no uneasiness; he knew they could not do without him. He was still the only doctor in California. The Boston skippers to whom he sold his hides at the embarcadero, several miles from San José, liked him as little. He too was a Yank and knew how to drive a hard bargain. Not one of them ever got the best of him.

But morose as he was, he was by no means dejected. He was realizing his ambition to be the first American cattle king, admired and envied by every Yankee in the province. The time came when he could renounce medicine and surgery and devote himself solely to his ranch, in which he took an increasingly absorbing interest. He could whirl a lasso with any of his vaqueros, and it amused him to brand his own cattle occasionally.

He was more popular with the Indians than with the whites, for his fees to them were moderate, and he had installed a handsome squaw in his adobe.

He had accomplished another object. In 1841, three years after he had taken possession of his ranch, he had written enthusiastic letters to his friends in Independence expatiating upon the virtues of California: its salubrious climate (he failed to add, if, indeed, he knew, that California in its eight hundred miles from Oregon to Mexico proper, had at least sixteen different climates); its fertile soil (omitting all reference to swamps, sand, droughts, and floods); its freedom from disease of all kinds (saying nothing of the fortune he was making as a doctor); the cheapness of the land; the hospitality and careless generosity of its inhabitants; the many and varied possibilities of acquiring wealth. In short, the earthly paradise.

He even gave minute details as to the route over plains and mountains, a route that would involve the minimum of danger and fatigue, and that led to the northern part of the province, where the immigrants would have the benefit of his advice.

These letters found their way into the local newspapers, were copied in newspapers all over the West, and eventually reached the eastern states.

Covered wagons began to pour over the Sierras. Mexico was furious and did all she could to harass the travelers; she had lost Texas and feared a similar fate in California. But still they came.

Marsh was almost happy. The time was nigh when the United States Government would be driven to protect its own in California. A stable government at last!

5

In 1842, California underwent a period of excitement that surpassed anything it had known for several years, and in those stirring events John Marsh played a dominant part.

Juan Bautista Alvarado, who had been governor since 1836, was anxious to retire as his health was failing, and, in 1842, in order to prevent another "war" between the north and the south, he asked the Mexican government to relieve him of his post. General Manuel Micheltorena was sent from the capital as Gobernador Propietario. He infuriated the north by arriving in Los Angeles and announcing that during his administration it should be the capital of California. Moreover, he brought with him an army of three hundred and fifty men, Mexico having decided that it was time to reinforce a province coveted by the United States. It was a dilapidated and tattered army, the scouring of prisons, with morals and behavior on a par with its uniforms.

Nor was this all. He announced his intention of restoring the Missions to the Church, thus dislodging a number of rancheros who had claimed or bought the properties after secularization. He gained further disfavor by reducing the salaries of certain high officials, who, it must be admitted, had done little but draw them. And what he left undone to make himself unpopular, his ragamuffin army accomplished. They forced their way into the adobes and stole clothes and food—the latter a daily performance—and so terrified the women that daughters and young wives were conveyed secretly by night to far-off ranchos.

The Californians stood him for two years, but in November, 1844, they revolted. Alvarado was called upon; he emerged from his retirement, and, with General Castro, collected an army. General Vallejo took no part. He had confided to John Marsh that it was his fervent desire to see California pass under the protection of the United States, and, as Mexico was too weak to send further reinforcements, the turmoil into which this local war would throw the province might be her opportunity.

Marsh's sympathies were entirely with the Spanish Californians. At least they were gentlemen; he had a strong liking for Vallejo, and admired Alvarado and José Castro. Moreover, Micheltorena had arrived with a decree to expel all foreigners from California, and although he had not yet enforced it, the Americans were in a constant state of apprehension. And no one more so than John Marsh.

The army of Alvarado and Castro included many Americans. John Marsh would have been the first to enlist but found himself in a dilemma. Micheltorena had appointed Sutter Commandante Militar over all the forces he could assemble in the Sacramento and San Joaquin Valleys, and Marsh received orders to join that section of the governor's army. At first he refused and in no measured terms. Sutter sent him word that he could take his choice: fight for the governor, or be arrested, confined in the fort, have his property confiscated. Marsh submitted, and laid his own plans.

He joined Sutter's army, which included many of the first American immigrants, and marched in the ranks, Sutter having refused him a command. He immediately began to sow dissension. With the Americans he could accomplish nothing at first, for they had been promised land grants from Micheltorena, but he persuaded the Mexicans and other foreigners that, if they were captured, they would be massacred by the governor's cutthroat army. The Spanish rancheros who had been forced into the ranks needed no persuasion. They knew Marsh's force of character and believed in his infinite resource.

The small army of ninety men under Alvarado and Castro was in camp near the pueblo of San José and it was Sutter's intention to liquidate them forthwith. He led his forces on horseback; the others walked.

Alvarado, Castro, and their army retreated down the valley. Sutter followed in a pouring rain. By this time the American immigrants, footsore and weary, had lost their enthusiasm and were more willing to lend an ear to Marsh, who, although as fatigued as his comrades, never lost sight of his purpose and talked a steady stream of propaganda.

Micheltorena joined Sutter at the Salinas River. There was now an army of eight hundred against ninety. Alvarado and Castro retreated farther south. The progress of the governor's army was slow. He was ill and, unable to sit a horse, led his army in a wagon. The roads were bad, the weather abominable. Morale steadily diminished. A number of the Americans deserted and went home. The others trudged on, unwilling to renounce the prospect of land grants. Still, it was a formidable army for California, and Marsh worried. Failure now would be the death of all his plans and ambitions. In treachery lay his only hope.

Alvarado and Castro retreated as far as Los Angeles, where their insignificant army was reinforced by a respectable number of Americans and Spanish Californians who detested Micheltorena. The rebels turned north again, and encamped in the San Fernando Valley not far from Los Angeles. Micheltorena's army was in camp on the other side of the valley. At dawn on February 19th, there was cannonading from both sides. No one was hit. Both armies advanced. There was more cannonading, the only casualty being Castro's horse, whose head was blown off. When the rebels' ammunition gave out, they filled their cannon with stones. Finally Micheltorena gave the order to advance again. By this time his Mexican recruits had had enough and deserted. When the two armies were close enough for musket fire, Marsh saw the Americans in the rebel army; they outnumbered those in the governor's. During a pause while Micheltorena and Sutter were conferring, Marsh gathered the "loyal" Americans about him, ran forward waving a white handkerchief, and asked his countrymen to come over for a conference. They came and the Americans on both sides all but fell into one another's arms. Many had been friends in Missouri. Marsh harangued his own men, who were dispirited by days of marching, scant rations, and still wet to the skin from a violent storm that had raged the night before. Marsh reminded them once more that if Mexico won this battle every American would be expelled from California.

Micheltorena gave the order to charge. His own army, which had been refreshing itself with aguardiente and cigaritos, rose leisurely and examined its muskets. The Americans resorted to a ballot to determine whether they would fight or desert. Sutter galloped up to ascertain the cause of delay. He was dumbfounded, but lingered long enough to learn that desertion had carried the day. He lingered too long, and was surrounded, taken prisoner, and delivered to Alvarado.

Micheltorena was a brave man, and, ill as he was, he fought on. But the next morning, when he looked down on the battlefield and realized that his supplies were cut off and that even the Spanish had gone over to the enemy, leaving him alone with his ragamuffins, he raised the white flag. A few days later he was deported to Mexico City. He never knew that he had been defeated by one man, John Marsh, an American refugee who had arrived in California without a penny in his pocket but who had the devil's own gift of getting his way.

Marsh had also made three friends: Alvarado, Castro, and Pio Pico.

6

Marsh was exultant, as happy as it was in him to be. It was he and he alone who had won that war, who had inspired the Californians to defy Mexico and elect their own governor. Mexico was humiliated and impotent, for the present at least. But there was more to be done, and he, John Marsh, would accomplish it. And this supreme confidence in himself was to lead him to the bitterest disappointment of his life: a visitation that, ironically enough, might have been spared him had Micheltorena never been appointed governor of California.

He conceived the truly great idea of detaching California from Mexico, annexing Oregon, and forming one great republic, which, free of internal wars, would be governed by Americans alone. He knew that the more intelligent Americans now in the province would hail the prospect with delight, that the Spanish Californians, with few exceptions, would offer no opposition, that the Americans in Oregon resented the British penetration and the arrogance of the Hudson's Bay Company.

He believed that his purpose could be accomplished without bloodshed. Mexico had had her lesson. She knew the mettle of the Americans in this province and would hardly care to risk another humiliating repulse—her finest general ignominiously driven out and his tatterdemalion crew with him! Her sullen acquiescence when the Californians elected their own governor, ignoring her right of appointment!

But Pio Pico would never bestir himself to the point of secession. A John Marsh was needed for so radical a step. He knew himself to be a born leader of men. His seventy thousand acres, his thousands upon thousands of livestock, were forgotten for the moment, save as they gave him an admitted importance in the province—no other American had achieved one-tenth of his success. Politics swamped even his passion for gold. He would convert every Californian, every American in the province to his purpose—and become the first governor, perhaps president, of the new republic, with his capital in Yerba Buena, whose great future he foresaw: the queen city of the Pacific coast, as important as New York or Boston. Then when he had accomplished his purpose and was firmly established, his authority unchallenged, he would, with a magnificent gesture, present his conquest to the United States of America, as Texas had done. Texas! What was that sprawling wilderness in comparison with California? California, with what was perhaps the greatest harbor in the world, her thousand other attractions and advantages? California! Who knew but that beneath her fertile soil there might not be an even greater wealth? Had not some man in an idle moment pulled up a bunch of onions and found gold at its roots? But the sensation had been momentary. These Californians were too lazy to dig and prospect. If that find had only been on his ranch!

But meanwhile. . . .

He was on friendly terms with Captain Weber, an able and enterprising merchant of San José, who had flatly refused to join Sutter's army and been confined in that autocrat's Fort while the war lasted. He was ripe for any adventure that would benefit the Americans and humiliate Mexico. Marsh invited him to Los Meganos and unfolded his plan. Weber slapped him on the back and vowed he was the "greatest American in California." It was decided to invite all the Americans in the north, from Monterey to Sonoma, to as-

semble in San José on the Fourth of July. A barbecue would
be the excuse and such a gathering would excite no suspicion
among the Californians, Spanish or Mexican, for it was the
custom of the Americans to celebrate their most famous an-
niversary in one way or another. It was thought best not to
invite Larkin; if he suspected their purpose he might think it
his duty to inform the United States Government.

The party was a hilarious success; besides steers and hogs
roasted whole in pits, there was abundant aguardiente, the
fiery Spanish brandy. Food and drink were paid for by
Weber.

Only a few were taken into their confidence. Marsh harangued the crowd, admonishing them to take no part in
those everlasting wars between the north and the south; by
refraining they would make no enemies among the Californians, but assure them that if Mexico attacked again the
Americans would fight as a unit to free them from the yoke.
There was no hint of conspiracy, of treason; nor was there a
Mexican within a mile of the barbecue.

To a chosen and enthusiastic few Marsh and Weber confided their purpose, and it was agreed that within two years
at most so many more immigrants would have arrived that
the time would be ripe for an open revolution; with a sudden *coup* they would seize both Oregon and California and
proclaim an independent republic. Meanwhile, they would
collect arms and ammunition.

Shortly afterward, Marsh received a letter from Larkin
telling him that President Polk was determined to have California; by peaceful means if possible; if not, then after Mexico had declared war, as in the case of Texas. Larkin had
written the President that John Marsh was the most important, intelligent, and highly-educated man in California, an
adept with the pen, who had already done more than any
other man to encourage immigration to this desirable province. Would Mr. Marsh, asked the wily Mr. Larkin, write a

series of letters for newspapers of the eastern states setting
forth the thousand and one attractions of this strip of land
more blest by nature than any on the continent? Send the
letters to him and he would see that they were published in
the most widely circulated newspapers on the Atlantic seaboard and inland. More and more immigrants and, no doubt,
of a higher class.

Marsh was flattered, but hesitated. The idea ran parallel
with his own, but he had no desire to see the President get
there first. The California-Oregon territory was to be his,
wrested from Mexico and Britain by him alone; to be presented to the United States Government in his own good
time.

Finally he decided that the scheme would suit his purpose
well enough. Immigration would be hastened, and Mexico,
he knew, would hesitate to declare war, not only because she
had lost Texas, but because she was ever dilatory—*mañana*
might have been her official motto—and divided by internal
dissensions. Marsh could accomplish his purpose, his ambition, before either side had made up its mind to fight—two
years, at most. Then he would have full credit for the conquest, be summoned to Washington to be commended and
honored; and be the first American governor of California.
He wrote the letters.

Two years!

Six months later Commodore Sloat ran up the American
flag on the Custom House at Monterey. John Marsh was forgotten.

7

Stunned at first, almost unbelieving when a courier
brought the news to Los Meganos, he soon fell into melan-
cholic despair. And youth had been reborn in his hard nature! Hope, ambition, high ideals; for his ambitions had

been not only for himself but for California—destined to a great future under his guiding hand.

He had been a regenerated man—and now! He knew that such an opportunity comes to no man twice. His own destiny was to be merely a rich cattleman and rancher for the rest of his life. He was only forty-five and he felt old, tired, disillusioned; and only a short time before he had been bursting with youth and energy! Despondency gave way to explosions of wrath so violent that his servants cowered in their huts. Then he subsided into a bitterness that filled him with psychic poison. He hated all men. He hated life. He paid no more visits to Monterey or Yerba Buena—or San Francisco, a "city" of several hundred inhabitants. His mayordomo and his vaqueros feared and hated him. When he saw one of his former associates approaching, he locked himself in his house and ignored the loud knocking on his front door. Bitterness poisoned the blood in his veins, the cells in his brain.

Marsh was born under a malignant star. If the fates had been as kind to him as they were to Henry Miller, he might have been a great intellectual, a great statesman, a leader of men to some great and perhaps noble objective. The defects in his character could have withered and died as achievement and recognition softened and ennobled him. And several biographies would have been written of him, instead of the long wait before Dr. Lyman unearthed him almost by accident and gave him a belated fame. It is easy to retort that if he had possessed true greatness neither disappointments nor misfortunes could have submerged it. Perhaps. But human nature is human nature, and John Marsh was but one more of its victims.

8

"The life of a modern man is not so much the history of a single soul; it is rather a play of many characters within a single body. . . . He is one man today and another tomorrow . . . he does not feel he knows himself. . . . The human character is a complicated thing, and its elements do not necessarily march in step." Those lines of Walter Lippmann's apply to no one better than to John Marsh. They might almost be his epitaph.

Marsh occasionally took refuge in the classics. The old Greeks knew! Man was but the plaything of fate. Blest only to be the more relentlessly cursed. A child of doom, with no escape but through the portals of death.

The great tragic poets had immortalized a few of them, and themselves as well; and modern man could find a brief respite in their magnificence—and—perhaps—sometimes—achieve balance in their philosophy.

On a certain day in April, 1848, Marsh was sitting under a sycamore tree beside his house reading the *Agamemnon*, completely absorbed in that most awesome of tragedies, blinding with splendor, throbbing with hate.

He heard the sound of shouting, the racing of a horse's hoofs, and looked up impatiently. Another courier. What now? What next? The most blasting news of his life had been brought by a courier. He hated the sight of them.

This man was waving a newspaper and shouting a word that made Marsh sit upright. "Gold! Gold! Gold!" As he passed the recluse of Los Meganos he flung the sheet at him and raced on. It was a copy of Sam Brannan's newspaper, the *California Star*. Marsh took in the headlines at a glance. Gold as abundant as the sands of the sea had been discovered in the foothills of the Sierras!

Gold! The very word had a magical effect on John Marsh. His old and fiercest passion blazed upward. Gold! Gold! The metal itself that he could handle and gloat over!

He flung Aeschylus into a tomato patch, ran into the house, changed into riding clothes, leaped on his horse, and rode furiously to San José.

The pueblo was seething with excitement. Men were running about, slapping one another on the back, pumping arms almost out of their sockets, pausing only to wipe the sweat out of their eyes.

Marsh had already made his plans. Before dawn the next day he had assembled four reliable citizens, pack animals, shovels and pans, and was on his way to the Sierras.

It was a long ride and they spent the night on the banks of the Yuba River near what is now known as the Marysville Buttes. The next morning they saw gold sparkling in the sands of the Yuba, and feverishly they set to work. From the first they panned out fifty dollars' worth of gold dust every hour.

Other settlers and Indians followed their tracks and encroached on "Marsh's Diggings," but there was enough for all.

Panning out gold dust and digging for nuggets is backbreaking work, nor was Marsh content with his trove. He made a trip to San José and returned with colored beads and other gewgaws more beloved by the Indians than mere gold would ever be. He also brought pack mules laden with stores of all kinds which he sold at exorbitant prices not only at his own diggings but at neighboring placers. The Indians paid for the beads and other trinkets anywhere from one to five hundred dollars' worth of gold dust.

Never, even in his youth, had Marsh known such excitement, such pure joy. But the time came when his overtaxed body demanded rest. His cool calculating mind asserted itself; he had no intention of breaking down. What good would his wealth do him if he were too enfeebled to enjoy it? He yielded to nature for the present, loaded his saddle bags and pack mules with his new fortune, and returned to Los Meganos. There were no banks in California yet, and he trusted no man but himself. He buried his gold.

A brief rest restored him to health, but he concluded not

to return to the diggings. There was an easier way of increasing his hoard.

He built a slaughter house and sold sides of beef and mutton at his own price to the mining camps along the foothills of the Sierras. He also built a smoke house and cured hams, for which the miners eagerly paid several times their weight in gold.

The site of his buildings on the San Joaquin River became known as Marsh's Landing. He also built a pier at which vessels plying up and down could stop and take on not only his livestock—either dressed or on the hoof—but grain from the farms on his rancho, fruits from his orchards, grapes from his immense vineyards, and aguardiente from his stills. For one shipment of cattle alone he received $10,000. His annual income from farm products, fruits, grapes, and wine never fell below $20,000. His close bargaining was resented by men in whom sudden wealth had bred generosity and reckless spending, but he got his price. He grew richer and richer. He was exultant and satisfied. He found no time to dwell upon the dissolution of great hopes and ambitions. The present was the greatest adventure of his life; he grew almost genial in manner. But still he trusted no man but himself, much less the banks in that money-mad city of San Francisco, full of murdering thieves when it wasn't burning to the ground, banks and all. He still buried his gold.

And then an incredible thing happened. John Marsh, at the age of fifty, fell in love again.

9

Miss Abigail Smith Tuck, a young school teacher from Chelmsford, Massachusetts, worried by an incessant cough, joined a party of Baptist missionaries and took the long voyage to California. In the salubrious climate of the Santa

Clara Valley she improved rapidly, and, in 1851, became the principal of a young ladies' seminary.

San José, always the most thriving of the pueblos, was now (temporarily) the capital of the state. The Legislature was in session and there were many festivities. Miss Tuck was taken by a friend to an evening party, and every man in the room asked her for a dance. Invitations were showered upon her thereafter. She was pretty and intelligent, both gay and properly reserved. A phenomenon. The only young American *lady* in California. Proposals of marriage were many, but she liked all the solons and cared for none. She was happy, free, independent. She gave no thought to marriage—until she heard of John Marsh.

His name was mentioned one night at a dinner, and immediately there arose a chorus of hate, admiration, contempt, envy, obloquy, defense. He was the cleverest man in California; he was a miser and a skinflint; he had done more than any man to encourage immigration; he soaked the immigrants as unmercifully as he did the miners; he had turned the tide against Micheltorena; he was a traitor to the man in whose army he had fought; he squeezed a penny till it squealed; if he did you got your money's worth; he was morose and ill-mannered; why had he, a Harvard graduate, come penniless to California and set up as a doctor in a Mexican pueblo when he might have practiced in Boston? Something shady in his past; no doubt of that.

Miss Tuck listened attentively. What a mass of contradictions the man must be. An interesting character, at least. Rather more so than any man she had ever met. When General Vallejo, who was a member of the Legislature, told her that tragedy and injustice in Marsh's youth had embittered and disillusioned him, that he found what compensation he could in material success, that, although brusque in manner, he was a gentleman, that he was a scholar and a brilliant writer who had been the first to discover California to the rest of the nation, and had joined Micheltorena's army with the sole purpose of driving him out and saving California for the United States, the interest of so intelligent a young lady accelerated, the more particularly as he was a native of her own Massachusetts and a graduate of Harvard, an institution she regarded with awe. He haunted her dreams.

The Reverend William Smith, brother of her friend Mrs. Appleby, with whom she boarded, visited Santa Clara and invited his sister and Miss Tuck to return with him to the town of Antioch, which he had founded in Contra Costa county. He mentioned incidentally that it was not far from Marsh's Landing.

Abby accepted demurely, lowering her eyelashes.

It was a long journey and they traveled not on horseback, as in the old days of which she had heard from General Vallejo, but in a wagon and over rough country roads. They spent the first night at the house of a rancher in Livermore, and started again at dawn the next morning. When they had traveled another twenty-five miles and there was no prospect of reaching Antioch before midnight, the Reverend Smith suggested that they ask the hospitality of the redoubtable John Marsh. "He will likely be as hospitable as a grizzly bear," said Dr. Smith, "but we may as well try it."

They received a surprisingly warm welcome at the big ugly adobe. Marsh often felt lonely during the long summer evenings and sometimes envied his neighbors who had all the comforts and pleasures of domesticity.

Marsh had a good cook and the guests were served an abundant supper. Afterward they sat outside in the soft balmy night and talked. Marsh and Miss Tuck found they had much in common. They both loved books, both were classical scholars, and, although Marsh had not read a novel since his youth, he was deeply interested in what she told him of those two remarkable young women who had set the

literary world of London afire with *Wuthering Heights* and
Jane Eyre.

They examined each other covertly. Abby saw a tall, erect,
imperious man with slightly grizzled hair, strong features,
and a saturnine face that could suddenly light up and radiate
charm. Marsh's eyes rested with supreme content upon a tall
young lady of about twenty-eight, with a good figure, black
hair, rosy cheeks, and a face both proud and animated.

The guests spent a none too comfortable night in beds of
swinging rawhide, and resumed their journey next morning
after a sumptuous breakfast of beans and coffee. Marsh accompanied them on horseback as far as Antioch and remained for the midday dinner. Two days later he paid them
a call and remained for supper. Then they visited him at
Marsh's Landing, where Mrs. Beemer, the Spanish wife of
the mayordomo, and the young lady from Massachusetts took
a great liking to each other. When Dr. Smith and Mrs.
Appleby were ready to return to Antioch, Abby accepted
Mrs. Beemer's invitation to remain for a week.

During that week she rode about the great rancho with
Marsh and gratified him deeply with her lively interest in
his immense herds of cattle, the fine horses of an imported
breed, the beautiful vineyards and orchards. He talked of
his youth in Danvers and Boston, his roving disposition, his
life at Prairie du Chien (omitting all mention of Marguerite
and Charley), of his subsequent adventures and struggles.
Abby found him the most interesting as well as the most lov-
able man in the world, and he could hardly believe in his
good fortune. A girl from his own sovereign state of Massachusetts, his equal in birth and intelligence, amiable, and
lovely to look at.

Two weeks from the day they met, the Reverend Dr. Smith
married them.

10

It was a happy marriage. For the first time in all the years since he had left Prairie du Chien, Marsh knew what it was to have a home in the exact sense of that much-abused word. He had the constant companionship of a woman who filled every want in his nature, who knew how to make him comfortable, and whom he loved sincerely and deeply.

He refurnished the old adobe and Abby no longer had to sleep in a swinging rawhide. There was no penuriousness in his dealings with her, and when business took him to San José, Sacramento, or San Francisco, he always returned with a handsome present, often with valuable jewels. Moreover, together they drew the plans for a new house which was to be the finest, the most spacious, the most elegant in all California.

Cattle and Marsh's Landing were not his only sources of wealth; minor farm products brought high prices. Chickens sold for five dollars each, eggs for three dollars a dozen. Butter was a rare delicacy both at the mines and in the towns. Marsh presented Abby with his dairy and a hundred and fifty cows. Vaqueros milked and squaws churned. The income from Los Meganos butter should be her pin money henceforth. It was sold for fantastic prices, and Abby sent the money to her parents in Chelmsford.

Once he took her to San Francisco, where they had the best suite in the best hotel, and again she was impressed; not by the giddy-pated city which she had seen upon her arrival in California, but by the deference paid to her husband. He might be cursed for his parsimony, his craftiness, his general unfriendliness, his brusque and arrogant manners, but he was one of the richest and most important men in the state, one, moreover, who had played a vital part in its history, and, as such, other able men respected him.

Upon this occasion they found him astonishingly mellow, and they were enchanted with the pretty, vivacious, intelligent wife "that old curmudgeon had managed to corral. How in thunderation—"

Such leading citizens as William C. Ralston, William T. Coleman, John Parrott, Sam Brannan, and even that proud Southerner, William Gwin, called and invited them out to lunch and dinner—in restaurants; few of these men newly risen to eminence were married, or if they were they had not yet sent for their families.

Abby, who already thought her John the most wonderful— as he was the most adorable—of nature's creations, could have danced for joy at the deference paid him; for the first time she wholly realized that he was a man of consequence beyond the San Joaquin and the Contra Costa Valleys. Her mind as well as her heart bubbled with gratification.

She also enjoyed herself. The men who paid court to her as well as to her husband took pains to interest her with their talk of the city they were building, of the great future they predicted for it, of the Vigilance Committee that had rid the city of "Hounds" and "Sidney Coves."

She experienced a more purely feminine delight in replenishing her wardrobe with fashionable garments out of real shops; hitherto her own deft fingers had sufficed. Marsh gave her a bag of gold pieces and told her to "go ahead." Boston skippers furnished the San Francisco shops with gowns and hats of the latest fashion. There might be a dearth of respectable women in San Francisco, but there were plenty of the other kind; Abby was horrified at their painted faces and flaunted jewels as they paraded Montgomery Street with dreadful-looking men. But she reminded herself that she was now a married woman and therefore "a woman of the world," and must accept the inevitable.

Moreover, she was too happy to care.

After this whirl of gaiety and their return to the rancho,

she had little use for her finery, but she could exhibit it to the many friends she had made among the squaws and to Mrs. Thompson, the wife of the new mayordomo at the Landing. Occasionally they paid a brief visit to Santa Clara or San José, where she was complimented and congratulated by her old friends.

How wonderful life was!

11

Marsh could hardly believe in the complete happiness that had come to him, and there was an odd sprinkling of humility in his gratitude. But, alas, the fates were never kind to him for long, and, after a little girl was born, Abby's health began to fail; eventually she went into a decline and, when the child was four years old, she died.

It was her last wish that little Alice should be sent to Mrs. Thompson, where she would receive proper care, and Marsh in his misery indifferently complied.

Once more he was a lonely and bitter man, and if his distractions were many they were as intolerable as his sorrow. Immigrants were insolently squatting on his ranch and stole his cattle and horses. He could get no redress from the courts. His vaqueros demanded higher wages and, when he brusquely refused, cursed him for an old miser, and—at least so Marsh believed—connived with the squatters.

He made an enemy of the small farmer who branded his cattle at the yearly rodeo, one Ygnacio Sebrian, a lawless creature who had a strong following known as "Sebrian's Gang." For years the man had been content with the payment of twenty-five cents for every calf he branded, but, in 1856, he took advantage of Marsh's negligence in the usual contract and demanded a dollar a head, his fee running up into the neat little sum of $1,200. Marsh laughed in his face. Sebrian sued him. The court decided in Marsh's favor. Sebrian left the courthouse vowing vengeance. When another of his gang, a Mexican with a strain of alien blood, named Olivos, also demanded four times the usual price for his services and threatened to sue him, Marsh shouted: "Sue me? You can't. You are a nigger." There was another cursing enemy. It was known that Sebrian had proclaimed he would pay $500 to anyone who would kill John Marsh; but though all the Los Meganos vaqueros were in ugly sympathy with the two scoundrels, none was inclined to commit murder.

Meanwhile Marsh had another brief period, not of happiness—all capacity for that greatest of life's compensations was in the grave with Abby—but of a certain pleasure and content.

He had been living for some time in his grand new house, that great stone mansion which was the wonder of the north, with its peaked roof, seven gables, carved lintels, its tower sixty feet high, its long glass windows. One night as he lay in bed reading Johnson's *Lives of the English Poets,* one of the books he had brought from Prairie du Chien, a young man pounded on his door, was ushered in, and announced himself as his son, Charles Marsh.

For a time Marsh, very naturally, was incredulous: California was full of impostors and braggarts; but when a number of searching questions had been answered satisfactorily, and the webfoot displayed, he opened his arms.

The explanation of his son's long silence was simple. Charles's guardian had moved to another part of the country and it was believed that John Marsh had gone to South America. Only recently had Charles heard that he was living in California.

The next day Marsh drove his son about the country and introduced him with obvious pride as "my son by a former marriage." He was heartily congratulated. Charles, externally a youthful replica of his father, was a fine young fellow with a lively and happy disposition. He loved books, and

once more Marsh had a companion. Charles was also interested in everything about the great rancho, and took a daily
gallop inspecting the livestock, although the scowls of the
vaqueros made him uneasy. He begged his father to increase
their wages, but this was the one wish of his son that Marsh
would not grant. In all else he was the indulgent parent. He
showed him a chest filled with gold that he kept on hand for
business emergencies and told him to help himself. He also
told him of the buried treasure and promised to take him to
the spot, but never did.

12

Then came the fatal day of September 14th. Marsh was
obliged to go to San Francisco on important business. Before
leaving, however, he went to the rodeo grounds to sell a number of his cattle to a butcher, who selected his steers and
paid Marsh $5,000 in gold. Two of Marsh's new vaqueros,
Juan Garcia and Felipe Moreno, were witnesses to the trans-
action. These men were members of Sebrian's gang, but this
Marsh did not know.

He rode home, buried his gold, asked Charles to bring him
$400 from the chest and a bag of silver, and arrayed himself
in his best clothes as he always did when about to visit the
young metropolis: a suit of black broadcloth, black satin
stock, white linen, an embroidered waistcoat further embellished with a massive gold watch-chain. At the age of fifty-
six he was still erect, muscular, ruddy, as strong and active as
any of his vaqueros. Charles watched him proudly as he drove
off in his buggy drawn by a spirited bay horse.

The next morning Marsh was found in the dry bed of a
creek half a mile from Martinez, his throat cut, his body
bruised and stabbed.

Marsh had left no will. A long-drawn-out law suit ensued.
James Marsh, a nephew who had arrived in California

shortly after Abby's death and received no welcome from his famous uncle, claimed that Charles was illegitimate and demanded half the estate.

The eminent San Francisco firm, Crockett and Crittenden, took the case for Charles, Colonel Baker for James. Affidavits were brought from Prairie du Chien and Danvers. Dr. Cameron, an old friend of John Marsh, testified that Marsh and Marguerite had lived together for seven years, that she had been received everywhere as his wife, such "marriages" being considered legal enough in that frontier town. Practically every white man had a squaw under his protection.

Colonel Baker produced a letter from John Marsh to his father written shortly before Marguerite's death, asserting that he had never married anyone. Colonel Baker was one of the orators of that era and Charles watched the jury anxiously as he poured forth a torrent of eloquence.

Fortunately, Judge McKinstry, preeminent in his profession, and a man whose integrity had never even been discussed, was on circuit at Martinez and the case was tried before him. He listened patiently to the mass of testimony on both sides, and then disposed summarily of Colonel Baker and James Marsh.

"It is of no consequence whether there was a marriage ceremony or not," he said when charging the jury. "If John Marsh lived with this French-Canadian girl as his wife, and if he introduced her to all his acquaintances and friends as his wife, she was his wife by the laws of France and by the laws of the United States."

The immense estate was divided between Charles and Alice.

The buried gold was never found—at least by his heirs. Ten years later Charles, who had already hunted down Olivos, captured Moreno, who was sent to San Quentin prison for twenty-five years. In 1891, Olivos was pardoned by the Governor, and soon after began to live the life of a man of unlimited wealth. Almost simultaneously, a recent excavation was discovered on the property that had once belonged to John Marsh but had long since passed into other hands. Suspicion was rife, but nothing could be proved.

PART TWO

5. San Francisco Is Born

IN 1847, the name of the old Battery down on the western shore of the Bay was changed from Yerba Buena to San Francisco by the first American alcalde (mayor), Lieutenant Washington A. Bartlett. In 1848, its population numbered one hundred and fifty sober industrious citizens: merchants, traders, exporters and importers, shopkeepers, artisans, and mechanics. There was a church, and a newspaper owned and edited by Samuel Brannan. On the outskirts were warehouses and temascals (sweat-houses) for the Indians.

Sam Brannan was the liveliest citizen of San Francisco. He had arrived in 1846 with a shipload of Mormons, intending to found a colony. However, the Californians would have none of polygamy, and the voyagers were allowed to remain only on condition that they conformed to the moral standards of American civilization. A few remained in San Francisco, the rest scattered throughout the territory and excited no further disapproval. Brannan had brought a printing press and published the first issue of the *California Star* in January, 1847. The "yellow press" of the 1890's was a pale reflection of that tinctorial sheet. His account of the vicissitudes of the Donner party, with every hideous detail, deprived San Franciscans of any desire for their midday meal. So vivid and detailed was the account that it traveled all over the state, and copies even reached New York and Boston.

The houses of San Francisco were either of adobe—left-overs from the Battery—or two-story frame buildings. There were several boarding houses, one or two billiard rooms, poolrooms, skid-rows. Besides these temperate amusements, there were many fandangos to which rancheros rode in from the north, General Vallejo and Doña Francisca among them.

At that time the Bay lapped the principal street, named for Captain Montgomery who had run up the American flag on July 8, 1846, in the Plaza—whose name was promptly changed to Portsmouth Square in honor of his ship. There were two other streets behind it and several running east and west. It was some time before anyone ventured to build above the lower slopes of those rugged hills; nor did the little city spread away from the cove and out into the great valley once the proud possession of the Mission Dolores, where the bear, the coyote, the deer, elk, and wildcat still roamed. In 1850, my father-in-law visited San Francisco and hunted bear with General Vallejo in the region where the Palace Hotel now stands.

The San Franciscans were growing rich slowly. They transacted business with the large cities on the western coast of South America and with the Sandwich (Hawaiian) Islands. Life was rather slow, the only excitement being the arrival of mail from the Atlantic seaboard, when the entire community ran to the top of the lofty promontory, later to be known as Telegraph Hill, to watch the ship sail through the Golden Gate—the name given to "The Straits" by John Charles Frémont.

It is futile to speculate upon what the future of San Francisco would have been if John Augustus Sutter had not sent one William Marshall into the Sierra foothills to build a sawmill.

In 1849, it was almost deserted. In 1850, it threatened to become one large gambling hell.

2

Marshall found his nugget in January, 1848, but gold had been found in small quantities before, and it was long before the eastern states took seriously the tale of California's new source of wealth. Not so Sam Brannan, who could "smell news" a hundred and fifty miles away. One day he sprang on his horse and galloped out of town. A fortnight later he electrified the little city by running up and down Montgomery Street waving a bottle and shouting, "Gold! Gold! This bottle is full of gold dust! There are *placeros* in the Sierras that are the richest in the world! Hurrah for California!" Then he dashed into his newspaper office and got out an extra—and sent it by Indian couriers the length of California and far into the midwestern states.

There was no immediate rush by the San Franciscans; they had seen Sam excited before, and they had more serious business to attend to. But several hundred men from other parts of the territory went to the *placeros,* and captains of the trading ships from Lima and Valparaiso saw the gold dust they left in the shops of San Francisco. In the least possible time there was an influx from Peru, Chile, and Mexico. Then the solid citizens caught the fever and departed.

For almost a year it looked as if the excitement would be confined to the Pacific coast. Thomas O. Larkin wrote to Mr. Buchanan, Secretary of State, without result. He visited the mines and wrote a second time; he had watched men dig or pan from one to five thousand dollars' worth of gold a day each. Governor Mason followed with a report that the yield in the rapidly developing placer mines was from twenty to thirty thousand dollars a day. President Polk included this report in his next message to Congress.

Then indeed the East took fire. The newspapers of New York, Albany, Boston, Philadelphia, and the South came out with what for that era were flaming headlines. The great stampede began.

In 1849, some twenty-five thousand covered wagons crossed the Sierra Nevada Mountains into California. The sailing vessels traveling by way of Cape Horn took from eight months to a year to reach the harbor of San Francisco. Another line took its passengers to Chagres, whence they crossed the Isthmus to Panama, where they were fortunate if another ship awaited them and if they did not die of fever meanwhile.

Married or single, the men were all young, but they suffered from the long trip " 'round the Horn." The food was bad, the water little better, they were seasick, they were tossed out of their bunks by storms. And the monotony was insufferable. They were depressed, disgusted, the lure of gold faded; they heartily wished themselves back in their comfortable homes.

On one occasion, however, they were cheered by some nonsense verses which they sang lustily to the tune of *O Susanna*. As these verses were sung on every ship thereafter, it is worth while to quote them here.

The California Immigrant

I

I come from Salem City
With my washtub on my knee.
I'm going to California
The gold dust for to see.
It rained all night the day I left,
The weather it was dry.
The sun so hot I froze to death,
Oh, brothers, don't you cry.

Chorus

Oh, California
That's the land for me.
I'm going to Sacramento
With my washtub on my knee.

II

I jumped aboard the 'Lizzie ship
And traveled on the sea
And every time I thought of home
I wished it wasn't me.
The vessel reared like any horse
That had of oats a wealth.
I thought it wouldn't throw me, so
I thought I'd throw myself.

Chorus

III

I thought of all the pleasant times
We've had together here.
I thought I ort to cry a bit,
But couldn't find a tear.
The pilot bread was in my mouth,
The gold dust in my eye,
And though I'm going far away,
Dear brothers, don't you cry.

Chorus

IV

I soon shall be in San Francisco
And then I'll look all 'round,
And when I see the gold lumps there
I'll pick them off the ground.
I'll scrape the mountains clean, my boys,
I'll drain the rivers dry.
A pocket full of rocks bring home,
So, brothers, don't you cry.

Chorus

These verses swept California, the middle and eastern states, and finally crossed the Atlantic Ocean to be embalmed in the *Edinburgh Review*.

3

For a while San Francisco looked like a ghost town. The citizens were all out at the *placeros* looking for gold. The shopkeepers soon returned, however, as they found they could make a comfortable nest egg more agreeably by selling goods for bags of gold dust than by straining backs and skinning knees. During the first sixteen weeks after their return they sold $850,000 worth of foodstuffs and other necessities to the miners. They also fitted out shipload after shipload of the immigrants, who were willing to pay any price for camping outfits, picks, shovels, pans, and rockers.

As time went on, there were three hundred ships at anchor in the Bay from Chile, Peru, Australia, and the East, their sails furled or hanging limply: every sailor had deserted and followed the stampede. The few women who made homes for their husbands in the city patiently waited for the fever to subside. They knew their houses were quite safe; no man was interested in petty thievery when he could fill his hat with gold dust in five minutes.

These women watched with amusement the young men from the East as they left the ships and strode through the town. They wore red shirts, trousers tucked into high boots, two pistols in their belts—dressed for the part! Those that had come by way of the Isthmus wore broad Panama hats, and were envied by the others.

One small community, however, was flourishing. In 1848, Sutter's son, John, Jr., who had arrived unexpectedly some time before, at the suggestion of Sam Brannan and in the absence of his father, laid out the little town of Sacramento, a square mile beside the fort, with streets now shaded by transplanted trees. Lots were sold to Mormons and other Americans who preferred the warmth of the interior to the fogs and winds of the coast; later to a number of the gold-diggers, who vowed they would "live and die in California." Sutter's Indians built houses for them and furniture as well. There were few of their needs he was unable to supply. His blanket factory had equipped every bed in San Francisco. His grist mill ran day and night. His warehouses were always stocked with tea, coffee, chocolate, sugar, and other groceries. His vaqueros supplied beef and mutton from his innumerable herds. The miners rode to and from the "diggings" on fine horses they had bought from their benefactor. When their ardor had somewhat diminished, they took a day off and planted flowers in their little gardens.

Such were the humble beginnings of Sacramento, now the most beautiful little city in California and the capital of the state.

4

Sutter seldom visited the mines, but gold dust and nuggets filled his coffers nevertheless. He demanded high prices for his horses, cattle, and sheep bought by the miners who had pitched their tents in the Sierras, but met with no remonstrance, for what were casual bags of "dust" and "lumps" to them? Although he gave generously to the unfortunate, he sold the lots in Sacramento and small farms on his vast estate at high figures. Before the end of 1849, $23,000,000 worth of gold had been taken out of the placers, and both the lucky and the unlucky liked this lord of the great Sacramento Valley, so genial, kind, generous, handsome, and grudged him nothing. He entertained many of those bewhiskered, mahogany-colored gentlemen clad in red or blue flannel shirts, pants pushed into hobnailed boots, slouch hats almost concealing their uncut hair; many of them were educated men, and he enjoyed their society. He was now forty-six, ruddy and erect, his blue eyes beaming a welcome. His conversation was always interesting, for he had traveled widely. Moreover, he and his son were always meticulously dressed, and the men were grateful for the sudden transition from savagery to a replica of the civilization they had left behind them. And such men worship success. Here was a man who had won his way from Old World insignificance to untold wealth; when he stood on the top of his Fort, he must feel indeed monarch of all he surveyed. He had won the allegiance of the best of the Indians—routing the others—whom he had taught the mechanical trades and cultivation of the soil; he had even established primary schools.

And to those American immigrants who had come before the Gold Rush and to whom he had sold small farms or whom he had directed where to "squat" on government land, he was the one and only nabob in California. He was their benefactor and friend; he had furnished them with seeds and cuttings, sold them groceries at a moderate price, and his Indians dug their wells.

Many of them had arrived in a pitiable condition, whole families weak from hardships, malaria, malnutrition. He had put them to bed in his Fort, dosed and fed them until they had been able to take up the burden of life again.

He was very happy for a short time during that famous year of '49, and not only for himself but for his beloved California. She was the most famous member of the Union, and Europe had none to compare with her. When the *placeros* were exhausted, thousands of these fine Americans would remain in California and develop her magnificent resources, neglected by the Spaniards, and California would not only be the thing of beauty bequeathed by nature, but she would teem with enterprise, and be studded with great cities. Great men would be sent to represent her in Congress.

And he, John Augustus Sutter, would be California's most illustrious citizen. He was already world-famous, for had it not been for him those fabulous placer mines might not have been discovered for a century. Pictures of Sutter's Fort had appeared in half the newspapers of the world. Even Marshall, when he had brought that first nugget for his inspection, had only a vague idea of its portent. It was neither Marshall nor that wildcat Sam Brannan who was the author of the great Gold Rush. It was he, John Augustus Sutter, and the world knew it. He would serve his California in the governor's chair, in the Senate of the United States. His future would be glorious, and he would, humbly as ever, give thanks to Almighty God.

Poor Sutter!

5

Among the thousands who had come to California from the eastern and middle states, there were, during the first "Rush," few inferior characters. They were well-bred, well-educated young men inspired as much by the love of adventure as lust for gold. But 1850 told a different story.

Gamblers, sharpers, crooks, came by the shipload. Some remained in San Francisco, for many of its inhabitants, laden with wealth, had returned to their city, and brought others, equally satisfied and tired of backaches and roughing it, with them. But the majority of those bad characters went to the mines, and soon every camp had its faro tables and dance halls—loose females followed as a matter of course. The weaker men were soon demoralized and became gamblers themselves. Occasionally there was retribution, and scoundrels either obeyed orders and betook themselves to other fields or left camp at the end of a rope.

In 1850, there were almost as many gambling houses, saloons, and houses of prostitution in San Francisco as there were dwellings and business establishments. It is not to be denied that the estimable citizens who laid the foundations of one of the great cities of the Union amused themselves occasionally at the gaming tables, for they missed the excitement of the mines, but most of them drank little and worked hard. The weaker succumbed and gambled all day and all night. Many lost their all, and either blew out their brains or trekked back to the mines in the vain hope of retrieving their fortunes.

Every day someone was shot in the frequent brawls.

But on the whole the pioneers were a sturdy lot. They had strong heads, strong characters, decent morals. They were men of initiative, ambition, and inflexible will. Their number was steadily increased by men who had "made their pile," and, having no love for the land, settled in San Francisco. Late-comers from the East, after one visit to the mines and after pocketing a few nuggets for souvenirs, found the conditions intolerable and decided to grow up with the new city whose future on that harbor they had the wit to foresee. In the first months of 1850, the population of San Francisco had increased to 1,500. Before 1851 had dawned, it numbered 30,000. They bought lots for homes and business houses. In due course there were office buildings for lawyers, a bank, a merchant's exchange, wholesale and retail business houses, a courthouse, a city and county jail, respectable places of amusement including a bullfight arena and a circus; also seven churches and seven newspapers.

The city spread up and over the nearest hill and across Market Street—a street as wide as the Champs Elysées, running from the Embarcadero to the San Bruno Range. The sand dunes swept down by the steam paddies filled the shallows of what was once known as Yerba Buena Cove, and two new streets were added, running north and south: Sansome and Front. There were also eleven wharves.

After the first of the 1850 fires, a sewer system of sorts was installed, but the streets were rivers of mud in winter and

ankle deep in dust during the long dry season. These draw-
backs to perfect living were regarded as negligible, as were
the winds and the fogs. The city burned down five times in
its first year of high prosperity.

Men who could rebuild a city almost overnight were not
likely to be dominated by gamblers and sharpers. A strong
city government had been formed early in the year, consist-
ing, in the first group, of mayor, recorder, marshal, treasurer,
attorney, street commissioner, and collector. There were also
nine aldermen, three officers of the Superior Court and their
clerks, a sheriff and five deputies, thirteen police officers, and
twenty-two policemen.

The saloons and gambling houses still flourished, the
gaudy ladies of commerce promenaded Montgomery Street,
but these were regarded as necessary evils and were unmo-
lested unless they became too obstreperous; then they were
run out of the city or herded onto a ship and sent whence
they came.

There were many and various costumes to be seen on the
streets of San Francisco. The eminent citizens were no dan-
dies. Black pants and blue jackets sufficed. The miners, when
they came to town, wore their unvarying uniform of red
shirt, high boots, six-shooters, and bowie knives. Californians
of the old régime clung to the gay serape and silver-laden
sombreros. The gamblers, who would have scorned to be
mistaken for eminent citizens, made themselves conspicuous
in black broadcloth, starched white shirts studded with large
diamonds, and wide, rakish, black hats.

One fashion reigned supreme in female attire. Both ladies
of fashion and ladies of commerce wore flounced skirts over
hoops, and coal-scuttle bonnets. The "fast women" might be
distinguished only by their paint and powder, and their billowing skirts were never brushed by the wives and daughters
of eminent citizens.

6

Despite the best efforts of its leading men, San Francisco was often in a state of turmoil. In the latter part of 1849, the Australian "Hounds," an organized band of cutthroats, thieves, and bullies, made up their minds to "get rich quick" independently of mines and hard work. Avoiding a clash with the sturdy Americans, they descended every night upon the tents of the foreigners encamped outside the city, men who had accumulated a reasonable quantity of gold and awaited ships to return them to their homelands. These unfortunates they beat and robbed. They tore their tents to ribbons and threatened to kill them if they resisted. The victims clamored for protection, but San Francisco was very busy and slow to wrath at any time.

But although San Franciscans may be philosophical and good-natured, when they do awake their wrath is red-hot. Sam Brannan called a mass meeting in the Plaza (the old name was in familiar use for many years) and exhorted the "decent citizens of San Francisco" to get rid of this cancer before it was too late; a murder had been committed the night before and it might well be the forerunner of many.

They responded as vehemently. The "Hounds" were rounded up by a large body of determined citizens, flourishing pistols, horsewhips, and clubs, and they were confined, because of the inadequacy of the jails, to the U.S.S. *Warren*. They were granted the formality of a trial, during which Hall McAllister, soon to become the most distinguished lawyer in California, won his first laurels as Prosecuting Attorney. The miscreants were found guilty with little or no opposition, but as there was no prison in the metropolis, they were set at liberty with a stern warning. Thoroughly cowed, they either returned to Australia or went to the mines, where they were even more summarily disposed of.

But San Francisco's respite from crime was brief.

7

In 1850, a second hundred thousand immigrants had arrived in California. It was easy for any number of criminals to enter the port without receiving more than a casual glance from San Franciscans, to whom expectant gold-diggers were an old story. As the population swelled to 30,000, those who remained in the city were unremarked as long as they behaved themselves. Moreover, when a number of ticket-of-leave men arrived from Australia they were engaged in rebuilding the city after one of the fires.

The ex-convicts bided their time; they even helped to cart away the débris and usefully occupied their time, for idleness would have excited indignation and inquiry. They also annexed a number of dissolute Mexicans to their band.

When the city was flourishing again, they began their career of crime. It was not long before San Francisco recognized the fact that she had an "underworld."

Unlike the "Hounds," these criminals did not parade defiantly through the streets, nor did they at first herd together in a headquarters to which they might easily be tracked.

Where the "Hounds" had dared to kill upon one occasion only, these desperados murdered every man who resisted them, and if a good citizen ventured out at night they shot him for the fun of it. Growing bolder, they raided the gambling houses in broad daylight and made off with the sacks of gold dust, shooting right and left as they departed.

Many were arrested, but, although there were lawyers as honorable as Hall McAllister, there were many shysters, the scum of their profession in the eastern states. The majority of the judges were equally corrupt. A bag of gold dust and a promise of votes could buy the freedom of any criminal. Another shipload from Australia increased the number of the "Sidney Coves," and now, openly contemptuous of both law and the police, whom they greatly outnumbered, they fore-

gathered on the slope of Telegraph Hill, calling their headquarters Sidney Town; and when not looting and murdering,
made night hideous with their yells of derision. Even the
prostitutes trembled, for they were often torn from their
establishments and carried off screaming to Sidney Town.
Sometimes they were found with their throats cut in the
morning.

"The eminents," busy and slow to wrath as ever, were
finally persuaded that their city was in danger and bestirred
themselves again. Prodded by Sam Brannan's editorials and
mass meetings of indignant citizens, in June 1851 they
formed the first of the famous Committees of Vigilance.

One hundred and eighty-four of the most determined and
influential citizens met in secret in Brannan's offices and
formed the Committee. The more conservative were for giving the legal authorities one more chance to operate, and
they appointed a guard for two prisoners accused of murder,
lest they be lynched by a mob. But the fiery Sam thundered
that they were wasting precious time. "I am very surprised,"
he told the Committee, "to hear people talk about grand
juries, recorders, or mayors. I'm tired of such talk. These
men are murderers as well as thieves, and I will die or see
them hanged by the neck. I'm opposed to any farce in this
business. We are the mayor and the recorder, the hangman
and the law. The law and the courts never yet hung a man in
California. . . . I want no technicalities. Such things are
devised to shield the guilty. . . ."

Sam had his way, for the majority agreed with him. It was
decided to choose a jury from their number, as well as a
sheriff, judges, a clerk, and public prosecutor. Men of the
highest standing were immediately elected for these offices:
William T. Coleman, prosecuting attorney; Hall McAllister
and D. O. Shattuck, counsel for the prisoners; others of the
same caliber.

Those two criminals escaped from the calaboose, but the

Committee functioned nevertheless. They were determined to rid the city of the "Sidney Coves" and restore law and order.

They made their headquarters in rooms on the corner of Battery and Pine Streets. The Monumental Fire Company was to toll the bell (not ring it furiously as for a fire) as a signal for the Committee to meet and try a prisoner. It was on the night of June 12th that the bell tolled for the first time; its deep solemn note shook the very vitals of the city. Thousands of men leaped out of bed, dressed hurriedly, snatched their firearms, and ran to the street below the lighted windows of the Vigilance Committee, whose organization and purpose was an ill-kept secret. A "Sidney Cove," one John Jenkins, they learned, was on trial for his life.

Within, twelve solemn men sat about a table and listened to the attorneys for the defense, determined to give the wretch a fair trial. Others of the Committee stood against the wall or guarded the doors and the stairway without, six-shooters in hand. The trial was brief. There were several witnesses to the murder, and the shaking "Cove" did not deny his guilt. At midnight the bell tolled again; a signal that the sentence was death and the execution would take place at once.

Brannan went out on the porch and informed the crowd that the evidence had been conclusive and asked for their approval. Eight thousand cheers drowned the bell.

A clergyman was summoned to talk to the condemned man, and at two o'clock, pinioned and hooded, surrounded by members of the Committee, he was marched to the Plaza, followed by the crowd. Not a word was spoken. The bell tolled until the noose had been adjusted and the body, after horrible gyrations, hung limp from the impromptu gallows.

Within a short time the summoning bell had tolled three times, three more murderers were hanged, this time from a wharf at the foot of Market Street. Two of these men were temporarily rescued by the legal sheriff from the Committee headquarters and taken to the jail. The bell tolled. The Vigilantes broke into the jail, brushed aside the sheriff, hustled the prisoners into a coach. The driver applied the whip and the horses galloped down to the wharf. By the time the crowd arrived two bodies were swinging.

The rest of the "Coves" promptly disappeared and never were heard from again.

The Vigilantes disbanded and peace reigned once more; that is to say, such peace as San Francisco ever knew in those days, for it was always in a state of excitement of one kind or another. Politics, business panics in which millions were lost and had to be made over again, fires, and smallpox epidemics, are not conducive to holy calm. But at least a fair semblance of law and order prevailed, and it was five years before the Vigilantes reassembled and the deep, solemn note of the Monumental Fire Company bell made every citizen, good and bad, drop his work or tumble out of bed at night and run to the corner of Battery and Pine Streets.

And meanwhile there were other changes.

8

After the last of her fires (until 1906), San Francisco rose from her ashes a handsome and substantial city. The business houses, office buildings, banks, stores, churches, and hospitals were built of brick, granite, or stone. There were fine hotels; French, Spanish, Chinese, plain American restaurants; theaters; music halls; large shops with tempting wares displayed behind plate glass windows; a public library; book stores; public and private schools; the proud little headquarters of the Pioneer Society, of which Sam Brannan was one of the founders and the second president; a Hall of Justice; an adequate Courthouse and a formidable jail. The plank sidewalks were still dilapidated and the streets rivers of mud (infested by rats) in winter, and in summer so thick with dust blown down from the hills and in from the valley that little whirlwinds capering up and down the streets were a familiar sight.

The Plaza, as ever, was the focal point of the city. It covered about an acre, and on the four sides of its green lawns and flower beds were some of the finest buildings in the city; all, however, quite overshadowed in interest and elegance by the famous gambling establishment whose name, known from coast to coast, was El Dorado. Newcomers visited it before they secured their hotel accommodations or left for the placers.

Its front of one hundred and twenty feet was set with plate glass windows reaching from sidewalk to ceiling and the curtains were never drawn. Those that dared not venture beyond those hospitable doors stood for hours gazing, fascinated and envious, at the dazzling scene within. On one side, running its entire length, was a bar laden with silver and crystal, magnums of whiskey, brandy, champagne, French vermouth, Spanish mescal, and aguardiente. Behind it were tall mirrors that reflected the six immense crystal chandeliers, blazing at night; the fifty tables piled with bags of gold dust, nuggets, and, as time went on, minted golden coins; the hard, intent faces of the gamblers (many with six-shooters at their elbows); dense throngs wandering up and down the narrow aisles or leaning against the marble pillars that supported the ceiling.

At the lower end was a platform where musicians played lively tunes and Mexican girls danced.

All sorts and conditions of men sat at those tables; judges, lawyers, merchants, doctors, artists, rancheros, miners from the placers, professional gamblers, broken-down members of the more lauded professions—men of college education but weak character and general inefficiency who had come from the East to the land of gold with the hope of picking up a

few thousand grains of "dust." Lacking physical strength for
the mines, they tutored, taught school, clerked in San Francisco, and squandered what they made under the bright lights
of El Dorado.

San Francisco was still a magnet for rapscallions, but they
knew better than to work in gangs, and what crimes they
committed were taken care of by the police—for a time.

9

The men who had married "back East" or "down South"
sent for their families. A number of the young bachelors
married lovely señoritas, others went home for a visit and
returned with "the girl I left behind me."

The residential quarter of the city was south of Market
Street. Folsom, Harrison, and Bryant Streets had long rows
of houses set well back, with gardens before them. Rincon
Hill and South Park, however, were the proud centers of
fashion.

The houses on the hill made no pretensions to architec-
tural elegance, but were large and well-built, with long
double parlors for entertaining, and surrounded by trees and
fine gardens. South Park, at its foot, an oval enclosure
between Bryant and Brannan Streets, was lined with ugly
brown houses as alike as lead pencils in a box; like many of
the buildings in Montgomery and other business streets, they
had made the journey " 'round the Horn."

The interiors of those houses, needless to relate, were Vic-
torian: horsehair or velvet furniture, Brussels carpets, four-
posters, washstands with bowl, pitcher, and slop jar. A
marble-top table was in every front parlor adorned with a
bowl of goldfish, wax flowers under glass, or the family Bible.
Antimacassars were on every chair.

But there was family silver on the dining tables and many
family portraits on the whitewashed walls; portraits of

bearded men—not a few in uniform and white wig—and stiffly appareled women—several by the famous Stuart who had painted Washington and Hamilton. Libraries, the books bound in aging calfskin, and conservatories were not uncommon, particularly on Rincon Hill where the houses were more spacious than in South Park.

Society for many years was dominated by the "Southern set," possibly because those Southern matrons were more numerous, more accomplished in the art of entertaining, more rigid in their standards of propriety. Theirs was the unique opportunity to create a society of elegance and decorum in a raw and money-mad community on "the edge of nowhere." And they took their mission as seriously as the Vigilantes.

No woman, no matter how wealthy, could hope to become a member of that sacrosanct group unless she possessed the three requisites of breeding, "family," and unblemished virtue. Not a shadow the size of a humming bird's wing must have drifted across the fair fame of even one of their own. And divorce meant ostracism. The husband may have been a brute, a drunkard, a lecher; such pleas might serve in a court of law, but not with the Vigilantes of SOCIETY. The very word divorce made them shudder. Anathema maranatha!

These laws were understood and enforced, but the ladies were informal among themselves. They ran in and out of one another's houses at all hours of the day, had gay little parties in the evening, called one another by their first names, were godmothers to one another's babies. If one of their number made a sudden descent into poverty (no infrequent occurrence) her position was unaffected. Money-madness had not poisoned SOCIETY.

They tore the bosoms of those beyond the pale with envy and hate as they drove through the shopping district in open barouches, their handsome gowns (made in the house by

itinerant sewing women, for dressmakers were among the last
of the immigrants) billowing over hoop skirts, coal-scuttle
bonnets framing patrician features.

A woman must have been an authentic beauty to survive
the fashions of that era. They wore their hair looped over
their ears and netted in a "waterfall" behind. Nor did they
dare resort to the faintest ministry of art: women who
"painted" were hussies; even powder was denied them. They
anointed their faces with olive oil at night and washed it
off with castile soap in the morning.

Several times a year one or more of their number gave a
grand ball, and upon these occasions they wore their gowns
astonishingly low for such devotees of all the proprieties; for
some reason, beyond even a psychologist's comprehension,
displayed bosoms (often opulent) were *summum jus,* while
rouge was *infra dig.* But life would be drab without its
charming inconsistencies.

They did not confine themselves to indoor diversions.
Before they grew too stout, they rose early and rode horseback beside their husbands (in long flowing skirts, tight
jackets, and neat little stovepipe hats), sometimes hunting
quail or deer in the still deserted upper valley (bears and
coyotes had retired to the mountains), more rarely shooting
snipe or ducks on the marshes at night.

They had their inevitable sorrows and tragedies, but on
the whole they were almost as happy and carefree as the Californians of a bygone day. They formed an odd little oasis in
the turbulent life of San Francisco, for which their men—who
never "took their business home with them"—were devoutly
grateful. No doubt it saved more than one from suicide.

TELYGRAFT HILL

BY WALLACE IRWIN

O Telygraft Hill she sits mighty and fine,
  Like a praty that's planted on ind,

And she's bannered wid washin's from manny a line,
  Which flutther and dance in the wind.
O th' goats and th' chickens av Telygraft Hill
  They prosper all grand and serene,
For when there's short pickin' on Telygraft Hill
  They feed their swate sowls on the scene.

For the Irish they live on the top av it,
And the Dagos they live on the base av it,
And every tin can in the knowledge av man,
Is scattered all over the face av it.
Av Telygraft Hill, Telygraft Hill,
Nobby owld, slobby owld Telygraft Hill!

O Telygraft Hill she sits proud as a queen
  And th' docks lie below in the glare
And th' bay runs beyant 'er all purple and green
  Wid th' ginger-bread island out there,
And the ferry boats toot at owld Telygraft Hill,
  And th' Hill it don't care if they do
While the Bradys and Caseys av Telygraft Hill
  Joost sit there enj'yin' th' view.

For th' Irish they live on th' top av it,
And th' Dagos they live on the base av it,
And th' goats and th' chicks and th' bricks bats and shticks
Is joombled all over the face av it,
Av Telygraft Hill, Telygraft Hill,
Crazy owld, daisy owld Telygraft Hill!

Sure Telygraft Hill has a castle from Wales
  Which was built by a local creator.
He made it av bed-slats wid hammer and nails
  Like a scene in a stylish the-ay-ter.
There's rats in th' castle o' Telygraft Hill,
  But it frowns wid an air of its own

*For it's runnin' th' bloof that owld Telygraft Hill
 Is a sthrong howld of morther and shtone.*

*For the Irish they live on the top av it,
And th' Dagos they live on the base av it,
And th' races they fight on the wrong side and right
To th' shame and onendin' disgrace av it,
Av Telygraft Hill, Telygraft Hill,
Windy-torn, shindy-torn Telygraft Hill!*

*And Telygraft Hill has an iligent lot
 Of shanties and shacks, Hivin knows!
An' they're hangin' on tight to the jumpin' off spot
 Be th' grace av th' Saints and their toes;
And th' la-ads that are livin' on Telygraft Hill
 Prefer to remain where they're at,
And they'd not trade a hen-roost on Telygraft Hill
 For a mansion below on th' flat.*

*For th' Irish they live on the top av it
And th' Dagos they live on th' base av it,
And th' owld sod-gossoon sits as high as th' moon
And there's nawthin he'd take in th' place av it,
Lumpy owld, bumpy owld Telygraft Hill!*

6. The Despoiled

Sutter

SUTTER'S exultation soon veered to dismay. Gamblers invaded his little town.

For one man who made a fortune in the mines and either took it "back home" or became a banker or merchant in San Francisco, hundreds were unlucky, or, stricken with malaria, rheumatism, or dysentery, were too weak for the strenuous life of a gold seeker, and, having neither business training nor desire for a farmer's life, pitched their tents in Sacramento. Their numbers increased. The pretty little town grew into a long straggling ugly settlement, not to be redeemed for many years. Many of these men were dissolute, but more were sober and industrious. All were reckless and unprincipled.

Sutter's garrison had been withdrawn, and he appealed to the governor in vain. The successive governors of California were hostile to great landholders; they were altogether too powerful. Let them take care of themselves.

These new inhabitants of Sacramento elected a mayor who laughed at Sutter's pretensions of ownership, but did what he could to preserve order. His success was moderate. Saloons and gambling houses flourished. The interlopers made periodic visits to the mines, picked up a nugget or two or managed to gather or steal a small bag of gold dust. The more enterprising set up little shops and stocked them from San Francisco. In time these establishments grew in size. The miners, out of a perverted sense of loyalty, or perhaps because they found more congenial company than at the Fort, patronized them. Sutter's stocks were undepleted.

He reasoned with their leaders in vain: the land was his and as honorable men they should pay him rent. They treated his arguments with contempt. What were obsolete Spanish and Mexican grants to a Government that owned every square inch of California? Hadn't the United States licked the daylights out of Mexico? America for the Americans.

2

No more gold flowed into Sutter's coffers. And his tanneries, his factories, his wineries were deserted; every employee, even the Indians, had fled to the mines. No more did skippers from Boston, traders from South America, sail up the Sacramento River for his hides and tallow, his wines and brandies.

But worse was to come. His richest acres were seized by squatters, and their argument was the same: America for the Americans. Moreover, they slaughtered his cattle and sheep and stole his horses.

Once more Sutter appealed to the Governor, and was reminded that the validity of the Spanish and Mexican grants was doubtful. He was advised to take his troubles to the Government of the United States.

One thing above all else saddened him: his wife and three younger children, after seventeen long years of separation, were to join him at last. He had reveled in the thought of conducting them proudly over an empire, that vast expanse between two mountain ranges, with its rivers, its woods of ancient oaks with their soft gray "beards," its acres of golden poppies in springtime, its orchards, farms, its great ranges, its vaqueros swinging their lassos amidst vast herds of cattle. Why, oh, why, could he not have sent for them five years earlier?

It must be remembered that before the Gold Rush Californians had transacted business, domestic and foreign, entirely by trading. There was little or no currency in the Department. They traded hides and tallow with the Boston skippers, foodstuffs with the Russians at Sitka, for such necessities and luxuries as they could not make themselves.

Sutter, despite the fact that he was regarded as the wealthiest man in California with the possible exception of Vallejo, had rarely seen a bit of paper money, much less a pile of minted gold. There was no one to whom he could sell land in sufficient quantities to cover the expenses of travel from Switzerland to California until San Francisco became a veritable American city and he could exchange his nuggets and "dust" for coin.

Moreover, he had been deeply in debt. He had bought the Russian grant and all it contained in 1841 for $30,000, and had never been able fully to discharge the debt; he had incurred other debts in order to make payments from time to time.

But in 1850, he did send for his family, and knew that it would be nearly two years before he could expect them, for mail and travel were slow.

3

The Fort, barren and uncomfortable, was no place for women; moreover, he was now bitterly ashamed of Sacramento—and he had written of it to his wife in such glowing terms! One of his richest properties, as yet uninvaded by the miners, was Hock Farm on the Feather River. The ground was elevated and therefore safe from floods. There he built a fine spacious house and furnished it lavishly. He moved into it, taking three cannon with him. His powers wrested from him, the Fort was but a mockery and he never wanted to see it again. He rented it for three hundred dollars a month. He might spend the rest of his life in litigation, but at least Hock Farm (its ugly name derived from a neighboring tribe of Indians) should be his haven. There, amidst the beauties of nature, he would live peacefully with his family.

They arrived late in 1851, and for a time he was happy and forgot his wrongs. His daughter, Anna, now twenty-three, was as beautiful as her mother had been in her youth; his two younger sons, Emil and William, were well-mannered and affectionate. Not only were they happy to be with their father again, but delighted to be in this fabulous land of which all the world was talking.

His family life was brief, however. His eldest son, John, married and moved to Acapulco in Mexico. Anna married and followed him. Emil, who had inherited his father's roving spirit, drifted away in search of adventure. William also married and left the valley.

Sutter was left alone with his wife, who, unless maligned by the artist who painted her, had a mouth as hard as an Indian bow drawn for action, small suspicious hostile eyes, and a long prying nose. No doubt she henpecked him.

4

Sutter sent an attorney to Washington to plead his case before the Supreme Court of the United States; if his grants were confirmed all would be well. Meanwhile, he employed lawyers to deal with the squatters, and they fleeced him unmercifully. He gave his power of attorney to friends who were either careless or dishonorable. Sutter, the most honest of men, was no match for high-class sharpers. Despite the adventurous life he had led, the immense power he had wielded for long years, he never became a "man of the world"; he had never learned business as it is practiced in cities where men sharpen their wits upon one another and money is god.

During his brief tenure of office, the Mexican governor, Micheltorena, had given Sutter an immense rancho as a reward for supporting him in his war with Alvarado. Despite all that Alvarado had done for him, Sutter had believed that his first duty was to the accredited governor of his Department; a mistaken sense of loyalty he regretted as long as he lived. The Supreme Court finally confirmed the original Spanish grant, New Helvetia, but decided that the title to the twenty-two leagues known as the Sobrante Rancho was illegal.

The squatters on the New Helvetia grant refused to budge, and the government declined to interest itself further. Sutter had no recourse but the courts of San Francisco. Moreover, since he had sold many farms on Sobrante, and since their owners were too proud to "squat" and demanded recompense, he was obliged to give them farms on New Helvetia.

He still had Hock Farm, however, and there at least he could live in peace and comparative plenty. But that, too, was lost through the chicanery of one of the men to whom he had given his power of attorney; it was attached in 1865 for a debt of which he had known nothing, and he found himself without an acre of land and very little money. And before he could move away the house burned down and with it went the valuable records of his pioneer days.

In 1870, totally impoverished, he appealed to the Governor for help and in that year and again in 1875 the state Legislature passed a bill appropriating $250 a month for his support. On this he managed to live and keep his case before Congress; his demand being as much of the unsold public lands as the Supreme Court of the United States had taken from him, or its equivalent in money, estimated as close to $100,000.

Meanwhile, thoroughly disgusted with California and all its works, he moved to Lititz, in Pennsylvania. Though he was still healthy, he suffered from rheumatism at times and a friend had told him of the healing waters of Lititz. A second recommendation was its admirable schools. There he lived for the rest of his life with his wife and the three children of his son, John.

And there at last he found peace; what little he had would not be taken from him, and, always the optimist, he believed in the integrity—and gratitude—of the United States; believed that he would leave a fortune to his beloved children. His new life was very pleasant. He read many books, and was held in great esteem by his fellow citizens, who pronounced him the most interesting conversationalist they had ever known.

He went to Washington every year, always hopeful, always disappointed. On June 17, 1880, he died in a Washington hotel.

California and the United States treated Sutter with the basest ingratitude and should blush whenever they see his name in print.

When Vallejo was state senator from the Sonoma district, in 1850, he was a member of the committee appointed to divide the new state into counties, and he named one for Sutter.

San Francisco has honored him with a street.

Sutter's Fort has been restored and is a show place for tourists.

At least he is not forgotten!

Vallejo

For a time after his return to Sonoma from Fort Sutter, Vallejo gave himself up to the pleasures of family life, to long rides over his ranchos with his children, to indulgence in dreams of a glorious future for California, and would have been completely happy had it not been for the death of one of his brood. A few months later, however, another infant arrived—the tenth. Before beneficent nature called a halt, Doña Francisca presented him with sixteen, of whom nine survived; and no other cloud ever darkened his domestic life.

Doña Francisca, reserved and often haughty in public, was an amiable and intelligent companion to her husband, a devoted mother and admirable housewife. She had a charming voice and sang to her own accompaniment with the guitar. But perhaps the most remarkable of her achievements, considering that she had married at fourteen and added to the Vallejo clan at brief intervals, was the retention of her good looks. At this time she was about thirty and looked like a young girl, but even in her old age she was handsome, erect, and stately. Spanish women mature early and are middle-aged at thirty, but Doña Francisca was the notable exception, and the more so as in her day the human race knew nothing of the laws of health, diet, exercise, vitamins, and beauty parlors.

Vallejo was now thirty-nine and in the full vigor of his manhood, ambitious and eager for action. As time passed, however, his complacency was shadowed; he began to wonder if California's new godmother was much of an improvement on the old. Except for the magnificent harbor of San Francisco and the steady stream of gold flowing from the placers, she appeared to take no interest in what Vallejo believed to be the brightest jewel in her crown. The United States Congress should have provided the new territory with a definite set of laws, a stable government, but it did not. Since the military governors knew nothing of the conduct of civilian affairs, the result was confusion, almost chaos. The squatters were becoming a menace, the land grants of the Spanish and Mexican régimes had not been confirmed, no Legislature had been called, there seemed to be no prospect of self-government in local affairs.

Vallejo, always generous and lavish, had taken pity on a number of the wretched immigrants who had arrived in the years before the gold rush and rented them small farms on his ranchos. He had also clothed and fed them as long as it was necessary, given them cows, sheep, chickens, seeds, and cuttings. They professed to be grateful and gave no trouble.

But, in 1849, others who had met with ill luck at the mines or gambled away their "dust" in San Francisco, began to straggle into the great ranchos of the northern and central valleys and "squat"; Sutter was not the only victim. Remonstrance was futile, the Governors were indifferent, and there was no other law to appeal to. Vallejo would not have hesitated to employ force, but he was no longer Commandante Militar of Sonoma and his barracks were empty.

Rumors came to him of agitation and disorder among the Americans and he decided to go down to San Francisco and investigate.

2

The Americans in the territory, those who took no interest in the mines and had come to California for other purposes, were uneasy and wrathful. Among them were many who were destined to play a leading part in the history of the future state: William Gwin of Tennessee, a subtle, brilliant intellectual and suave politician; David Broderick, who had been a fireman and ward politician in New York, a man of little education but of immense native ability and unbounded political ambition; William T. Coleman; Horace Hawes; Eugene Casserly; Peter H. Burnett; James King of Wm.; Joseph B. Fulsom; John W. Geary; Thomas B. King; Robert Semple; our old friend Samuel Brannan; and that future Associate Justice of the Supreme Court of the United States, Stephen J. Field.

Gwin and Broderick had not been in San Francisco a month before they were declared enemies and rivals, and other men had begun to bet on their political futures. Gwin, handsome, stately, patrician, was the favorite, but, although Broderick looked like a chimpanzee and dressed like a roughneck, he was by no means despised; he had an eye of remarkable penetration and power, he was magnetic and kind, and there was no political trick he had not learned in the purlieus of Manhattan.

Personal preferences aside, the two men led opposite factions. Should California become a slave state or should she not? Gwin said, "Yes." Broderick thundered, "No!" Although there was already a considerable number of Southerners in San Francisco, they were still numerically inferior to those able men from the North who were determined that slavery should never disgrace California. Both parties were indignant that their adopted "country" was not given statehood at once, that they might elect their own governor and Legislature, and settle the hundred and one problems that confronted them.

When Vallejo arrived in San Francisco, he was told that the United States Congress was responsible for the turmoil in California. It was rocking on its foundations over the slave question; the free and slave states were evenly balanced at present and both North and South were determined that California should tip that balance in its favor and increase its power. For a time it looked as if the Civil War would begin in 1849 and California be the precipitating agent.

Vallejo was told that these men of San Francisco, whose careers were at stake, had besieged General Mason, the fourth of the military governors, to call a Constitutional Convention, but Mason, although sympathetic, refused to take so radical a step. Vallejo informed his new friends, Gwin, Sam Brannan, and others, that he had written to a number of the rancheros advising the same course and had received a favorable response from the more energetic of them. Laws must be drawn up and enforced in California or no man would know whether or not he owned an acre of his inheritance. If the United States, quoth Californians old and new, continued to ignore them, they would make their own laws and to the devil with the consequences. News traveled slowly, Washington was three thousand miles away and too busy to know or care what they did.

While these men were debating what step to take first, Brigadier General Riley arrived in California to replace Governor Mason. He was advised by the latter to accede to the demands of the territorials and call a convention. Otherwise he would have no peace day or night; Mason was thankful to get out while there was still some flesh left on his bones.

Riley ordered a general election on August 1, 1849. Even the discovery of the *placeros* had not thrown the Californians into such a state of excitement and confusion. The Americans, who knew how to organize their forces, elected twenty-eight of the thirty-seven delegates; the "natives," who had never heard of polls nor electioneering technique, sent but nine to the convention; Vallejo and Don Pablo de la Guerra of Santa Barbara were the only delegates of distinction.

The convention assembled in Colton Hall, Monterey, on September first and sat for a month and a half. Semple was elected chairman, and Vallejo spokesman for the Spanish-Californians.

The burning question of slavery was disposed of first. The majority of the Americans were Northerners, and the gentlemen from the South accepted defeat gracefully (after a grand display of oratory), and devoted their talents to the framing of a constitution that would ensure order and the safety and prosperity of their new homeland.

The state constitution of New York was finally accepted as a model, and submitted to the people in November. It was ratified without dissension. Peter H. Burnett was elected governor of California, John McDougal lieutenant governor. On December first the Legislature met in San José, and Gwin and Frémont (who had turned up again) were elected United States Senators, Edward Gilbert and George W. Wright to the House of Representatives. They had a lively time in

Washington as there was some question as to their status, but on September 9, 1850, California became the thirty-first state in the Union.

3

Vallejo served in that first Legislature, but he soon retired from politics. It was evident that the Americans intended to rule the state and he was too proud to play a minor part. Moreover, private affairs claimed his attention. The men sent to Congress had orders to press the claims of the rancheros for immediate confirmation of the Spanish and Mexican land grants; but nothing had been accomplished by the end of his first term, and the Governor and Legislature refused to take action of any kind. Vallejo knew that their secret sympathies were with the American squatters, although this they volubly denied; they both liked and feared the still potent Lord of the North and heartily "wished him well." He returned to Sonoma with a low opinion of politics in general.

4

Vallejo forgot the squatters for a time. His eldest daughter, Epifania, was betrothed to a young naval officer, Captain John Frisbie, and in the old adobe mansion on the plaza no one had time nor thought for anything but preparations for the wedding. And not only was Casa Grande filled with guests, but aunts, cousins, and friends from San Diego to Sonoma overflowed the houses of Leese, Prudon, and Salvador Vallejo. The male guests, when they arrived, would camp in the barracks.

And all these women from morn till eve worked on the trousseau. Captain Frisbie, being a mere American, could not be expected to supply the *donas* of old, and every thread of the deshalados was drawn by the expert fingers of ladies accomplished in all the domestic arts. They cut and fitted innumerable gowns of silk, satin, lace, white and colored lawn; undergarments and nightgowns so fine they could have been drawn through the bride's wedding ring. The Indian maids had nothing to do but weave blankets and draw the threads of bed linen.

Presents arrived daily: mantillas, fans, Roman sashes, Chinese shawls, jewels, and a dozen pairs of silk stockings direct from Paris.

Epifania was that rarest of all Spanish beauties, a brown-eyed blonde, her golden hair an inheritance from those Visigoth invaders of Spain in the fifth century. Her features were regular, her body tall, slim, rounded, and graceful. But her liveliness and wit had attracted the American as much as her beauty; he paid her the highest compliment in his repertory—although he knew better than to utter it: she might almost have been an American girl with her quick wit, her sauciness, her frank careless gaiety. He was a lucky man, Captain John Frisbie, and, to do him justice, he never forgot it.

The house was in a constant state of uproar, particularly when the presents arrived. Doña Francisca, who must have possessed an enviable set of nerves, placidly presided over the infinite variety of the trousseau and the decorations for the wedding. Vallejo beamed with paternal satisfaction, and when the laughter and chatter (mingled with the squalls of his latest offspring) reached too high a crescendo he took refuge in his library and read *Don Quixote* or the latest newspapers and reviews from Boston. Sutter arrived on the day before the wedding and they took a long walk and found comfort in cursing the United States Congress.

He was well content that his daughter should marry a man of the dominant race, a fine young fellow, and of good family to boot. But that was not the only cause of his satisfaction. He might no longer be Commandante Militar, but he had informed the governor, in his genial but lordly manner, that

the first of the new generation of Vallejos to marry demanded
the pomp and ceremony of a military wedding: it cost the
governor nothing to order a regiment to arrive in Sonoma on
the day before the greatest social event in the history of the
north, and camp in the barracks with the other male guests.

5

The great day arrived. From all the windows in the
plaza hung fabrics of every hue: rugs, serapes, shawls. The
patio was equally colorful with oleanders, roses, geraniums,
branches of apple blossoms, golden poppies. The military
stood at attention in two rows on the north side of the plaza.

The band of the San Francisco Presidio played a wedding
march as the bride appeared on the arm of her father. She
wore a high-necked, long-sleeved gown of white satin, its
many lace flounces billowing over a small hoop skirt, and a
veil of white chantilly lace, worn by her mother and many
grandmothers before her. She held her head very high but
her eyes were modestly downcast.

Don Mariano, the proudest father in all California, was in
full regimentals. The bridegroom, escorting Doña Francisca
(in pale gray satin and many jewels), was also in full uniform.
The guests following displayed every hue as yet invented by
art or nature.

Epifania's two younger sisters, Adela and Natalia, had
woven a great wedding bell of jasmine flowers, magnolia
buds, and orange blossoms, and under this work of art and
love the wedding party passed to cross the plaza and enter
the chapel.

The wedding took place at ten in the morning, and when
the nuptial high Mass was over and the thunder of artillery
that greeted the young couple as they left the church had
died away, there were many hours for the entertainment of
guests. They sat at tables in the house and the plaza and

partook of venison, tamales, chicken smothered in cream, quail fried in oil, vegetables and fruits, dulces, and mellow Mission wines.

The young people danced in the sala for a time, but the fun was in the plaza. There was a bull-bear fight; there were rooster fights, feats of horsemanship, horse and foot races beyond the walls. They kept it up with no sign of fatigue until late in the afternoon, when the guests departed amidst a chatter of congratulations and appreciation. Captain Frisbie had married into a sturdy race—and it may be mentioned in passing that his Epifania outdid her mother and enriched the population with twenty-two boys and girls, some of whom survived.

6

At the foot of a mountain not far from Sonoma was a spring with a romantic history. Once upon a time an Indian maiden whose lover had fallen in one of the tribal wars retired to a secluded spot to weep alone. She wept so long and so abundantly that her tears seeped down between the rocks, and that accumulated wealth of sacred water boiled upward into a spring that was famous throughout California.

The old adobe house in the Fort was too small for his ever-increasing family, and, in 1851, Vallejo selected this spring site for a house double its size. It came " 'round the Horn" (in sections) from Boston, a large, frame, gabled mansion with a living-room forty by twenty-five feet, a big square dining room, the General's library for his many books in Spanish, French, and English, and a bedroom on the ground floor. Two of the rooms had fireplaces with marble mantels, and the walls were papered with colonial patterns. Above the circular staircase were rooms for the rest of the family—and a bath!

The waters of the spring were diverted into a lake, where

the children paddled, sailed their toy boats, and even had a little gondola of true Venetian pattern.

The grounds, already abundantly supplied with trees, were laid out with orange and olive groves—golden fruit and silver leaves!—further embellished with fountains and statuary. At one end of the park was a Swiss chalet, also imported, and beyond were orchards, vineyards, the usual grist mill and warehouses, the servants' quarters, and a corral for the horses.

Vallejo christened his new home Lachryma Montis—tear of the mountain; rather a sad name for so happy a household.

Adela's wedding to a brother of Captain Frisbie was even grander than her sister's. Adela was a brunette beauty (all the Vallejo children were handsome) and her husband was as fair and good-looking as her brother-in-law. Vallejo invited many of his new American friends, including the Governor, and the wedding march was played on one of the three first pianos to arrive in California.

7

Vallejo built a house in San Francisco on the street named for him and was warmly welcomed by the Southern set. But despite his harmonious family life and social popularity, his mind was seldom free of anxiety. The squatters seized more and more of his land, and those whom he had befriended before the discovery of gold now refused to pay rent. Their ingratitude at first stunned, then angered, him, and he told them that when the grants were confirmed they should go with the rest. They laughed and told him to do his worst and be damned.

He took his case to the San Francisco courts and became involved in endless and expensive litigation. He was forced to mortgage or sell tracts of his ranchos to pay the fees of lawyers who knew when they had a good thing and resorted to every legal device to prolong the suits.

He also had two claims against the United States Government and was obliged to keep a lawyer in Washington to press them. One was a bill of $117,000 for damages, loss of stock, grain, and other properties consequent upon the Bear Flag Revolution. In 1852, the Claims Committee paid him $48,000, which barely covered his lawyers' fees. Another disputed bill was $20,000 for rent of his buildings in Sonoma for seven years. In 1856, the case was settled for $12,500.

There had been nothing in Vallejo's life to teach him even the academic definition of the word economy, and little heretofore to disturb his faith in the honor and justice of his fellow men. Brilliant and versatile intellectually, he had no head for business, and the men of his own race, whatever their faults, were too proud to cheat and deceive. So were a number of his good friends in San Francisco.

But he was rapidly becoming disillusioned.

One of the men he befriended was an Irish immigrant whom we will call Tim Flanagan, who arrived in California without a penny in his jeans. Hearing of Vallejo's careless generosity and sympathy for the unfortunate, he tramped to Lachryma Montis and asked for a job. He was a clever and entertaining fellow; Vallejo took a fancy to him and appointed him town constable of Sonoma. Several years later, when the Nevada mines were discovered and Flanagan expressed a wish to seek his fortune there, Vallejo staked him with several thousand dollars, accepting his note without hesitation; by that time he was convinced that Flanagan was a man of uncommon abilities.

His belief was justified. The Nevada mines were unbelievably rich. Flanagan became a millionaire. But it was long since Vallejo had heard from him; it was evident that Flanagan had forgotten that loan, without which he might still be constable of Sonoma. But Vallejo was not disturbed; Flanagan was his friend, and, he was convinced, as honorable as he was able. Any man might suffer from lapses of memory while accumulating millions in that madhouse, Virginia City.

But the time came when he needed the money, and he wrote Flanagan an elegantly worded letter asking his former employee if it were convenient to repay the loan—without interest, of course. It was a difficult letter to write, for his haughty spirit hated the mere mention of money between friends. But he was trying to become a realist.

Flanagan ignored the letter. Vallejo, angry and disgusted, took the matter to court. Time had outlawed the note. Vallejo was heard to declare that "laws were made for scoundrels."

But Vallejo's genial nature could not harbor bitterness for long, and life was teaching him an accommodating philosophy.

Moreover, he had other interests and consolations. His eldest son, Platon, graduated from Saint Mary's College in Baltimore at the age of eighteen, carrying off all the honors. He entered the College of Physicians and Surgeons at Columbia University, but his studies were interrupted by the Civil War, during which he served in the Union army as a volunteer surgeon. When the war was over, he returned to the University and graduated first in his class, receiving the Faculty Prize. For a time after his return to the Pacific coast he was surgeon on a Pacific Mail steamer plying between San Francisco and Panama, but, in 1868, he married Miss Lillie Poole Wiley of New York and settled in the now flourishing town of Vallejo. Although he received many offers to practice in San Francisco, he preferred the life of a country doctor and became famous throughout the north for his exceptional skill, his benevolence, and his professional enthusiasm. Very often he had to ride ninety miles a day on his rounds, but, like all the Vallejos who managed to grow up, he had a constitution of tempered steel. He also had their lavish generosity, and merely smiled when his poorer patients paid a bill with a load of hay, a turkey, or a brace of ducks.

While he was still at college, another event occurred to

divert Vallejo's attention from interminable litigation and shrinking acres. In 1860, Colonel A. Haraszthy, a Hungarian wine expert, arrived in Sonoma, his object being to ascertain if the famed climate and fertility of California were myth or fact. He arrived in the spring when the climate was on its best behavior, and as he galloped with his host, Don Mariano Vallejo, over the beautiful valleys between two ranges of high hills magnificently wooded, the land, where not under cultivation, such a carpet of wild flowers as he had never seen even in Greece, he concluded that here was the place above all others to convert grapes into champagne. He came to an agreement with Vallejo, returned to Hungary to settle his affairs there, and came back to California with his sons, Attila and Arpad. These handsome and ardent young gentlemen promptly fell in love with Natalia and Jovita Vallejo, and there was a grand double wedding, as magnificent as if Vallejo were still a man of potential millions.

The large tract of land chosen for the vineyards was several miles south of the squatter colony, and Colonel Haraszthy and his two stalwart sons let it be known that they would shoot any man who encroached upon their preserves. They were not molested.

Such was the beginning of the great champagne industry of California. The "Golden State champagne" became famous throughout the world—and often came back to the United States in bottles ornamented with French labels. Its prosperity continued until Prohibition. While that disastrous law was still impending, Senator James D. Phelan offered to buy up all the stock on hand, only to discover that France had already bought two-thirds of it.

8

Only one of Vallejo's land grants was confirmed and, between the squatters and litigation, his great estate shrank to three hundred acres. But thanks to the Haraszthys, he was not reduced to poverty; his daughters had married well, his younger sons were prosperous, and Platon had the largest practice in California.

He retained his vigor and good looks, his erect military carriage to the last. Nor did his social popularity wane. He sold his house in San Francisco, but after the Palace Hotel was built he became a frequent visitor at that famous hostelry and met all its distinguished guests. One of them, the exiled Mexican poet Guillermo Prierte, wrote of him: "General Vallejo is now a man of over seventy, but broad-shouldered and active as any youth, with not a trace of white in his hair and stormy whiskers. Laughter comes easily to his lips and his speech is salty."

As he was a brilliant and accomplished speaker, he was chairman at many public dinners at the Palace Hotel, and equally sought after in private.

And he was happy with his Doña, his children and grand-children—whose number I dare not venture to enumerate. One of his favorites was Francisca Carillo Vallejo (daughter of Platon), now Mrs. McGettigan, and a poet and composer.

His death, on January 18, 1900, had a quaint touch of modernity, and nothing could more strikingly illustrate the aeons that had elapsed since "The Days of the Dons."

His illness was brief, and when it became known that he had but a few hours to live the editor of the Sonoma *Tribune-Index* held up his presses in order to be the first to proclaim the news and get ahead of his San Francisco rivals. He sent his daughter, a girl of twelve, to sit up all night if necessary on the veranda of Lachryma Montis. The poor child, nearly frozen, fell asleep, but when a weeping member of the family ran out of the house and shook her, sobbing that the great man was no more, she ran all the way to Sonoma. The presses clattered and two hours later every newspaper in California had an extra on the street.

Vallejo is the name of a street in the fashionable Western Addition of San Francisco. Vallejo had once fondly hoped that the town he founded, and which was named for him, would be the state capital. But it was not to be. As he figures largely in every history of California, however, he needed not those small tributes to his fame.

Vale, Vallejo, the last and the grandest of the Dons.

The Peraltas

In 1820, the Viceroy of New Spain gave Luis Peralta a grant of land on the east side of the Bay, a region known as Contra Costa, and comprising forty-eight thousand acres. Today those acres are covered by the cities of Oakland, Piedmont, Berkeley, Alameda, San Leandro, Albany, and half of Richmond; but at that time it was a beautiful expanse of rolling hills and irregular valleys green in winter and spring, golden in summer, brown in late autumn; woods of live oak, sycamore, and laurel; creeks; thousands of acres of good grazing and farm land—bounded on the east by the Contra Costa Mountains.

In 1826, Don Luis, who preferred to live in San José, divided the San Antonia rancho between his four sons, Vicente, José Domingo, Ignacio, and Antonio. There, in four large adobe haciendas, they lived the usual life of the California rancheros, and raised many children and great herds of cattle, horses, and sheep. Vaqueros took care of the livestock, Indians tilled the land. The brothers traded hides and tallow with the Boston skippers for silks, satins, slippers, shawls, and other luxuries, and had little themselves to do but gallop about their property for exercise, entertain other rancheros, visit Monterey to race their blooded horses and enjoy the lively society of the capital. So they expected to live to a ripe old age: a life of ease, pleasure, and plenty. So would their children after them. Viva California.

They regarded the American occupation without alarm, for all they knew of the United States were its honest skippers and the Americans already in the province. They had little or no contact with the *placeros,* and looked upon the mushroom growth of San Francisco with satisfaction. More pleasant gentlemen, a steady market for wheat and lumber. When several of the newcomers made handsome offers for "a hundred acres or so," they laughed inwardly but declined with flowers of speech.

But in 1850 they ceased to laugh. One Edson Adams deliberately staked a claim of a hundred and fifty acres on Don Vicente's rancho, slaughtered his cattle and felled his trees. Two friends of his, Andrew Moon and a man named Carpentier, squatted on either side. Don Vicente sent his vaqueros to drive them off, but lassoos and a torrent of Spanish invective were no match for shotguns.

Three men, all named Patten, had the grace to ask for the lease of a tract for eight years, and Don Vicente, grown wiser and less optimistic, signed the lease. In 1851, the unjust "Squatter's Act" was passed and thereafter they paid no rent. Don Vicente and his brothers, who were also having trouble with squatters, took their cases to the San Francisco courts, with the usual results. The laws were American.

2

Adams, Moon, and Carpentier were able and ambitious men. Here was the site for a city that should rival San Francisco. They called in a surveyor and proceeded to lay it out: a business section on the flat near the Bay, a residence quarter on the rolling hills. A map of the embryo city of Oakland was displayed in San Francisco and advertisements in the newspapers invited those who would enjoy life in a region free from fogs, winds, sandy and rocky hills, to come over and settle; prices for every purse.

The response was enthusiastic. Dwellings, business houses, shops, rose with the rapidity of that era. Before 1853, there were a mayor, a board of aldermen, a church, a public school, and a college. Trees were planted along the residential streets. There was a garden plot before every house.

Lake Merritt, near the center of the city, was surrounded by handsome houses, the country homes of wealthy San Franciscans. The gardens were almost as imposing as the mansions with their statues, fountains, graveled paths between the flower beds, and ornamental trees. Weeping willows trailed over the verge of the lake, which was lively in summer with rowboats and canoes, pretty girls and fine-looking young men. These summer months were the delight of the young people of San Francisco, and many a proposal which had hung fire in the tempestuous atmosphere of the city was whispered on moonlight nights under the protecting shade of the willows. On the north side was a small tavern known as "Old Blaze's," where the young men could refresh themselves while the girls waited patiently in boat or canoe.

3

In due course the other towns were founded, and flourished. The Peraltas sold what land they could and retired from the scene. There is a Peralta Street in Oakland. Others of the despoiled were similarly honored.

No one can dispute the fact that the Americans accomplished a great work; that Contra Costa if left to the Californians might be just one more big rancho today, that Oakland, the second city of the north, would never have been born, that there would have been no Berkeley, one of the beauty spots of the state, to surround the University of California.

No one cares that "the lazy, pleasure-loving, unenterprising Californians" were robbed and practically wiped out. Would the north have possessed Mills College or the University? Would they have built beautiful cities with hotels and shops that New York might envy?

No. But if the Peraltas and others like them were bound to go down before the irresistible Law of Progress, the Congress of the United States would have fewer blots on its 'scutcheon if it had compelled the invaders to pay for their grabs. But, as we have seen, Congress was too occupied with the verbal war between the North and the South to give heed to the conquered in California. They were of no account anyhow. They'd had their day. Let them take their medicine. The race was to the strong.

It is true that the skull content of those old rancheros and caballeros, with a few notable exceptions, may have been inferior, but they contributed a chapter of elegance, romance, and beauty unsurpassed by any other state in the Union; they knew how to *live;* they knew the meaning of contentment and happiness, an achievement denied to mortals in general. Congress violated the Constitution and the Bill of Rights in its treatment of Californians of Spanish blood, for they were citizens of the United States and entitled to the protection of its laws.

A Lopsided Romance

The southern rancheros suffered less than their northern counterparts from the squatters, but they were despoiled in another fashion. Several hundred of the meanest Yankees in the U. S. A. swarmed into the south and opened stores in Santa Barbara, Los Angeles, San Diego, and the smaller towns, displaying every luxury and necessity to tempt the always self-indulgent and extravagant hidalgos and their ladies. The Californians had no money to pay for these desirables, but the shopkeepers were very accommodating: just a little mortgage on a little piece of land; they were in no hurry.

The Californians, whose only business transactions had been with the Boston skippers, believed that all Americans were as honest as they were clever; they signed the documents without hesitation, assuming with their usual careless optimism that the money would come from somewhere before the final payments were due; no doubt many of those men who had made fortunes in the *placeros* would come and buy little ranchos in the south, preferring it to the less salubrious north. And if not, what matter? They had thousands and thousands of acres; if a few had to go they would never be missed. And never had the old Boston skippers brought them such satins and silks, such dainty ready-made costumes, such hats, such laces and jewels, such superb furniture—even pianos—such crystal and silver!

The shopkeepers charged exorbitant prices for their wares and a high rate of interest. More and more acres were mortgaged. More and more.

2

It must have been some time during the 1860's that a wealthy and distinguished lawyer from the East paid a visit to Southern California. Let us call him Mr. Abel Eustace Harrison.

He brought a letter to Don Diego Vibora who owned a rancho of two hundred and fifty thousand acres, every furlong of which was mortgaged. Nevertheless, Mr. Harrison was entertained with the elegance that became one of the great hidalgos of the south. Horses as gaily caparisoned as of old, American buggies, filled the courtyard. There was a dance every night. Never had Mr. Harrison seen horses so beautiful, golden in color with manes and tails like flowing silver. Never had he seen such beautiful girls, eaten such delicious food, breathed such balmy air. He made up his mind to spend the rest of his life in California.

Don Diego had several daughters. The eldest, Erlinda

Benicia Rosario, was not a beauty, but she had a fine pair of black eyes, a tall graceful figure, and she was the most vivacious and charming girl Mr. Harrison had ever met. He fell in love with her and asked her hand of Don Diego like the courtly gentleman he was. The ruined lord of two hundred and fifty thousand acres drew a long breath of relief: one, at least, of his daughters would be provided for, and no doubt a rich son-in-law would be generous to himself.

But when he summoned Erlinda to his office and informed her of her good fortune she repudiated the offer with scorn. What! Marry that old thing? He must be forty—and she but seventeen. And did she not love José Mendito, the handsomest of the caballeros? She would marry him and none other.

Don Diego roared with disappointment and anger. How dared she defy the wishes of her father, she a well-brought-up California daughter? And would she throw away an opportunity that might never come again? For what? A penniless caballero whose every acre was mortgaged? To live with him in a hut? Would she live to see her father and mother, her sisters and brothers, begging their bread—or clerking perhaps to those damnable shopkeeping robbers—marrying them perhaps and living on her father's stolen ranchos?

But Erlinda was adamant. She was a high-spirited girl and was moved by neither arguments nor roars. Never would she marry Don Abel Harrison nor any other American. She hated them all. She would marry José Mendito. Did he wish to make her the unhappiest of mortals? Was that paternal love? She ran out of the room and slammed the door.

Don Diego, despite his tempers, was a soft-hearted man and loved his children, this clever, willful, independent girl most of all. His younger daughters were prettier and more amenable—true Spanish maidens who never would have dreamed of defying the will and judgment of their father; perhaps he loved Erlinda the more for that very dissimilarity (thus resembling himself) which now plunged him into the well of despair.

He sent for Mr. Harrison and told him sadly that Erlinda loved another and refused the honor of his hand. Don Abel could not be more disappointed than he was. *Madre de Dios!* What was the world coming to when a California girl refused to obey the will of her father? Possibly he was an old fool to submit to her imperious will, but he loved her and would die rather than make her unhappy.

Harrison had expected opposition, for the lady of his choice had made no secret of her indifference. But he was a man of inflexible will and determined to marry her. Don Diego had confided his desperate financial situation to this clever and congenial American, and Harrison had offered to "look into" his affairs. He studied them thoroughly.

As they sat in Don Diego's office, in deep comfortable chairs unknown to an earlier generation, and smoking the friendly cigaritos, Harrison appeared to ponder deeply. Finally he spoke.

"Don Diego," he said in a voice carefully charged with emotion, "I love your daughter and must marry her. She is too young to know her own mind, and it was natural for her to fall in love with a caballero—they are, assuredly, handsome fellows. But Don José is destined to be a clerk or a vaquero; he is a young man of neither brains nor energy. He would lead Erlinda a miserable life.

"Erlinda is a girl of intelligence and character. Married to a man who sincerely loved her, whom she could respect, who would give her the position of the greatest lady in the south, who would gratify every wish, she would learn to love her husband and forget her childish romance. You must persuade her, Don Diego."

"But I cannot! I cannot!" wailed poor Don Diego. "She has a will as hard as a diamond, that niña. She won't even speak to me. *Ay triste de mi!*"

"You must show her that your will is stronger," said Mr. Harrison firmly. "Moreover—" He hesitated a moment, then went on, his voice apologetic. "Do not be angry with me, Don Diego, if I seem indelicate—but this is no time for squeamishness. The future, the happiness of Erlinda as well as mine is at stake. . . . Compel her to marry me and I will buy up all the mortgages on your estate and present them to you on the day of the wedding."

Don Diego dropped his cigarito on the floor. *"Madre de Dios!"* he gasped. *"Dios de mi alma!* Do you mean—do you mean that I shall be a wealthy ranchero once more—carry on the great tradition of my family? My two hundred and fifty thousand acres! All mine again! *Dios de alma! Dios de mi vida!"*

"All yours again, Don Diego. Will you persuade her—"

"Persuade her!" roared Don Diego, bouncing to his feet. "I'll shut her up in her room on bread and water and keep her there until she comes to her senses." And he stumbled— he was a large heavy man—out of the room.

He kept his word. Erlinda was marched into her room forthwith, despite her mother's tears and her own fury.

"Here you stay!" he shouted, flourishing the key. "And not a bite shall you have to eat but dry bread, not a drop to drink but water. No sweet angelica, no tamales, no chicken con carne, no dulces. I will bring the bread and water myself twice a day."

The days passed. Erlinda grew hungrier and hungrier, thinner and thinner. She shuddered when she looked at herself in the mirror; her face was gaunt, her once rosy cheeks yellowish. For a time she was consoled by the voice of Don José warbling the love songs of Old California at her grating. But when hunger gnaws at the vitals and the mirror is unrelenting, romance expires. Moreover, what was the good of a man who could do nothing but sing? Why didn't he rescue her? Caballeros! She despised the whole lot of them. She ceased to go to the window, but lay on her bed too weak to storm up and down the room. She wept until her tears dried up, and those tears had been inspired not by the heart but by a clamoring stomach. She endured the ordeal for a fortnight, then sullenly yielded.

The wedding was the grandest that had been held in California for a generation. Harrison, who had heard of the *donas,* sent East for a magnificent trousseau. It included a wedding dress of Spanish lace and a diamond necklace. She was married in the old Mission church, crowded with family, relatives, and friends from every rancho in the south. There was a reception at the hacienda, a sumptuous breakfast at tables in the sala and courtyard. The bride looked handsome, stately, and well-fed. Her spirits had never been gayer. She was a sensible girl and accepted her fate. Don Diego beamed; he knew that every mortgage on his ranchos had been paid off.

When, after hours of feasting and the usual variety of entertainment, the company had gone and the bridegroom and his bride were about to depart on a honeymoon to San Francisco, Harrison nodded to Don Diego and they went into the office together.

"My dear father-in-law," said Harrison solemnly, "I have, after deep thought, come to a decision that I hope you will not question. To turn this great estate over to you would be the height of folly. Not one of your race has known how to protect his inheritance from squatters and sharks. You would have it mortgaged again before the year was out. I shall therefore keep it for your grandchildren and give you a handsome yearly allowance in cash—an allowance that will give you the comfortable feeling of security for the rest of your life. You are welcome to live here in the old house. I prefer to live in town and shall build a house there."

And he made a hasty exit, closing the door on the speechless Don Diego; but as he and his bride drove out of the courtyard, in a fine new open barouche, a loud and prolonged roar followed them.

In every other respect he kept his word. The don and his family were more comfortable and carefree than they had been for long years. He built for his bride the finest house in California, sent to Paris for a man to fresco it and decorate the walls, and furnished it with both comfort and elegance. Nor was it long before she became accepted as the Great Lady of the south, its unquestioned and envied leader.

She bore him a large family of handsome sons and daughters, was increasingly devoted to her aging husband, and after his death managed his affairs as well as he had done. The Spanish, despite their youthful aberrations, are not a sentimental nor a romantic people. Erlinda got all out of life there was in it for a clever, popular, charming, and wealthy woman. As far as is known, she never regretted her submission.

7. Hangtown

(and Grass Valley)

HANGTOWN, eight miles south of the placers, was founded by men of more modest ambitions than lust for sudden wealth. Its first name was "The Diggings," for fugitive gold flakes sprinkled the creek and neighboring ravines; the more ominous name was adopted later.

These pioneers—they were covered-wagon immigrants— lived in tents for a time while they felled trees and built cabins large enough to hold their families. Thereafter they tilled the land, planted orchards and vegetable gardens, bought cattle, sheep, horses, and chickens from Sutter, and looked forward to a life of peace and plenty.

Among the original settlers were men whose names were to be better known many years later: Mark Hopkins, who supplied his neighbors with groceries; Johnny Studebaker, blacksmith by trade, but who also made hundreds of wheelbarrows for the miners; Phil Armour, butcher.

The dwellings were on the two steep hillsides of a ravine, one of many in the Sierra foothills. Main Street, on either side of the creek on the broad floor of the cañon, was lined with stores, warehouses, a church, a saloon, and, in due course, a hotel—the Cory House, where Mark Twain, at a later date, spent a year or more and was visited by Horace Greeley. There was also a small building known as the Courthouse, and a jail, both of which were usually empty. The schoolhouse was perched on top of a hill.

The hills beyond their own, rising to the mountains above,

were a forest of pine, scrub oak, poplars, laurel, and the famous Sequoia gigantia.

No more charming spot was ever chosen by men with an eye for beauty as well as for fertile soil; a pleasant place to begin life over again and dwell in peace forevermore.

But peace, like the dove, hath wings.

The first shipload of gold-diggers were, as we know, a fine lot of men, but in the following year came the scum of the eastern cities, men who had never made an honest dollar and who swarmed into the land of gold with no intention of digging for it. They won dust and nuggets from the miners at the gaming tables or got them drunk and stole it from the tents at night.

They soon invaded The Diggings. Word had drifted north of the flakes of gold that had been found in the ravine by those who cared to look for it; not enough to cause another "rush" by honest miners, but easy money nevertheless; the scoundrels let nothing escape them.

One night three of them entered a cabin on the hill where a man lived alone, robbed him of his hoard, and threatened him with death unless he "kept his mouth shut."

But the man, although forced to yield at the point of three sharp knives, was not a coward. As soon as it was light he ran down the hill to Main Street and shouted his story, demanding vengeance. The good citizens of The Diggings, stunned at first that such an outrage should have been visited upon their peaceful God-fearing community, rallied and started in search of the miscreants. They rounded them up in a saloon where they were brazenly refreshing themselves, kicked them out, kicked them up and down Main Street, and lashed them with reatas. They yelled with pain and begged for mercy.

Grim justice, not mercy, was to be their portion. While the fun was at its height, a sheriff and his posse in search of three horse thieves rode down Main Street. They recognized their prey, dusty and bloody as the hounded were. And horse thieving in those days ranked in the crime calendar with murder.

On one side of Main Street was a great oak tree with a branch projecting across the creek, as stout as a man-made gallows. After an impromptu trial, demanded by the etiquette of the time, the men were formally pronounced guilty, and three bodies swung from the branch.

The citizens changed the name of their community to Hangtown and were proud of it.

Many more bodies dangled from that tree. If those respectable citizens could not have peace, at least they could mete justice to its destroyers and possibly throw fear into the hearts of others. And they had their own sheriff. Hangtown won a fearsome reputation, and in time was given as wide a berth by criminals as if the yellow flag of smallpox waved at either end of Main Street.

But Hangtown had more pleasant diversions. The first Pony Express rider raced down Main Street, waving his hand to the cheering inhabitants. Once a week Hank Monk drove his stage and six galloping horses up to the post office and delivered the mail. A great day in Hangtown, for all had left behind them relatives and friends whom they hardly expected to see again. And much as they loved California and Hangtown, they longed for news of the world beyond the Sierras. They also wrote enticing letters to the younger members of the communities they had left, but advised them to avoid "the trail" and come by ship to San Francisco; Hank Monk would deliver them safely to Hangtown. A number responded, and, in 1854, the town having grown large enough to be incorporated as a city (with a secret ambition to become the county seat), they changed the name to Placerville. But although duly recorded, in common speech it remained Hangtown for a generation. Historians have kept the name alive.

In 1846, it had been destroyed by fire, but the citizens, undismayed, at once set about rebuilding it. Even by that time they had a bank whose deposits had fortunately been rescued and conveyed by an armed guard to Sutter's Fort. This time they determined to have a real city, one of which northern California would be as proud as it was of San Francisco. Houses and buildings of all sorts came around the Horn, others were designed by a San Francisco architect. In 1859, after the discovery of the Comstock Lode in Nevada, the "Placerville Road" was hewn across the Sierras. Nevada was a semi-barren state, and Placerville supplied most of the edibles demanded by the miners growing rich with a velocity that for the time being wiped out the memory of the exhausted placers.

Placerville is still flourishing. Great quartz mines were discovered in the vicinity and they appear to be inexhaustible. Like other towns of its kind so fortunately close to the Sierras, Placerville has grown not only in wealth but in elegance. It has handsome hotels, shops, banks, and stately homes on the hills surrounded by gardens.

And the old name, of which it is still proud, is kept before the modern public by the *Pony Express Courier,* edited and published in Placerville by H. S. Hamlin, descendant of one of its first pioneers.

Grass Valley

If a stranger visits Grass Valley, at the northern tip of the Mother Lode, is he immediately and proudly informed that he is walking over or adjacent to some of the greatest quartz mines in the world: the Empire, the North Star, and the Idaho-Maryland, richer than the old placers and mined for nearly a century?

Not at all. He is led at once to the show spot of the town, a plain small cottage where Lola Montez lived for two years in the fifties, and where she raised cacti and flowers in a good-sized garden. "They do say she wore an old calico dress and a sun bonnet and got down on her knees and troweled. And there was a shanty where she kept a pet bear."

"They do say, too, she was a trollop and had a mighty bad reputation back in Europe, and once after the parson had preached against her and bade the decent citizens run her out of the town, calling her a 'scarlet woman,' what does she do but dress herself up in a flaunting Spanish outfit, burst into his house and dance a fandango before him and his good wife. They almost fainted, they were so scandalized, but somehow she made friends with them as she did with everybody else. Just irresistible she was. Hundreds of beautiful women, mebbe thousands, came to the mines in those days, but who remembers their names? There was only one Lola Montez."

2

There is, as far as I know, only one other house associated with the name of Lola Montez, and that is in Munich. It is larger than the one in Grass Valley but equally unpretentious, and is—or was—quite overshadowed by the British Legation next door. It, too, has a garden, but I doubt if she worked in it. In the tourist season, guides mentioned it casually in passing, but no Münchener ever referred to it in conversation. The Lola Montez episode in the annals of that beautiful and kingly city on the Isar were best forgotten. She was younger then and of an extraordinary beauty, but no woman was ever more hated; she made a fool of the old King and was the cause of a revolution.

Lola was born in Ireland of a good and highly respectable family. The name was Gilbert and she was christened Marie Dolores Eliza Rosana. Her mother was half Spanish, and to her Montalvo ancestors she owed her exotic beauty.

Her immense black eyes were as variable in expression as her moods, her dusky hair had a large natural wave, her complexion was rosy and fair; and her figure was so perfect in its curves and grace that her eyes were sometimes forgotten. She was an authentic beauty, a gift for which she should have burned incense to Aphrodite, Diana, and Juno, for she had little else save, to be sure, her abounding vitality charged with a thousand magnets. She was an indifferent dancer and a worse actress. Her mind was quick and audacious, but she had no intellect and less common sense.

She married several times, but the names of these casual husbands are not worth mentioning. Her lovers were almost as numerous as nuggets in the old *placeros*. They, too, had brief innings; she could fall wildly in love and cool off as abruptly. Nevertheless, she was gay and kind and sweet—to all but her frantic and too persistent lovers in the discard— and these qualities were not the least of her fascinations and won her many friends even among women.

The historic episode of her stormy life was played in Munich. She had danced in various capitals on the European continent and in London, but it was her beauty and magnetic charm, her fantastic reputation, that filled the theaters. The critics gave her meager praise, sometimes ridiculed her acting unmercifully, and she horsewhipped two of them.

Her gnawing ambition was to be the ballerina of Munich, the art center of Europe and the one capital to which she had not been invited.

Whether agents were employed in those days I know not, but certain it is that Lola would never have employed one. She drove into Munich in her traveling carriage, wearing a suit of pale blue English tweed with hat to match, sitting very erect but bowing graciously to staring passers-by, and put up at the best hotel. On the following day, dressed in a Parisian costume of blue-gray and cherry-red, a large hat covered with feathers tipped coquettishly over one eye, she presented herself at the door of the palace and demanded to see the King. The lackey was stunned no less by the dazzling vision and regal air than by the unconventionality of her demand. He stuttered that no one could have audience with His Majesty without the usual formalities. If the *Gnädiges Fräulein* would ask the English Minister to intercede—

Lola, looking more imperious than the Queen and all the royal family combined, brushed him aside, swept into the palace with a loud swish of her long skirts, and ordered him to announce her to the King at once. At once!

The flunkey, wondering if the world had turned upside down, so bereft was he of all power to resist, tottered into the royal presence and stammered out that a young lady in the most unorthodox and unheard-of manner had forced her way into the Residenz and demanded to see His Majesty at once.

"What does she look like?" asked Ludwig I characteristically. "Is she beautiful?"

"She is, Your Majesty. I have never seen anyone like her. She has big black eyes that flash like two suns; they scorched my own eyeballs. Her mouth is redder than her gown. Her form is like the goddesses in the Pinakothek. I had not the strength to deny her. I humbly crave pardon of Your Majesty."

"Show her in," said Ludwig.

Lola came; she was seen; she conquered.

3

Lola was quickly installed in a sumptuously refurnished house in the Barestrasse. She drove about Munich in her new carriage behind a spanking team of horses as black as her hair. She was given credit at all the fashionable shops, and her jewels rivaled those of the Tsarina, before whom she had danced in St. Petersburg.

But her new triumph was brief. She incurred the hatred of the clergy (she was a Protestant and Munich was the most Catholic of German cities); of the cabinet, for she presumed to interfere in politics; of the aristocracy, who resented her arrogance and the fact that she had made a fool of the old King; of the people, who were taxed that she might be covered with jewels like some heathen idol; finally of the students of the University, who were infuriated that she induced the King to dismiss two of the professors who had incurred her displeasure. The students mobbed her house; she dared not appear on the streets; the police, who liked her as little, swore they were unable to protect her. The King was forced to yield, and she departed for London, carrying her jewels with her and a small fortune in marks.

Her continental notoriety had preceded her and she danced to crowded houses and added guineas to marks, and more jewels.

She was tried for bigamy in London, but the learned judge was so moved by her plaintive plea that she had "forgotten all about the other husband," to say nothing of her bewildering self, that he dismissed the case. An American producer offered her a New York engagement and she accepted.

After a long series of successes and failures in the United States, she arrived in San Francisco in 1853.

Once more she had a triumph. Not only was she as beautiful as ever, but San Franciscans, always avid for sensation, welcomed the new diversion. She always made a little speech when her famous "Spider Dance" was finished, and they flung great bouquets and garlands at her feet, sometimes silver and gold in the good Old California fashion.

She was less successful in the mining towns, and horsewhipped another critic; she also excited disapproval for throwing out of the window a husband she had picked up in San Francisco, and his wardrobe after him.

The time came when she longed for peace and seclusion. She was tired of dancing, tired of crowds, sick of men.

The little town of Grass Valley, nestling in the gentle hills at the foot of the towering pine-clad Sierras, appealed to her and she bought a cottage and settled down to a quiet life with her garden, a bear, a monkey, and a parrot. Despite one or two indiscretions, she made many friends, the sincerest perhaps she had ever known. The women, at first excited by her flaming reputation, finally decided to disbelieve it. Undoubtedly her affair with the old King had been purely platonic, and as for the other "lovers," who were they anyhow? Could anyone mention a single name?

They had never met anyone so charming, so lovely, so amusing, so simple and friendly. She also gave liberally to the church and even attended service occasionally. And she taught little Lotta Crabtree how to dance, assuring the delighted friends of the Crabtree family that the child was born to be one of the greatest dancers of her time. Lola was a better teacher than dancer, and she knew whereof she spoke, for Lotta, a few years later, became the idol of the American public.

But her seclusion was not unbroken. In time, traveling artists, actors, singers, painters, and writers heard of her "romantic life in a cottage in the Gold Rush country" and sought her, at first from curiosity, and again because she fascinated and entertained them so charmingly. Her "salon" became famous. She danced for them and with them. Opera stars sang, poets recited, authors coyly read chapters from forthcoming novels, actors mouthed Shakespeare, the bear growled, the monkey chattered, the parrot screeched. A good time was had by all.

In 1855, after two years of Grass Valley and off-and-on peace, she felt a sudden longing for the world with its footlights and more varied excitements, and returned to it.

But the world was tired of Lola. Even her lectures upon how to be beautiful met with no success, for her own beauty had waned. In 1861, after she had given away, lost, pawned, or sold the last of her jewels, she died penniless and penitent in New York. She lies in Greenwood Cemetery and the name carved on her tombstone is Eliza Gilbert. Had she never sailed through the Golden Gate and won for herself a page in California history, she would be as forgotten in America today as are the thousand other stage beauties who have flashed and faded. Grass Valley was the one inspiration of her tragic life.

8. *"The Wickedest City on Earth"*

William T. Coleman

SAN FRANCISCO had improved in appearance if not in morals since 1851. The city was racing over the hills and up the valley, two new streets had been added to the waterfront on "made ground." Telegraph Hill was no longer a promontory, but still the chief landmark to mariners sailing through the Golden Gate. A semaphore on its top announced the approach of mail, passengers, cargo for shopkeepers; and many still ran through the streets and up the steep slope to watch the welcome sight. Where "Hounds" and "Sidney Coves" had once made their nefarious headquarters, Peruvians and Chilenos camped when not at the mines. The Irish and goats came later.

Telegraph Hill looked down with pride upon the city of which it was the guardian. Large blocks of business houses, banks, hotels, buildings of all kinds, including theaters, shops, and restaurants, had risen in Montgomery, Sansome, Front, and intersecting streets. Wealth poured into the city from the mines, the ranchos, from South America, the Sandwich (Hawaiian) Islands, and even from the East, for a lively business was done with hides, tallow, cereals, and other farm products. Importers of necessities and luxuries, merchants and shopkeepers—all accumulated wealth almost as rapidly as the golddiggers.

And spent it as freely. Prices were exorbitant, but no one complained; extravagance was a natural sequence of sudden prosperity in a young community that had leaped from adolescence into maturity almost overnight. Nor was it tempered by the electric climate, the excitements of this strange new life lived by men so recently come from older and more tranquil states.

They speculated wildly on the Stock Exchange. They were rich today and ruined tomorrow—and on the way to riches a month later.

In 1854-55, they paid the penalty of their recklessness with a panic during which banks failed, business houses crashed, and few escaped ruin. But after a period of depression during which there were many suicides, they pulled themselves together and began life over again.

2

As is often the case after a spectacular period of reform, the good citizens of San Francisco, having given their city a thorough purification, dismissed the subject from their minds and returned to the conduct of their own affairs. The underworld, cowed for the time being, bided its time. But not for long. Its numbers were augmented by every ship that anchored in the Bay. California was the land of easy money, and not only in the mines. Before a year had passed, more and gaudier gambling houses surrounded the Plaza. Prostitutes outnumbered the respectable women by a hundred to one. They claimed lower Dupont Street, now the fashionable Grant Avenue, as their own. By night their brothels flamed with light and were raucous with music. There was a long row of cottages where French women, scantily gowned, heavily painted, their hair dressed high on cushions, sat behind the open slats of shuttered windows by day and solicited the passers-by. But the majority promenaded Montgomery Street at the fashionable hour, and, in that uncomely costume of the era—flounced skirts over immense hoops, coal-scuttle bonnets, to say nothing of hair parted in the middle and plas-

tered over each ear—they were hardly to be distinguished
from the ladies of South Park and Rincon Hill. Many were
escorted by the professional gamblers or *maquereaus,* wearing fancy waistcoats, stovepipe hats, diamond studs, and carrying gold-headed canes. Nor could these women be kept out
of the fashionable shops; their twenty-dollar gold pieces,
fresh from the mint, rang temptingly on the counters and
the best was theirs.

And it would seem as if all the shyster lawyers in the eastern states had taken refuge in San Francisco to escape prison
or disbarment. Any one of those buzzards could be bought
by the highest bidder.

And the judges! They presided in their shirtsleeves with
their feet on the table, chewing tobacco, spitting, swearing,
shouting, and even cutting their corns. They were as venal
as the lawyers. To obtain a conviction for the most abominable crimes was almost impossible. Between 1851 and 1856, a
thousand murders had been committed in San Francisco, and
only one man condemned to death by law. (There were several impromptu lynchings down by the docks.)

Such men as Hall McAllister, Judge McKinstry, and a few
akin to them in honor if not in greatness, were like lone
green islands in a phosphorescent sea.

Another contribution from the East to the West, and to
San Francisco in particular, were professional politicians of
the lowest class, the spawn of great cities, who knew every
trick of the political game, and never permitted their minds
to be diverted by legitimate business. They soon obtained
control of San Francisco. It was they who "protected" the
shyster lawyers and appointed judges. They stuffed the ballot
boxes, and gangs of bullies were on hand to prevent honest
men from voting. They corrupted the police, the sheriff and
his deputies, the prosecuting attorneys; gamblers and prostitutes were their boon companions.

The decent citizens were outraged and often met in private

to discuss ways and means to save their city from complete rottenness before it was too late. But they were too absorbed in making money, or losing it, to spare several months from their personal affairs to reform San Francisco a second time. Some day—of course—let those scoundrels beware. . . .

During the panic of 1854-55, when banking and business houses failed, appalling scandals came to light in the following litigation. Men of the better class had engaged in dishonest practices, the treasury had been looted by officials. The press was equally corrupt—Sam Brannan had long since retired from journalism and, already California's first millionaire, had come unscathed through the panic. These newspapers had known of the rotten spots in the financial and business world, but had been bribed to silence. When at liberty to make their revelations, the good citizens, who, although reckless on the stock market, sometimes equally reckless in their business ventures, cursed volubly, wrung their hands, and mopped their brows.

Sam Brannan loudly demanded another Vigilance Committee, but still nothing was done. Not until 1856.

3

One of the leading citizens of San Francisco, one of the most liked and honored, was James King of Wm. (He had appended the given name of his father, when a schoolboy in Georgetown, D. C., to distinguish himself from another James King among his fellow students, and the habit persisted.) Shortly after his arrival in San Francisco, he had opened a banking house in partnership with one Jacob Snyder. The firm prospered for four years, and then, nearly ruined by the speculations of his partner, James King merged his bank with that of Adams and Company, which proved to be one of the houses doomed to failure and scandal.

Although he personally was above suspicion, he neverthe-

less wrote a series of pamphlets in which he explained to
the excited public his connection with Adams and Company
and how a new partner might be kept in ignorance of fraudu-
lent dealings for even a longer period than a few months.
These articles were so vivid in style, so lucid, so convincing,
that the public read them for their interest alone, and when
it became known that he had surrendered to the bank's credi-
tors every penny he possessed and desired to edit a newspaper, the money was raised at once. Heaven knew if there
was one thing San Francisco needed more than anything else
at this time it was an honest, fearless, authoritative newspaper so interesting that virtuous and wicked alike would
read it.

The San Francisco *Bulletin* was born on October 6, 1855.

In no respect was the public disappointed. A staff of clever
young men reported the news of the moment (and there was
always plenty of it), the dealings on the Stock Exchange, the
shipping news, such news as came in from other parts of the
state: all that a man was accustomed to read at his breakfast
table, although presented in more select prose, and inter-
spersed with as much humor as was consistent with dignity.
San Francisco still "had a murder every morning for breakfast," but even these were served up in a manner both dramatic and acid.

All this was very pleasing, but it was King's editorials that
shook the town.

The banks were excoriated, and then King proceeded to
blast David "Cataline" Broderick, "Boss of the most dastardly
set of politicians that ever infested a city." He exposed election frauds in minute detail and accused Broderick of striv-
ing by corrupt practice to get himself elected to the United
States Senate, of complicity in the Jenny Lind theater swin-
dle, one of the spectacular failures of the panic. "If we can
only escape David C. Broderick's hired bullies a little while

longer," he concluded, "we will turn this city inside out, and expose the corruption and malfeasance of her officiery."

King was now a crusader in full swing. He knew that he imperiled his very life in that city of easy murder, but he was determined to clean up San Francisco single-handed if he must.

His vitriolic pen attacked the gamblers by name, and every man and institution given to corrupt practices. His friends were terrified and warned him of his danger; but, although he received many threats, no attempt was made upon his life for a time. The *Bulletin* had a circulation unequaled by any San Francisco newspaper since Brannan's *Star,* and even Sam had made no attempt to sway public opinion.

4

Six weeks after the first issue of the *Bulletin* and while the public was still in a state of righteous indignation, United States Marshal William H. Richardson was murdered by Charles Cora, one of the more notorious of the gambling fraternity and the *maquereau* of Belle Cora, queen of Dupont Street. The murder took place after a brief altercation in a saloon and was wholly without provocation.

For the first time since 1851, San Francisco was in an up-roar over a murder, further inflamed by the eloquence of James King of Wm., who demanded speedy vengeance. The thought of an upright citizen whose only weakness was an occasional indulgence at a bar—one weakness never criticized in San Francisco—murdered by the most contemptible of his kind, one, moreover, who would command all the corrupt machinery of the law in his defense, sent hot blood to every head and a simultaneous roar went up of "Lynch him! Lynch him!" from the crowds that quickly gathered in the streets.

Charles Cora was rushed off to jail and locked up under a heavy guard. That night, for the first time in five years, the deep ominous note of the Monumental Fire Company was heard throughout the sleepless city. But although many of the Vigilantes of 1851 answered the call—the first, needless to relate, being the redoubtable Sam—still nothing happened. After several hours of serious deliberation, the Committee agreed to give the law one more chance to redeem itself.

The trial was a farce. Belle Cora retained lawyers whose abilities exceeded their virtue, and the inflamed oratory of these accomplished gentlemen swayed all but a few of those on the jury who had not been "fixed." The result was a disagreement. Charles Cora was returned to jail and the citizens once more collected in the down-town district and expressed their bitter resentment.

James King of Wm. implored the heavens to drape themselves in black. Day after day he poured forth his indignation. He knew there was no hope in the law unless it could be shamed into action; he flayed both the lawyers that had defended the wretch and the judge who had presided until they dared not show themselves on the street. He called upon the members of the old Vigilance Committee to foregather and take the law into their own hands.

Once more his friends begged him to desist; the denizens of the underworld were apprehensive and, beyond a doubt, plotting to rid themselves of the one enemy they feared. But King must have had the blood of the old martyrs in him. What was the life of one man to the regeneration of a potentially great city?

But the climax did not come until May 15th, four months after the trial. On the previous morning an editorial in the *Bulletin* was devoted to one of the supervisors, an ex-convict named James P. Casey, whose elevation to the board was one more disgrace to the city. The man's past was laid on the dissecting table, and it stank.

The streets were deserted when King left his office that afternoon; a soft white fog had floated down from the tule lands of the north and King held his long cape across his chest with both hands. As he was crossing Montgomery Street diagonally between Washington and Clay, Casey, who had been hiding behind an express wagon, stepped out of the fog and pointed a large navy revolver at King. "Are you armed? Defend yourself! Come on!" he cried excitedly. But the victim had no time to draw his pistol. Casey fired as he spoke. He ran for the jail and gave himself up, thinking it wise to take shelter with his friends.

King staggered into the Pacific Express Building on the corner. A surgeon, hastily summoned, pronounced the wound mortal.

In an incredibly short time the town was ringing with the news that James King of Wm. had been foully murdered, and a howling mob was gathered in the Plaza and the downtown streets demanding that Casey be lynched at once. The prison officials, knowing that the jail would be rushed, sent for a carriage, and Casey, accompanied by the captain of police, several police officers and the city marshal, ran down an alley behind the jail and entered it at the corner of Washington Street. The coachman lashed his horses into a gallop and the hack, swaying perilously, dashed down Kearny Street toward the county jail on Broadway near Dupont Street. The crowd, yelling "Hang him! Hang him!" ran after, but the murderer was safe within the stronger walls before they could catch up with the horses.

The mob attempted to rush the jail but were held at bay by three of Casey's friends, a leveled gun in each hand. Before they could gather for a second rush word flew about that the Vigilantes were organizing. Mayor Van Ness harangued the crowd, and three separate companies of armed civilians, hoping to see Casey hanged but opposed to violence, surrounded the jail, stationed themselves in the corridors and on the roof. The mob, on a high note of derision, turned about and marched to Montgomery Street and the building where King

lay dying. For hours ten thousand men stood there waiting
for the bulletins issued every few minutes by the surgeon.
These were increasingly hopeless, and once more the crowd
ran to the space in front of the jail. Three hundred men, all
armed, were on guard. At eleven o'clock two of King's
friends, Frederick W. Macondray and John Sime, entered the
jail, and when they came out, they informed the crowd that
it was impossible for Casey to be rescued. Their assurance,
supplemented by the arrival of a mounted battalion consist-
ing of the California Guards, the First Light Dragoons, and
the National Lancers, finally induced the mass of indignant
men to disperse. Casey, cowering in his cell, was safe for the
moment.

5

The next morning the same crowd of citizenry, all business neglected, marched down to Sacramento Street and stood
in front of the American Club Building where, they had
learned, a Vigilance Committee under the leadership of
William T. Coleman, one of the city's most honorable, energetic, and highly respected men, had assembled. While Sam
Brannan was haranguing the crowd from the balcony before
a second-story window, Mr. Coleman wrote out an oath of
fealty to the organization pledging life, liberty, property, and
honor, and swore in all that were present.

Before the day had passed, the applications for member-
ship were so numerous that when the Committee was finally
established in larger quarters on Sacramento Street between
Davis and Front, the enrollment had reached thirty-five
hundred.

At the same time, several hundred equally eminent citizens,
who objected to illegal practices no matter in what worthy
cause, formed the "Law and Order" party; others as influential but having no wish to ally themselves with Lynch Law,
covertly supported the Vigilantes. Among them were two

sound bankers, John Parrott and William C. Ralston—the latter also destined for fame and tragedy. As may be imagined, many families were divided during that time of high passion. My grandfather, who revered the law whatever its exponents, was a member of the Law and Order group. My father was one of the Vigilantes. Upon one occasion my grandfather called my father a murderer, and relations were strained.

Summoned from Sacramento by the mayor, the Governor remonstrated with Mr. Coleman, who gave him such an eloquent report of the abominable condition of the city of San Francisco that he was almost convinced. But during his second interview with the Law and Order citizens he changed his none too stable mind and sent William T. Sherman, Major General of the Second Division of the California Militia, to "enter into a treaty with Mr. Coleman" and make him understand that law and order were of more importance in a city's history than temporary vengeance. Mr. Coleman replied that the Governor, if he wished, might place a guard of ten men about the jail, but he must accept the fact that there was but one law in San Francisco and that he, William T. Coleman, was the head of it.

Charles Duane, who had been elected chief marshal of the Vigilante Military Force, drilled fifteen hundred men, many of whom had fought in the Mexican War; the majority of the militia forces disbanded and joined his small army. Sherman resigned.

On Sunday, four days after King had been shot, Mr. Coleman gave formal notice to the Governor that the Committee was about to act. Marshal Duane's company started by three separate routes for the county jail. They marched up Kearny, Dupont, and Sansome Streets, and that slow tramp of many feet sounded as ominous to anxious ears as the deep bell that had summoned the Vigilantes to foregather.

When the three divisions met in front of the jail they fell

into position as precisely as if they had been trained for a month instead of three days, and awaited orders. They had a large audience. On the hills above, on all the roofs near by, in the adjacent streets, stood practically every male in San Francisco not on duty. There was no demonstration. They were awed into silence.

A cannon stood before the doors of the jail, a gunner beside it. Within the entrance stood Sheriff Scannell behind a wicket, a good friend of the murderer and of the underworld in general. When a carriage drove up and Mr. Coleman and Miers P. Truet descended, Scannell refused them entrance. Mr. Coleman took out his watch and gave Scannell five minutes. Every man in the company took out his own watch and counted the minutes. Four and a half minutes passed. The doors were opened and Mr. Coleman and Truet entered the jail.

Casey, who was running up and down a corridor brandishing a knife, surrendered when assured that he would have a fair trial. He drove off with his captors amidst the same profound silence. The carriage returned for Charles Cora, and the troops, led by Marshal Duane on a white horse, re-formed and marched to Sacramento Street to protect "The Fort."

The trial of Cora began at once. Mr. Coleman, a man of great dignity and imposing mein, presided in the center of a long table's length. The other members of the executive board, twenty-nine in number, were equally composed. There was no evidence of excitement in Cora's demeanor, although he must have quaked when a messenger entered and announced the death of James King of Wm. The Committee bowed their heads for a moment, then proceeded with the evidence.

Every business house was closed; every building draped in black; every man, save the maggots of the underworld, who went into hiding, wore crêpe on his arm. Every town and hamlet in California paid James King of Wm. a similar tribute. On the day of the funeral every respectable citizen in San Francisco, eminent and humble, with the exception of the Committee, Duane and his forces, followed the hearse through the city and out to Lone Mountain Cemetery—or almost everyone. Several thousand of those marching in the rear melted away and walked hastily back to Fort Vigilante. Some kind friend had brought them a sensational piece of news.

The Committee had sat almost continuously for two days and nights listening to the evidence for and against Cora and Casey, to the arguments of the counsel the miscreants had been permitted to hire. They were pronounced guilty and sentenced to death. Two priests administered the last rites, and one of them brought in the queen of Dupont Street and married her to the man whose name she had assumed. Belle Cora, although she wept profusely, no doubt congratulated herself that she was to be a more or less respectable widow.

A wooden platform had been erected before the second-story windows fronting on Sacramento Street, and, after the funeral procession had started, a gallows as well. In the hollow square below stood Marshal Duane's troops, muskets on their shoulders. There was also a detachment on the roof in front of the great alarm bell. Cannon were in place at each end of the street.

No attempt was made at rescue. The thousands that had rushed back from the funeral filled the streets or climbed to the tops of neighboring buildings. Again there was no demonstration.

The condemned men were led out of the window at a little after one o'clock. They wore shapeless white garments and their arms were pinioned. Cora, true to the gambler's code, was as expressionless as a clam, but Casey screamed for his mother until the white cap was drawn over his face and head. The priest who led them out begged him to pray, but he would not. Nor would Cora.

The nooses were adjusted. The signal was given. The bodies jerked for a moment, then dangled limply.

As they had repented and been received back into the Church, burial in hallowed ground could not be denied them. The bodies, escorted by Belle Cora and several friends, were taken out at night and buried in the cemetery of Mission Dolores.

6

The Committee sat in continuous session for six months. They executed two more murderers and expelled from California all on their famous "black list," packing them off wholesale on steamers and sailing vessels. All were given a fair trial. The Governor commanded Admiral Farragut, stationed at Mare Island, to bombard the city and cow the "insurrectionists." The admiral refused. Major General Wood, commanding the Pacific Division of the United States Army and stationed at Benicia, declined to supply the Governor with arms and ammunition.

By this time the building on Sacramento Street was surrounded by a barricade six feet thick and ten feet high of gunny sacks filled with sand. Cannon were in three embrasures. Cannon pointing in four directions were also on the roof, as well as on the roofs of neighboring buildings. Fort Vigilante became known as Fort Gunnybags.

The Vigilantes were the only law in San Francisco.

They were opposed steadily—that is to say verbally—by the Law and Order party, and not for reasons wholly virtuous. It was a party composed almost wholly of Southerners, able and ambitious men who had come to the new state to improve their political fortunes, to achieve eminence and power more rapidly than was possible in a section of the United States whose principal interest was politics. Their only obstacle to complete control of San Francisco hitherto had been David C. Broderick and his gang. And now they were confronted by an even greater menace. Those men making history in their impregnable "Fort" might develop into a strong political power, obtain control of the state.

But the Committee proceeded on its impassive way despite annoyances and threats. The shyster lawyers and the judges were told to reform or get out, and they did the one or the other. The same warning was given to the low-grade politicians, who had balked even the powerful and accomplished Southerners, and they betook themselves to greener pastures. Broderick was in Sacramento manipulating the Legislature and the Committee thought it wise to forget him.

When their work was finished, San Francisco was as respectable a city as Boston and remained so for nearly twenty years. The Colemans, Gwins, Thorntons, Crittendens, McKinstrys, Lafayette Maynards, Bowies, Howards, McMullins, Horns, McNutts, Maxwells, Franklins, Shorbs, Hitchcocks, Kelloggs, Louis McLanes, Athertons, Hollidays, Donahoes, Donahues, Ashes, Lathams, Peytons, Kings, Gordons, Thiebaults, Selbys, Parrotts, Reddingtons, Macondrays, Babcocks, Otises, Fairfaxes, Poetts, and the Hall McAllisters—either Southerners or at one with them in all important matters regarding the welfare of the city—became as powerful politically as they were socially.

And San Francisco at last had "tone." The ladies of commerce promenaded Montgomery Street no more, nor did they invade the fashionable shops. Belle Cora retired. Dupont Street externally was almost demure.

Even the sidewalks were reformed. Pedestrians no longer walked with lowered eyes to avoid stumbling over loose planks or into holes, nor did they make detours to avoid garbage cans where rats were feasting. Night street lamps of flickering whale oil were replaced by gas.

Even the Chinese peddlers, trotting over the hills, bamboo poles across their shoulders with deep baskets containing fruit or vegetables or trays of fish, swaying from either end, no longer had their pigtails pulled by loafers; and, although Chinese laundrymen might still draw a crowd to watch them distend their cheeks with water and then sprinkle the undergarments of ladies and gentlemen therefrom, their windows were no longer stoned.

Sometimes the good citizens sighed. True, it was pleasant to wake up in the morning and feel confident that you would not be shot or stabbed by a hired assassin, find your store looted when you went down town to run up your shutters, or hear yells and pistol shots in the saloons when you went out to lunch—but, still, life was just a trifle drab when you thought of the old days.

But San Francisco was to have its excitements.

Broderick

Mr. Coleman said to my grandfather one day, when they were indulging in reminiscence, "David Broderick was one of the most remarkable men this country has ever produced. And the greatest skinful of contradictory elements! The son of an Irish-American stone cutter with little schooling, he educated himself; not from any love of learning at first but because he was ambition incarnate. Later he read widely for the satisfaction it gave his eager inquiring mind and mitigated somewhat his loneliness—for with all his activities he was the loneliest of men. And somewhere along the line he picked up a fair knowledge of parliamentary law which made him a power in Sacramento as he was everywhere else.

"He had none of the common vices; he never drank, he avoided women, never even smoked. In politics there was no crooked wile to which he would not stoop to gain his ends, but he never told an unnecessary lie, never broke a promise except once, and then for reasons which he thought justified it. He never went back on a friend, and he helped many to fortune—his friends were men of worth; the others with whom he was forced to associate were his political tools. He was absolutely fearless; that cold piercing eye of his never wavered even when a pistol was thrust under his nose. He was ever ready with his fists—and as ready to forgive.

"His mind was the most brilliant and flexible I have ever known. He had the brain of a statesman, and despised and deplored the devious methods he was forced to employ—but his life was one long fight against the handicap of his birth. That was the day of the aristocrat's supremacy in politics, and his more fortunate rivals combined against the man of plebeian birth and did all they could to thwart him from the first—even when they did not fear him, and they generally did.

"He was the kindest and gentlest of men, and the most ruthless, the most domineering, the most blatant.

"He had what amounted to a passion for San Francisco, the city of his adoption, and did much to add to her beauty and importance. But he would have sacrificed her, if necessary, to accomplish his inordinate ambition. And his magnificent abilities justified that ambition. If he had lived he would have succeeded Lincoln as President of the United States. And when he entered the White House he would have left politics on the doorstep and become the greatest statesman of his time. But God willed otherwise," added Mr. Coleman piously. "No man was ever endowed with greater gifts, but he was doomed to frustration; not once but again and again."

2

Sacramento was already a handsome city; every street was lined with trees, and there were comfortable houses, two hotels, and good shops. But the streets themselves were dilapidated and filthy, and the state capitol had not yet been built. The Legislature met in churches—where fist fights were not uncommon—or in barns: wherever they could find shelter.

That itinerant body had traveled from town to town until Broderick put his foot down, announcing that Sacramento should be the capital of the state, and the capital it was.

Twice Broderick had striven for a seat in the United States Senate, and twice lost his fight, powerful in state politics as he was. The Southerners were numerically in the ascendant, and not above chicanery themselves.

The three political parties at that time were the Whigs, the Democrats, and the Americans—the latter better known as the Know-Nothings (owing to their reticence), whose leading principles were opposition to all foreigners (meaning the Irish), to all European and Asiatic immigration, and to the Catholic Church. The Whig party in California was bitterly opposed to Broderick and liked Gwin little better.

Gwin was the leader of the Chivalry Democrats ("Chivs"); Broderick of the opposite faction of the same party, whose pivot was anti-slavery. Many of those men were eminent citizens and personal friends of Broderick.

In 1857, when John B. Weller's term was about to expire, Broderick rallied all the anti-slaverites, and many of the indifferent, to his banner. He indulged in none of the oratorical extravagances of the day; he spoke with a rigid sledgehammer logic, in cold, incisive, implacable tones, and rarely failed to convince his audience.

He was possibly the ugliest man in California, but, despite the preternaturally long upper lip of his Neanderthal forebears and the short jungle of black hair that fringed his face from ear to ear, so great was the dignity and austerity of his bearing that he was no figure of fun. He had discarded the blue shirt and pants tucked into high boots that he had affected during his first years in California, for the boiled shirt, black frock coat and trousers, and tall silk hat of the everyday gentleman. Even Gwin, "king of the Chivs," was no better turned out.

When he returned to Sacramento, he entered into a deal

with Milton S. Latham, a wealthy man with a yearning for the title of United States Senator, promising him that he should succeed Gwin when the "Old Roman's" term expired if he would help him to secure the necessary votes in the Legislature.

The ambition of Broderick's life was fulfilled: he was elected to the Senate of the United States; he, the poor Irish boy, the plebeian, was elected to a body as exclusive and aristocratic (with one or two notable exceptions) as the Knickerbocker Club of New York. The social aspect, however, interested him little, save insofar as it humiliated and infuriated the Chivs.

And then for the first and only time in his life he broke his word. He wanted a malleable partner in the Senate and Latham was an obstinate man accustomed to have his own way.

Broderick believed that the great national issue, slavery, was of more importance than an election promise. He shrewdly suspected that Gwin cared more for his brilliant social position in Washington and the title Senator—which he hoped to retain for the rest of his life—than for any abstract principle, and that if promised re-election he would even renounce his immense Federal patronage—every Federal office in California was filled by a Southerner—and Broderick could keep his promises to his constituents.

And then occurred one of the most absurdly melodramatic incidents in the history of politics.

Gwin was in Sacramento at the Orleans Hotel. Broderick had his headquarters at the Magnolia. What secret messages had passed between the two men has never been revealed, but one night as the town clock struck twelve, Gwin, enveloped in a long black cape, a black slouch hat pulled down over his face, and looking for all the world like the villain in a play, stole from the back door of his hotel. He tiptoed to the street, looked furtively up and down, and, finding the coast clear, passed like a shadow through one ill-lighted street and alley after another, bent equally upon not falling over piles of refuse or slinking cats and avoiding his fellow men. Finally he arrived at the rear door of the Magnolia. A hench-man of Broderick stood within and whispered the password. Gwin, assuring himself that the back hall was empty, fol-lowed the man upstairs and into the Presence.

Broderick, whose manners were now excellent—when he chose—received him with elegant courtesy, dismissed his min-ions, and the two men came to terms with no further waste of time in formalities. Gwin wrote out a paper (afterward to be known as the "Scarlet Letter") promising to give up all the patronage of the state of California. There followed a mass of verbiage, in which it might with some effort be deciphered that he made this sacrifice in barter for another term in Washington, D. C.

The two men shook hands at parting and Gwin returned as stealthily as he had come.

3

Broderick's two years in Washington must be passed over briefly. His fame had preceded him and he was received by the Senate with both courtesy and admiration; even the Southerners were interested—and quite sure they could han-dle him.

No more picturesque figure had ever taken his seat in that august body, and he made many friends. He could have be-come a social lion, but he accepted no invitations to private houses. His intention was to spend his leisure hours in thought and study, for he was determined to become a states-man of the first rank.

But those hours were soon given over to bitter reflections, grave apprehensions, finally to rage.

Gwin was an intimate friend of Buchanan. The President

took an immediate dislike to the too independent young man from California and treated him with insulting disdain. Broderick's demands for Federal patronage were ignored. The Southerners in California retained their fat jobs, and there seemed to be no prospect of fulfilling his campaign promises.

It was long before he could bring himself to doubt the good faith of Gwin. He disliked the man, but he cherished the naïve belief that a gentleman never broke his word. Gwin avoided him in the halls of Congress and of course they did not meet socially. Observing the usual etiquette of the Senate, Broderick made no attempt to speak until his second term. The question agitating the Congress, the whole country for that matter, was the relation of Kansas to the balance of power between the North and the South. It had been decreed that the question of slavery in the territory should be determined by its citizens. Immediately hordes from free and slave states poured into Kansas, and United States troops were called in to prevent a minor civil war. Two Legislatures were chosen, one dispersed by the United States Marshal; the other framed a pro-slavery Constitution to be known as the "Lecompton," and it was endorsed at the polls.

When Kansas made her application to Congress for statehood, Buchanan, who was a Northerner with pro-slavery sympathies, urged Congress to ratify it, and once more there were torrents of eloquence and invective in both houses. Finally the Lecompton Constitution was sent back to Kansas to be digested again by the people and this time it was overwhelmingly defeated.

The Democratic party was now split into two factions, and the anti-Lecomptonites, declaring that their once-honored name had been disgraced, thereafter called themselves Republicans.

Broderick was now in his second year. He let loose all his vitriolic eloquence in scarifying Buchanan. Broderick was recognized as one of the outstanding forces in national affairs. Even his enemies admitted his remarkable abilities, and his fellow Senators never failed to be in their seats when he spoke. He had won the complete confidence of his own party. His poise, courage, above all his merciless powers of invective, soon made him the leader of his faction.

All over the country the enemies of the President delighted in Broderick, and there was no thin plate in Buchanan's armor that his fiery lance did not penetrate. He became known as the most powerful anti-slavery man in public life. The pro-slavery men writhed in their seats when he favored them with the more personal darts in his repertory. Gwin held his breath with apprehension; then his long face grew longer and longer with chagrin; Broderick ignored him.

Broderick secured the passage of several acts important to California, advocated a coast-to-coast railroad, and, if he could not secure Federal plums for his friends, he extracted some of the flavor from Gwin's. He introduced a bill to decrease the salaries of California officials paid out of the national treasury, demonstrating that the high cost of living in the new state which had been responsible for them was now reduced to normal. The bill passed.

Gwin was besieged with letters of lamentation, but he was helpless.

4

Then, slowly, the tide began to turn. Broderick's enemies both in California and in Washington became thoroughly alarmed, and, in the less elegant parlance of a later day, ganged up on him.

His deal with Gwin had long been an open secret in California, and the Chivs, knowing that the rumor had reached Washington and slightly darkened the reputation of their leader, made an effort to get hold of the "Scarlet Letter." Had Broderick taken it with him? Had he left it behind in a

strong box in some bank that might be looted? There were
still a few ruffians left in San Francisco, although they were
extremely wary, and their price correspondingly high.

By spying and ferreting, it was finally ascertained that the
note had been entrusted to W. I. Fergurson, a clever young
politician, devoted to Broderick, but not always discreet.

Fergurson made a speech in the Legislature in which he
extolled Broderick for his war on the Lecomptonites and his
attacks on Buchanan, adding his own unflattering opinion of
the President of the United States, whom he denounced as
a traitor for kowtowing to the Southern faction. When he
returned to San Francisco, a Buchanan Democrat involved
him in a quarrel and challenged him to a duel. But if the
man had expected to be placated by a gift of the compromis-
ing letter, he was mistaken. Fergurson confided it to a friend
and went to his death.

Broderick had no illusions when he heard this ominous bit
of news. The death of young Fergurson was meant as a warning to himself. Give up that letter, retire to private life, or
expect a similar fate.

The Southerners in Congress, or Lecomptonites as they
now called themselves, cared nothing about the "Scarlet Letter," nor about Gwin for that matter, but they had come to
the conclusion that Broderick was no longer merely a picturesque nuisance but a dangerous man, and they spelt the
adjective with nine capital letters. They could take care of
the Northerners to whom they were accustomed, but there
was no knowing what this wild man from the West would do
next—and, they admitted sourly, he was more resourceful,
more brilliantly endowed, than all of his enemies rolled into
one kicking mass.

Their first move was to oppose his plan for a transconti-
nental railroad. The United States might have its railroad,
but *not* to the borders of an anti-slave state. Broderick was
dropped from the Committee on Public Lands. They thun-

dered in the halls of Congress, and the press followed suit.
How dared a young Senator from the "jumping-off end of
the nation" oppose slavery? How dared he advocate free
labor, denounce corrupt Indian agents, jobbery by post-
masters and revenue collectors, demand reform and retrench-
ment in public affairs?

So great was the turmoil that even his friends drew away,
apprehensive for their own political futures.

Never had any man in the United States Congress stood
more conspicuously alone. But he was a born fighter and he
fought on. And no matter what their hatred, they always
listened to him. And every word he uttered was reported in
the newspapers—with stinging editorial comment. He knew
the fearful odds against him, knew that a powerful combina-
tion was in action, both in Washington and in California, to
force him out of public life, and that their hatred and fear
were augmented by the rising power of the Republican party,
of which he was a member in all but name. But grimly he
fought on.

5

When Broderick returned to San Francisco, at the end of
the term, he found California in a wild state of agitation over
the slavery question. The Kansas incident had reawakened
both factions and California heaved from end to end like its
own Pacific Ocean in one of its unpacific storms. This was
but three years before the Civil War; the Southerners hoped
that California might yet become a slave state, the Northerners feared the same thing. The former had attempted to introduce a large number of negroes into California—and had
been thwarted by Broderick.

Even the ladies of Rincon Hill and South Park, Harrison
and Folsom Streets, were infected, and the regnant Southerners cut many of their old friends dead when they met on

the street—heads thrown back, eyes blazing contempt from the depths of coal-scuttle bonnets.

The Kansas issue was dead, but the two warring factions even in far-off California still called themselves Lecomptonites and anti-Lecomptonites. Broderick immediately made a tour of the north, talking to immense mass meetings in every town and hamlet; traveling by horse, stagecoach, buggy, boat, wagons almost as springless as the carretas of Old California. Gwin spoke to other cheering or hissing crowds, but his suave polished diction, his elegant personality devoid of magnetism, were no match for the impassioned oratory, the cold convincing logic, the blasting invective of the man who was convinced that the life of a nation was at stake, and with it his beloved California.

But the crowning sensation of the campaign took place at Shasta, that beautiful, still prosperous little town named for the great mountain peak crowned with everlasting snow. A huge mass of blue ice and black lava, its white crest fourteen thousand feet above the Sacramento River not far from its base, Shasta towered above the lovely town amid the rolling foothills.

Broderick, whose rugged frame had suffered from his exertions and the hardships of travel—he had been too impatient to rest after the long jolting ride by stagecoach from Washington to San Francisco—was grateful for the hospitality of Major Pierson P. Reading, the first pioneer to settle in Shasta. The adobe house was large and comfortable, the Indian servants efficient, and for the first time since he left San Francisco, Broderick slept in a soft bed and ate palatable food.

Refreshed, he stood before the entire population of Shasta, some twenty-two hundred in number and not a Southerner among them. There was no proselytizing to be done here, and after a statement of facts to whip up their ardor and a pulsating sketch of his life in Washington, he sprang the sensation he had reserved for this all-out loyal community. He took the "Scarlet Letter" from his wallet and read it aloud to a breathless audience. Then he uttered his first public denouncement of Gwin, and his tones were so level, so cold, so deadly, so charged with contempt devoid of venom, that after a stunned silence a roar went up that, one good citizen averred, made the snow fly on Mount Shasta.

Reporters had followed him. They obtained copies of the letter, took horse, and galloped, with relays, to San Francisco to publish the "big news." Gwin's friends advised him to go into retirement until the excitement had subsided.

"I suppose I have signed my death warrant," said Broderick to a friend that night. "But they have long since made up their minds to get me, for I am the one anti-slaverite they fear and they know that only death will muzzle me."

He returned to San Francisco suffering from a heavy cold intensified by exhaustion, and went to bed in a friend's house at the military post, Black Point.

He expected a challenge from Gwin, but the challenge came from another quarter.

6

David S. Terry was probably the most anomalous figure that ever sat on a Supreme Court Bench. He had fought bravely in the war to free Texas from Mexico, and as long as he lived he retained the swagger, garb, and personality of the Texas Ranger. He was learned in the law and fair in his decisions. He blustered and shouted and bellowed down his opponents, used his fists upon the slightest provocation—and had been a member of the Law and Order party! He stabbed a man in a street row while the Vigilantes were sitting, and that august body found itself in the embarrassing position of trying a Justice of the Supreme Court of California. Only the recovery of his victim, however, saved him from making a final exit through the second story window of Fort Gunnybags. He ignored the Committee's order to leave the state, and the order was never enforced.

He was a vociferous pro-slavery man and Lecomptonite, and as fervently pro-Gwin and anti-Broderick.

Whether there was a deliberate plot to exterminate Broderick with Terry as the willing instrument will never be known, but in 1859, when he was a candidate for re-election, he delivered himself before the Convention of an insulting tirade against the junior Senator from California and, failing of re-election, left Sacramento at once and entered into an abusive correspondence with Broderick. It is needless to report that Broderick's replies were equally vitriolic.

The inevitable challenge followed—from Terry. Broderick, in whom the germs of pneumonia were developing, and who would infinitely have preferred to die on his feet, accepted the challenge with a grim smile. His friends, whose indignation overpowered their common sense, dragged him out of bed at midnight, dressed and put him into a lumbering hack, and the equally excited driver—all San Francisco was on edge by this time—galloped him into town to receive the cartel.

Where was his doctor? Or had he refused to call one in? But why was there not one level-headed man among his devoted friends to insist upon postponement of the duel until he was well again? Apparently they were all in the same state of excitement, and it occurred to no one that his hand might not be as steady, his aim as quick and sure as his opponent's.

Terry's seconds were Calhoun Benham, an eminent Chiv, and Thomas Hayes. David D. Colton and Joseph C. McKibben acted for Broderick.

The duel took place on September 13, 1859.

7

Lake Merced, the favorite dueling ground, lay in a small valley some ten miles south of San Francisco. The rolling hills at this season were parched and brown, the trees heavy with the dust of a long dry summer. The wild ducks were swimming on the blue lake and birds sang to the dawn, their liquid voices rising above the steady booming of the sea beyond the western range of the hills.

Terry, his seconds and surgeon, were the first to arrive. They had slept comfortably in a neighboring farm house, and Terry had never been in better condition—nor more sanguine.

Not so Broderick. His friends drove him down the night before to a road house several miles from the dueling ground. The place was crowded and the four men slept in one room in bunks furnished with "pula" mattresses, an importation from the Sandwich Islands and hospitable to vermin.

A heavy fog had rolled in from the ocean and the night was cold and raw, the blankets thin. Bedbugs feasted. No one slept. When they rose at five o'clock, they were unable to get a cup of coffee, much less an inspiriting breakfast. Shivering in their light overcoats, they entered the hack and were bounced over five miles of rough road to Lake Merced.

Broderick had summoned all his reserves. Pride and will power enabled him to stand erect and walk steadily to the spot where the seconds were measuring off the paces.

He was a dead shot, but his large hand was accustomed to the heavy dueling pistol in vogue. Colton and McKibben, after much rhetorical persuasion, had accepted the gift of two "famous Belgian pistols," the property of a friend of Terry.

Broderick turned the little weapon over and over in his big hand. Then he remarked to a friend who had driven down from the city to stand beside him until the last moment, "My seconds are children. As likely as not they have traded away my life."

He raised his eyes to the hills. They were black with people from San Francisco, determined to witness what might be the last act of a drama that never had been wanting in interest.

In defiance of dueling etiquette, many of them cheered and shouted, "Broderick! Broderick! Our bets are on you."

Broderick made no response.

The principals were ordered to remove their overcoats. They wore the formal dueling costume: full black suit, the frock coat tightly buttoned, and soft black hat. Both men were subjected to a pressure of hands by the other's seconds to make sure that neither wore a suit of mail.

The principals were told to move into position. Both were fine specimens of manhood, tall, upstanding, well-proportioned. But no two faces were ever more unlike. Broderick's, like his figure, was massive, prehistoric. Terry, handsome despite his chin whiskers, had delicate features, an amiable expression. His body was wiry and swift in movement. This morning he looked as amiable as always when not shouting at some unfortunate witness or reaching for his knife, and gave no hint of his deadly purpose. Broderick's face was black with rage. He, whose courage was famous, had been subjected to an insulting prodding by Benham while his own second had merely tapped Terry.

The men stood in position ten paces apart. As Broderick stared once more at the tiny pistol in his hand, his rage expired in apathy.

Colton asked: "Are you ready?" Terry replied: "Ready." Broderick adjusted the "Belgian" between his big fingers as best he could and nodded.

The duelists held their pistols vertically, their right arms hanging.

Colton droned: "One—two—three."

The men raised their pistols. At the word "One" Broderick's badly adjusted weapon went off and hit the ground. Terry, who knew quite well what had happened, seized his chance and fired before Colton could utter "Two." The bullet hit Broderick in the chest, puncturing the right lung.

Broderick shuddered and dropped his pistol, but for a few

seconds he stood upright. Then his body was shaken by a powerful tremor and he sank slowly, inch by inch, as if his will were protesting to the last. But when the surgeon reached him he lay in a heap, unconscious.

Terry stood with folded arms as both surgeons examined the fallen man. Then, discontented that he could not fire a second shot, he was persuaded to leave the field—after being assured that the wound was mortal.

Broderick was rushed to Black Point in the same lumbering old hack in which he had suffered tortures already. The blood was again gushing from his wound when his friend Colonel Baker hastened to his side, but he managed to gasp, "Baker, when I was struck I tried to stand firm, but the blow blinded me and I could not."

He lived for three days, a part of the time under the influence of chloroform. In his delirium he revealed plainly that all along he had known that he was marked for death, but as often he talked of the slave powers against which he had pitted all his resources and for which he was to die. His last words were: "I die. Protect my honor."

He expired on Friday morning, September 16, 1859. San Francisco, instead of indulging in one of its fits of unbridled excitement, was plunged into a gloom unique in its history. The bankers, the merchants, the shopkeepers, closed their doors and draped them with crêpe or black cloth.

The funeral took place on Saturday. The casket lay on a catafalque in the Plaza. Thirty thousand citizens were crowded into the square and adjacent streets. Colonel Baker, famous for his oratorical flights, had been chosen to preside, and surpassed himself.

Every male in San Francisco who was able to walk (except Terry) followed the hearse to Lone Mountain. Even his enemies joined the procession, for the Chivs were brave men themselves and willing to pay tribute to a brave man whom they silently admitted to be greater and perhaps better than themselves.

8

Terry expiated his crime more bitterly than was common in that era of frequent duels. Men shunned him. He continued to practice law, but his cases were second rate. What had promised to be one of the most brilliant careers in California was over.

Broderick was avenged.

In the eighties, Terry took the case of an adventuress, one Sarah Althea Hill, who claimed to have made a contract marriage with William Sharon, a man of many millions. The case was lost, but Terry fell in love with the woman and married her. In the legal tangle that preceded the marriage she appeared before Stephen J. Field, Associate Justice of the Supreme Court of the United States. He ruled against her, and when she screamed and called him names and he ordered her removed from the room, Terry drew a knife and attacked the bailiffs. Both were sentenced to a short term in jail.

Terry vowed vengeance on Judge Field, and, as he was a man whose resentments were permanent, the Justice never appeared in California save in the company of a guard employed by the government. On the 15th of August, 1889, while the two were on their way from Los Angeles to San Francisco, they left the train for lunch at Lathrop and sat down in one of those dirty, fly-ridden, dreary eating houses that disgraced the overland route for many years. Terry, with his wife, had been on the train. When he entered the restaurant and saw Judge Field, he flew into one of his uncontrollable rages, darted up to the esteemed Justice from behind, and slapped his face.

The guard shot him dead. Sarah Althea went insane. She died in the State Hospital at Stockton many years later, at the age of eighty.

PART THREE

9. Tossing Horns

Henry Miller

A MILLION acres of land, a million head of livestock! Such was the dream of a barefoot boy. Such was the realization of that dream not so many years later.

The life of Henry Miller reads like one of those success stories which, if the subject of a novel, would be treated with the disdain that gross exaggeration deserves by any conscientious critic.

Nevertheless, this is a true story. Henry Miller lived eighty-nine years and died with his millions intact, thus violating the laws of drama—real life drama in California at least. Many of his contemporaries made large fortunes and died in poverty, either through their own folly, the injustice of other men, or the inexorable law of causation. But not Henry Miller.

Heinrich Alfred Kreiser was born in the little German town of Brackenheim July 1, 1827. His father was the town butcher, and when Heinrich was not driving the cows to and from pasture, he helped to cut the roasts and steaks and arrange them temptingly in the window.

It was a narrow life, as narrow as the crooked streets, the individual pastures in that crowded land. Little Heinrich dreamed his compensating dreams; he had heard of a vast new country on the other side of an ocean, called the United States of America, where there was more land than there were people; a phenomenon almost unthinkable to the untraveled

173

German. But Heinrich had imagination. And the older he grew the more vivid became the dream of a vast farm with thousands of cattle all his own. Pastures always green. Running brooks. Tossing horns! Above all he loved that vision of thousands upon thousands of white horns tossing in the bright golden light of the sun.

When he was eighteen, avoiding the ordeal of farewells, he walked out of Brackenheim and made his way to England. There he worked at odd jobs until he had made enough money to buy a steerage passage to New York. He arrived there at the age of twenty with five dollars in his pocket, a limited knowledge of the English language, and the grim determination to remain in that great bewildering city until he had saved enough money to carry him to the sparsely settled West. He found employment with a butcher, and enjoyed a brief romance with a childhood sweetheart whose family had emigrated several years before. For a time he was very happy, his ambitions almost forgotten. They wandered all through the city during their hours of leisure—she was a servant—and their dreams and their talk were all of a blissful future together.

Then, one Sunday night after he had returned from a long day on the Hudson Palisades, a wave of revulsion swept over him as he closed the door of his little room behind the shop. He was an engaged man! He was about to hamper himself with a wife! What of his future? What of his dreams? A wife, perhaps children, would be a clog and a nuisance. What a fool he had been to let the emotions of youth obscure reason and judgment. Never! Never! But how could he extricate himself? What could he say to her? If he remained in New York how could he avoid her? Love shriveled and died.

And then the luck that was to follow him through life made its first offering that very night.

His intimate friend, one Henry Miller, a clerk in a neighboring shoe store, was to sail for California the next day; one of the thousands of adventurous young men bent upon making a quick fortune in the fabulous gold mines of which all the world was talking. Heinrich envied him deeply, but to sail with him was impossible. He had saved little, for every month he sent a part of his wages to his family.

Something, most opportunely for our hero, caused a sudden change in Miller's plans. He entered the little room behind the shop where Heinrich Kreiser was sitting disconsolately on the edge of the bed, and offered to sell him his ticket.

Heinrich had been paid a month's wages the day before. It was not enough for the ticket, but Miller could rest assured he would send the balance from California as soon as possible. Miller was satisfied. Heinrich Kreiser sailed the next day.

On his way to the wharf he looked at the precious ticket and noted that it was made out to Henry Miller and stamped "Not transferable." He changed his name to Henry Miller forthwith.

2

The mines had no lure for Henry. He thought San Francisco uglier than Brackenheim, but it was crowded with men, all busy, all intent upon making a fortune; men who had come from the eastern and southern states to grow up with the new city, men from the mines with their bags of "dust" to spend or gamble away, men from every ship that anchored in the harbor. All these men wanted food, above all juicy beefsteaks.

Henry received a warm welcome from the leading butcher, for capable young men were rare and, after a few weeks, deserted him to join the Rush. When Henry assured him that he had no intention of going to the mines and had demonstrated his ability to carve up a steer with the quick agile hand of an expert, he doubled his wages.

Henry served him faithfully. He gave the glittering gambling halls but a casual glance of curiosity; he never entered lower Dupont Street; the saloons had no attraction for him save as a rendezvous of cattlemen where he could pick up information about the interior valleys. He talked to many of the customers on the same subject—and he kept his wages in his pockets, for he heard of the fires that had destroyed the city several times.

Then came another of the fires (the last until 1906), and in the period of universal brotherhood that followed he was no longer a clerk in a butcher shop but a citizen who did his part in rebuilding the city. His stocky body with its big head and short legs was seen darting here, there and everywhere, clearing away débris, carrying timber and bricks, shoveling out foundations. Moreover, when the fire had broken out his first thought had been for the stockyards, malodorously situated within the city limits. He had driven the terrified cattle up the valley to a place where they could feed and drink. Then, when the excitement was over and the citizens were clamoring for meat, he opened a shop of his own and sliced steers into steaks and roasts for hungry men who had been living on groceries they had salvaged while the fire was raging, or vegetables brought in by the rancheros who charged them exorbitant prices. San Franciscans who had laughed at his thick German accent and queer ways now patted him on the back and regarded him as a valuable citizen.

San Francisco was quickly rebuilt, and although Henry had little love for cities, he regarded its handsome new buildings with pride as well as with a sense of personal proprietorship; it was to be his springboard to greater things.

The Mexican cattle which had been bred in California for a century were inferior in quality, but he managed to get the pick of them by rising early and being first at the stockyards— now beyond the city limits. Then one day a man who owned a rancho in the Santa Clara Valley and who wished to return "back East," drove three hundred head of first-class American cattle into San Francisco, and Henry Miller bought them all for $35,000—so greatly had he prospered.

But still he longed for the open country, and the time came when he determined to take a trip into the valleys and prospect. He had two well-trained trustworthy assistants who had failed at the mines and were glad of a steady job.

3

The San Joaquin Valley, an immense sweep of land, lies between the Coast Range and the Sierra Nevada Mountains. To Miller as he descended the Coast Range from the Pacheco Pass it seemed illimitable and he learned afterward that it was two hundred miles long and fifty miles wide. A great river swept an erratic course. He had been told that this valley was not favored by squatters, for, although the land was rich, it was subject to droughts during which crops withered and cattle died of hunger and thirst. Nevertheless, it made a stronger appeal to Henry than any of the valleys he had traversed on his journey; he made a vow that one day he would own not only acres but miles of it, and Henry Miller never broke a promise he made to himself.

He rode directly toward a small ranch of which he had heard. The cattle looked healthy but the ranch house was dilapidated. The corrals and granary, however, were in good repair.

He remained with the owner for several days, a welcome guest to a lonely man. Miller, who regarded the Americans as the most enterprising people in the world, was surprised to learn that it had never occurred to this one to drive his good American cattle to the San Francisco market. "What!" exclaimed the man. "Drive steers one hundred and fifty miles? They would die of exhaustion on the way." He sold them to the miners and made a good living.

Miller immediately thought of a way in which the cattle

could reach San Francisco in prime condition, but said nothing. The man was "sick and tired of ranching." He hated the sight of horns, and between droughts and floods life was not worth living. He'd like to sell out and try his luck at the mines.

Miller probed. Yes, the land was rich enough in good times. It was favored by several channels of the San Joaquin River, and when the water overflowed in moderation the grass was green and luxuriant. The man had bought his ranch, eight thousand, eight hundred and thirty-five acres, from the heirs of a large Spanish grant. Barring droughts, it was good grazing land. The cattle were Hereford-Durhams, the best there were.

Miller adroitly led him on until the man finally offered to sell him the ranch for $1.15 an acre, and his seven thousand five hundred cattle at $5.00 a head.

After the proper amount of hemming and hawing, Miller agreed to buy the ranch, paid the option, and promised to send him the remainder within a fortnight. On his way back to San Francisco he stopped at several small ranches in the valleys on the other side of the Coast Range and bargained to have his steers rested and fed on their journey to the city. Subsequently he bought these ranches.

He was short of cash, for not only had he paid out $35,000 for the cattle he already owned, but had recently sent a large sum to his family. But he was confident that he could raise the money.

This was the year 1856. The great Bank of California had not yet been founded, but William C. Ralston was the dominant partner in the banking house of Garrison, Morgan and Fretz. His personality had already impressed the town and a great future was predicted for him. Butchers and bankers did not meet socially, but Miller knew him personally. Ralston liked his famous sausages and sometimes stopped in at the shop and bought a bag of them to take home. If the shop was not crowded he would linger for a chat; the little man interested him, and he had sized him up as an original with a shrewd bold mind and a flare for success.

Ralston was as quick of thought as Miller; it was said of him that he could grasp a proposition and make up his mind in exactly one minute. When Henry arrived in San Francisco, he went directly to Ralston's bank and gave the presiding genius a rapid description of the Rancho Sanjón de Santa Rita, his determination to buy it, his plans for its improvement, and his intention of cornering the cattle market in San Francisco. Ralston lent him the money.

4

Henry Miller's only rival was Charles Lux, who had a butcher shop in the fashionable residence quarter of San Francisco, and a slaughter house of his own on the outskirts. Miller intended to live hereafter in the country with his cattle and needed a partner in the city to receive the steers, slaughter them, put them on the market, and attend to the business end in general. Miller had always found it profitable to turn business rivals into friends, and he decided that Lux was his man.

Lux was lively, energetic, honorable, and keen. An Alsatian by birth, he too had run away from home when he was a boy, but more for the sake of adventure than ambition. When he arrived in San Francisco he took the first job that offered, which happened to be in a butcher shop. The business interested him and in due course he opened a shop of his own and prospered.

When Miller expounded his somewhat grandiose plans, not only to corner the cattle market but to become the greatest cattleman in the history of the West, Lux, like Ralston, instead of laughing as the average man would have done, was deeply impressed; he too had imagination. Everything was possible in California. He agreed to enter into partnership, but insisted that the firm be called Lux and Miller, as he had arrived in San Francisco first and had his own shop some time before Miller opened his. Miller planted both feet squarely and stuck out his chin. It was his idea, wasn't it? Had Lux, or anyone else, ever thought of such a thing? Would not Lux have plodded along behind a counter with no prospect of ever becoming a millionaire if he, Henry Miller, had not offered him this opportunity to become one of the richest men in California? "I does all the work and I makes you a fortune like myself," said the future cattle king bluntly. "Yes! I does all the work. You sits here and does a little more than you haf done already. You takes it or you leaves it."

The stronger will prevailed. The firm, to become the most famous of its kind in the world, was duly recorded as Miller and Lux.

5

The cattle were in good condition. At once a procession of steers ambling through the Pacheco Pass to Gilroy and along El Camino Real (The King's Highway) to San Francisco became a familiar sight. But Miller needed more and better pasture. The other heirs of the Spanish grant had no cattle; at first he rented their land, then, gradually, at his own price, bought them out.

It was also necessary to improve the land. To quote from *The Cattle King*, the biography of Henry Miller by Edward F. Treadwell: "If it had only a little Spring feed, and was dry the balance of the year, he knew water would make it blossom if it had deep sediment built up from the overflow of the creeks. If it had hardpan or yellow maul near the surface he knew the most he could do with it was a crop of grain. If the land had black alkali he knew it was worthless. If by reason of years of non-use white alkali had accumulated on the surface, he would flood it and thus wash the alkali out, and by keeping the water fresh he could get water grasses started which were strong enough to withstand the alkali in the soil. Abundant crops of wild hay were thus produced. After several years of treatment the land might be made to grow grain or other crops."

With his usual thoroughness he soon knew land as well as he knew meat. His stocky erect figure was on horseback all day and in all weathers. He often drove his cattle to market himself; he galloped beside his vaqueros on the rancho, giving minute instructions; he superintended the moving of supplies, then was off in another direction to buy hay when necessary.

And his ambitions grew with the ample fare they fed upon. More and more cattle. More and more land. His first opportunity came when United States surveyors began running their lines over California and land speculators followed. He was always in the market to buy after title had been acquired —and he mastered the art of buying at his own price.

His next opportunity was when the United States Government issued "land scrip" to pay for certain obligations incurred. One hundred and sixty acres of scrip was worth $180.00 in California. Miller bought thousands of dollars worth of scrip, thus obtaining valuable land for a trifle, which added to his acreage and to the already formidable income of Miller and Lux. Before many years had passed he owned nearly all the land for fifty miles on both sides of the San Joaquin River.

To quote Mr. Treadwell again: "As fast as land was acquired along the San Joaquin River dams were thrown in the sloughs, levees were thrown up, and the water spread over large tracts for the production of grasses. The economy and effectiveness of this method of wild irrigation were remarkable. A few levees across low places would often spread the water over low areas of land, and the eye of Henry Miller was as acute and keen as a surveyor's instrument to determine where the levees should be placed. To prevent perpetual in-undation, the low places along the banks of the rivers were likewise filled. Crude but substantial boxes were placed in the heads of branch channels to regulate the flow of water. The basic principle was that water-loving grasses were de-sired. These were best produced by water reasonably deep on the surface, but kept fresh. This was best done by allow-ing water to fill the land behind the levee and then flow over and into the next check. By using almost unlimited amounts of water this was accomplished by a minimum of labor. . . . By these means a small outlay of money gave immediate results. The grass would stand well up on the sides of the feeding animal. It could readily be cut for hay, but as a general rule Miller was as economical in the harvest-ing as in the growing of crops. . . . The cattle did the har-vesting; they cut and ate the grass where it grew. They trans-ported it on the hoof in the form of fat. A piece of land would be bought and instantly it would be made to produce; this produce was automatically fed to the cattle, and they were automatically fed to the slaughter-house and carried to the meat block. The land was thus made to pay for itself and a profit besides. . . . His turnover was rapid and produced a constant flow of gold which was used to expand as the de-mand for meat grew."

Eventually, in order to control the water, he acquired land on both sides of the river for a distance of a hundred and twenty miles "so as entirely to control the flow of the water for a distance of fifty miles. The work was done largely with his own horses, mules, and scrapers during the non-harvest period and was done at an astonishingly low rate of cost."

6

But Henry Miller had his worries.

One day when riding about his ranch, he came upon a notice nailed to a sycamore tree at the confluence of the San Joaquin and the Kings Rivers, to the effect that one John Bensley had "appropriated" a large amount of water to be used—through a canal to be constructed—for irrigation, transportation, and mechanical purposes. Miller went to San Francisco immediately and consulted his lawyer, who "gave an opinion that he thought the common law of riparian rights, which made the water belong to the land, was in force in the state, and not the law of 'appropriation,' by which the first comer might acquire rights therein; but he was not sure."

This was unsatisfactory, but many laws in the new state were rather loose and could only be expounded by litigation. Shortly after, Miller heard that Bensley had interested certain San Francisco capitalists in his scheme. Such names as Isaac Friedlander, W. H. Talbot, Charles Webb Howard, Alvinzo Hayward, W. S. Chapman, and those of half a dozen other equally eminent, enterprising, and wealthy citizens of San Francisco, rang unpleasantly in Miller's ears. In 1871, the San Joaquin and Kings River Canal and Irrigation Company was organized with a capital of one million dollars. Public calls for subscription to the stock were made. "The point" —I continue to quote Mr. Treadwell—"was that not only would land be irrigated, but that transportation facilities would be afforded and stressed. The growing hostility of the farmers to the railroad was played upon, and the project was thus pictured as one of great public benefit. Chapman, who was himself a large owner in the San Joaquin Valley, invested heavily in the project and from all over the country money was raised for the great work."

But nothing daunted Henry Miller. He stood on his riparian rights, and to save time and trouble the company signed a contract which granted them the right of way over his property on condition they would furnish him with water at half the price demanded of others, free stock water, and water to overflow his grass lands.

Then he proceeded to guide matters in such a manner as would benefit himself.

He was well content to have a great canal built at no cost to himself; he persuaded the promoters that they could have no better advice than his and saw to it that the canal was built exactly as and where he wished it to be dug. He even showed them how to build it, and graciously permitted the use of his horses, men, and tools. He was on the ground himself constantly, and as he knew how to win the affection as well as the respect of men, the superintendent and engineers were soon worshiping him and following his advice in all things.

At the end of the year the canal was seventy-eight miles long and flowing toward the Pacheco Pass. "A dam made of brush and sand three hundred and fifty feet in length was put across the river which often carried upward of 30,000 cubic feet of water per second."

Meanwhile, "Henry Miller was putting his own land into shape to receive the water. Miles of lateral canals were constructed; thousands of acres were plowed; levees were thrown up. His figure on horseback, covered with dust, could be seen at any time directing the workers. Machinery, foodstuffs and lumber made up freight for trains of wagons drawn by horses and mules . . . sometimes sixteen horses to a wagon or string of wagons. . . . As soon as the river dropped in the Fall scrapers were placed in the bed of the river and sand was piled up, and alternating layers of sand and brush were put in the channel, allowing the water in the meantime to run through the collapsible wier. There was a small island in the middle of the stream and this was used as an anchor for the structure. Thousand upon thousand of yards of sand and acres upon acres of willow trees were hauled into place and cunningly interlaced so as finally to form a dam over 350 feet in length. . . . A few years later the canal was extended to its present length of 103 miles."

Henry Miller bided his time.

The promoters had their troubles with farmers and ranchers who rebelled at paying $2.50 per acre for water, and the "privately owned monopoly" became a political issue. They were obliged to abandon their plan of getting water from Kings River owing to "prior rights" and much money was wasted. But we are not concerned with the woes of the company save insofar as they affected Henry Miller. The promoters discovered that they had not read their contract with him as carefully as they should have done, and whereas they were obliged to provide him with water at half price, nothing was stated about his obligation to take a certain amount. He took very little. The promoters raged. Miller treated them with bland indifference. They filed a suit. Of no avail. Other worries and trials multiplied. Finally they threw up their hands in despair and sold out the controlling interest to Henry Miller for less than one-third of its cost. The financiers became minority stockholders. "Henry Miller not only had a canal system to irrigate his land, but to sell water to the entire community. . . . The canal was immediately put in condition and under economical management. Alfalfa was introduced into the territory, and it became a prolific dairy and cattle country. The water supply was the cheapest and best in the state."

7

More and more land, more and more cattle.

In 1850, the United States Congress had passed the "Swamp Act," by which California received two million acres of swamp land. In the early seventies, Henry Miller acquired a tract along the Kern River, fifty miles long and containing a hundred thousand acres, at a cost of $1.25 an acre.

He "conceived a huge reclamation project, including a new river channel on one side of the property. For this purpose a right of way for a canal was obtained from the United States over the adjoining land, and the new canal was put on government land which was dry and worthless. Horses, mules, plows, and scrapers were collected and the dust was made to fly. The canal was one hundred feet wide and fifty miles in length. Gates were constructed to control the flow of the river into this new channel and soon one hundred thousand acres of land were reclaimed."

Then came war with two Kentuckians, James B. Haggin and Lloyd Tevis, men who were destined to play a prominent part in the financial and social history of San Francisco. Both were short stout men, but whereas Tevis was "sandy" and genial, Haggin, who had a strain of Turkish blood, was dark, saturnine, and picturesque. They were clever, shrewd, ruthless men, growing richer with every revolution of the earth round the sun and highly respected in San Francisco.

The firm of Haggin and Tevis had acquired land farther up the river and their intention was to spread its waters over the plains of the valley and sell it to farmers to whom the land had no attraction in its present parched condition. But the land which they proposed to irrigate had been patented by the government in small parcels, and only a limited number were contiguous to the river. Of course they had planned to "appropriate" the water, but Henry Miller claimed that the river was part and parcel of the land touching the river. Once more riparian and appropriation rights locked horns.

In the litigation that followed, Hall McAllister, the most commanding figure at the bar, was counsel for Miller. Haggin and Tevis were represented by John Barber, another legal light. Lawyers less illustrious but able assisted both.

"The Battle of the Giants" was a long-drawn-out affair. It is needless to go into the multitudinous details, the legal tangles, the involvement of politicians, press, and public opinion. But money flowed faster than water over the dams.

The Miller counsel played up the fact that California was no longer a Spanish or Mexican province, but had been conquered by English-speaking people and their first act "was to carry to it the laws of England, which had been brought to almost all of the states in the Union and were considered a sacred heritage of English-speaking people. This argument appealed to judges who had come from various states where the common law of England was the rule of decision, and from colleges where Blackstone was the Bible of the lawyer, who were nurtured on the law of England and considered it as a law that automatically accommodated itself to every clime and every people, a law that was capable of ruling people in the cold climate of Massachusetts, the torrid climate of Arizona, and the semi-arid climate of California."

The Haggin and Tevis counsel argued that "the rule of law which existed in the British Isles where it rained every month in the year, and where irrigation was unnecessary for the production of crops, could not possibly have been intended to prevail in a state where the rainfall was slight and of short duration, and the land was incapable of growing the usual crops without artificial moisture."

There were decisions and rehearings, the suit went on and on but finally "it fell to the lot of Justice McKinstry to write the opinion of the court. A man of higher standing, morally or intellectually, could not well have been found, and if the whole world had been sought for a man of unimpeachable character, who was still the best suited to uphold the Riparian Doctrine for which the Miller interests contended, no one could have done better than to have selected Justice McKinstry for that part. He was born and bred in the common law, and knew his Blackstone forwards and backwards. He believed honestly and sincerely in the omnipotence of the law and the infallibility of the common law of England to solve every human dispute. His decision occupied two hundred pages in the California reports. It was a victory for the common law, for the Riparian Doctrine, and for Henry Miller; and through all the assaults that have been made upon it, it still stands as the recognized law of the state."

Once more Henry Miller had triumphed. But in lesser matters, especially if they favored his own interests, he was always willing to compromise. He joined forces with Haggin and Tevis. "Levees were hastily constructed and a reservoir built to impound one third of the water for Henry Miller, and the other two-thirds were permitted to be taken out and distributed over the arid land of Kern County."

8

Miller's passion for land was insatiable. Before the middle eighties his holdings had swept over into Nevada and upward into Oregon. He had realized his dream of a million acres of land and a million head of livestock. To him Lux was merely a business appendage; it was *he* who bought the land, fought the legal battles—and won them—*he* who bought the live-stock, which now included ten thousand hogs and two thousand horses. In 1881, Miller and Lux slaughtered 82,332 animals for the San Francisco market alone: 12,000 steers, 6,564 calves, 22,435 lambs, and 7,631 hogs. The aggregate value was $700,000.

As it takes ten acres to feed one steer, it may be assumed that his livestock sometimes straggled over state borders and grazed on government land; even a million acres will not support a million hungry cows, steers, sheep, horses, hogs. Sometimes he rented.

But not even his pride in being known throughout the entire Union as the "Cattle King," in being the greatest land-owner in the West, in the immense wealth he was piling up, in his legal triumphs, gave him such a thrill of sheer happi-ness as when he reined in his horse on a hilltop and gazed down at the great Santa Clara Valley, filled from border to border with his thousands upon thousands of tossing horns, as white as if polished with alkali, gleaming in the sunlight. A dream come true. The living symbol of his genius. And all flaunting his famous brand, a double HH.

9

In 1860, Henry Miller had found time to marry. He cared little for women but he wanted an heir to carry on his name. No doubt many a young woman had longed to marry him quite aside from his wealth, for although his body was ungainly he had a handsome face. His large luminous dark eyes had a farseeing expression in repose; they could blaze with anger, half close with contempt, sparkle with laughter. His head and nose were finely proportioned, his brow was broad and full, his well-cut mouth, save when smiling, registered the power and determination of his character. All in all, he was a romantic figure to the feminine mind.

But such young ladies as he met, all but one, sighed in vain. It was not until he was thirty-two that he married a sister-in-law of Charles Lux. Unfortunately, she died within the year; but an heir he must have, and in the following year he married his partner's niece. She bore him three children, Henry Junior, Sarah Alice, and Nelly. Their home was in Gilroy not far from Pacheco Pass, and the land for miles north and south was his.

Miller was less fortunate in his private life than in his worldly adventure. It was the old story: life gives with one hand and takes with the other. His son was a cripple; his eldest daughter was thrown from a horse and killed. Only Nelly lived to carry on the fortune if not the name. She married Leroy Nickel and her descendants are notable in the business and social world of San Francisco. But he had his compensations even in his domestic life. His wife was devoted and intelligent, and so were his remaining daughter and his son who attained middle life. Nor was it in his half-visionary half-realistic nature to remain for long in the Cave of Despair.

As ever, he spent the greater part of his time among the livestock on his various ranches, attending to every detail. And there were floods and droughts to contend with. Prolonged rains turned the rivers into roaring torrents that broke down the levees and covered the floor of the interior valleys. There were frantic hours of driving the livestock to higher ground. The wailing of the cows for their lost calves mingled with the shrieking of the wind. For days and nights the battle went on, a few hundred men against the relentless forces of nature.

But the droughts were even more dreaded. The streams dried, the grass withered to its roots. In one of the droughts more than a million cattle perished in the state. The plain looked like a forgotten battleground, strewn as it was with bleached skulls and bones. Many ranchers were ruined, forced to begin life over again on borrowed money.

But not Henry Miller. Always farsighted, he had accumulated stacks of hay from year to year and when the drought came, he had an immense stock on hand. He drove his cattle from one of his ranches to another, from county to county. Such as succumbed to the lack of green fodder and the scarcity of water, he slaughtered in vats already prepared. "They were skinned and the fats extracted, the balance made into chicken feed. In this manner he utilized not only his own stock, but the stock of his neighbors who had no means of salvaging it. The fat netted him thousands of dollars in lard. . . . The losses were staggering, but the prices of meat were high in view of the shortage. When all was over, most of his competitors were bankrupt while his resources enabled him to purchase their ranchos for a song and restock them. Droughts not only did not ruin him but were turned to his advantage. In the five years following the drought of 1888 he made a profit of $8,000,000."

And when he approached his end, at the age of eighty-nine, he had little to regret (having a well-disciplined conscience), sufficient happiness, and a long life of almost unbroken success to look back upon.

Graham Cranston

Gone are the great ranchos save for one or two in the southernmost part of the state. Gone are the cattle kings; since the death of Henry Miller none has held that proud title, received the deference of a monarch. Gone also are the "tossing horns" so beloved by Miller; the poor devils are now dehorned.

It is true there are more cattle in California than ever before, but the innumerable ranches on which they are raised rarely exceed five thousand acres.

And these ranches are as modern as skyscrapers. The owners—the more fortunate, at least—live in large comfortable frame or stone houses furnished with electricity, central heating, running water, and the ranchers rarely do their own slaughtering: butchers buy steers on the hoof. They drive their cars over good roads to the nearest town where they go to the movies or attend to business. They love the life and rarely desert it for another, even when they have accumulated wealth.

Of the many young men engaged in this agreeable and lucrative business, I have chosen Mr. Graham Cranston as typical of the best. His ranch of forty-six hundred acres in the Sierra foothills is ten miles from the small but important city of Auburn and one hundred and fifty miles northeast of San Francisco. His herd runs from four hundred to five hundred head of cattle; about one cow to ten acres. As this ratio is possible for seven months of the year only, he, like other cattlemen in the foothills, has a summer range high in the mountains—he rents forty-five thousand acres from the Tahoe

National Forest. This range is about fifty miles east of the home ranch and on it the cattle spend five months of the year.

In May Mr. Cranston starts rounding up the cattle on the home ranch. The calves are branded, ear-marked, castrated, and vaccinated against certain diseases. The bulls which have been with the cows since the first of March, are taken from the herd; they are kept at home the year round.

Every one of the grown stock is belled, for the mountains are rough and rugged, and the bells keep the cattle from being lost no matter how far they may stray.

The drive to the mountains is one of the high points of the year. Four riders (who would scorn to call themselves anything as old-fashioned as vaqueros) are needed, and a man to drive the pick-up truck, which takes the place of the old chuck wagon. Each rider has at least one cow dog (usually a shepherd) with him. Of course Mr. Cranston always accompanies his cattle on their yearly pilgrimage and is frequently joined by friends on horseback who go along for the fun of the ride, and incidentally give welcome help; four riders are none too many for five hundred head of cattle. At night they camp at corrals where the cattle get food and water. Arrived at the range, the cattle are split into small groups and driven to various parts of the range, a task that takes another five days.

One man with two horses is left on the range for the summer. He rides about, keeping an eye on the cattle, seeing that they have plenty of salt, keeping the springs and water troughs flowing, and killing such predatory game as he can; there is some loss from mountain lions, bears, coyotes, and wildcats. They seldom attack a cow but frequently get a calf. Mr. Cranston makes regular visits to the range, taking up salt, and food for the man, dogs, and horses.

The round-up takes place early in October. This again calls for four riders and one pick-up driver. It takes five or six weeks of long, hard riding before the last of the cows and calves are collected and driven down to the home ranch. Usually three drives are necessary.

Arrived at home, the cattle are again sorted out. The bells are taken off most of the stock, a few being left on the known leaders. The calves are weaned and the steers and such heifers as are not needed for replacement are sold. The cows are put into a number of small fields, where they spend the winter. During December, January, and February the new calf crop arrives and someone rides out every day to see that all is well. In March the bulls are again put with the cows, and the cycle of cattle raising is complete.

Many other things of importance occur during the year. The old cows that have ceased bearing—"cull animals"—and bulls that have been in the herd three years are sold in the late spring. Five bulls are sold and five purchased each year. The old ones usually go to slaughter, although sometimes to a neighbor. The new ones are bought from some reputable breeder of registered stock, and cost from $150 to $300 each.

The commercial industry of beef cattle is divided into three parts. In the first group, to which Mr. Cranston belongs, are the breeders and raisers of cattle. The second group takes the young stock at breeding time, or a little later, and, with extra good care and feed, raises them to maturity. The final group takes the mature stock and, in ninety to one hundred days, puts the final finish on the cattle by placing them in small pens where they are fed enormous quantities of concentrated feeds. Seldom does one outfit attempt all three operations, although sometimes the first two are found together, particularly in the central valleys where cheap and plentiful feed is produced. Due partly to labor shortage, there is an increasing tendency toward smaller units, with greater use of cultivated crops and irrigated land.

The Cranston ranch lies at an elevation of about twelve thousand feet. It has little level land but it does have about twenty-five acres of ladino clover and alfalfa pasture. It also raises about seventy-five tons of oats and vetch hay. On the irrigated pastures are kept, during the summer months, a few head of registered cows, the beginnings of a pure-bred herd. Hogs have proved a valuable side line. A few cows are retained for family use. Two men are kept throughout the year. If one is a married man with children, Mr. Cranston provides him with a comfortable house, electricity, water, and pasture for several cows and horses. The single man is lodged in a bunk house. These men take care of all the daily chores: milking, feeding the hogs, and such cattle as need extra feeding. They do most of the regular work of plowing and harvesting.

2

One would think that Mr. Cranston would have quite enough to do on his ranch, but he has taken on civil duties as well. He drives into Auburn, the county seat, two or three times a week, for he is or has been president of the Rotary Club and the Placer County Farm Bureau. He is also a member of The Grange and the California Cattlemen's Association.

Like John Marsh, he is a graduate of Harvard, but there the likeness ends. He is amiable, generous, neighborly, and popular. He has two children and a wife who was brought up in Placer County and knows almost as much about ranching as he does.

This ardent rancher started life as a playboy. When he left Harvard he intended to be a newspaper man. But to this his father would not consent. Mr. Cranston senior was a mining engineer of note and wished Graham to enter the firm. So Graham decided to do nothing and played about with the young people of San Rafael and San Francisco. By the time his father died, however, he was tired of society and idleness and decided to become a rancher. And a contented and successful rancher he has been ever since. He visits San Francisco occasionally, and his old friends visit him. Many of these young men, whose business or profession force them to live in the city, depart from the Cranston ranch envying its owner deeply. Californians, even when born and bred in San Francisco, are always longing for life in the open, but few of them are fitted for it. And city-bred wives have no longing for it whatever. Graham Cranston was wise in his choice.

10. *The Pageant of San Francisco Society*

Swells and Belles

SAN FRANCISCO SOCIETY (spelled with seven capitals) in the 1850's and sixties took itself very seriously. Like priests, clergymen, and social reformers, it had a mission. There must be one group in that turbulent city *sans peur et sans reproche;* elegant, virtuous, select, above all EXCLUSIVE. Today they would be called snobs, but they meant well.

Throughout the fifties and sixties, and the early seventies, Mrs. Hall McAllister was the leader of the group, the arbiter elegantiarum, as powerful in her small world as was her great husband at the Bar of Justice. She was a small woman but very erect, very haughty in public, but gracious, vivacious, utterly charming in her own circle. Her features, like her figure, were exquisitely modeled, and after the day of coal-scuttle bonnets had passed she wore her hair—prematurely white, which added to her distinction—*à la pompadour,* the erstwhile waterfall softly disposed on top of her head. Her hands and feet were tiny and she dressed with the instinctive taste of her French blood—she was a creole from New Orleans. Her mansion was on Rincon Hill.

But if she was the unchallenged leader of both society and fashion, there were others in her flock equally notable. Roberta Barron, the half-Mexican wife of one of the owners of the New Almaden mines, the greatest quicksilver mines in the world save their famous namesake in Spain; Mrs. Donahoe, Mrs. Friedlander, Mrs. Redington, Mrs. Cutler McAllister, Mrs. Crittenden, Mrs. Thornton, moved in an almost visible aura—wafted from the South, of course. Oh—many others. At the end of this chapter I will list the names of what outsiders derisively called the "ancient aristocracy," but these will do for the present. Their favorite author was Ouida, although a few read the classics: Thackeray, Scott, and Dickens. Their poet was Byron.

Of course there were many belles. Alejandra Atherton, born in Chile of a Spanish mother, had immense blue eyes— as Spanish as if they were ebon-black—which "talked" more eloquently than her tongue. Her features were regular, her hair a rich mahogany-brown, her body tall and slender; and she affected a complete indifference to dress. She was an accomplished flirt but, although her proposals were many, she married rather late. At one time she was engaged to a Mr. Sturgis of Boston, whom she had met on a sea voyage, but he died suddenly and it may have been that she cherished a secret sorrow. Eventually she married Major J. Lawrence Rathbone of Albany, a West Pointer who came to California on the staff of General Schofield, and her eyes talked to no other man thereafter. He retired from the army and became a good citizen of San Francisco and a notable sportsman.

And then there were the "Three Macs": Ella Maxwell, daughter of the physician who ushered all fashionable babies into the world; Jeannie McNulty; and Mollie McMullen, whose husband, Milton S. Latham, built her an enormous house in the fashionable suburb Menlo Park, furnished it like a palace, and gave her a standing order with a Paris dressmaker for two trousseaux a year. She was the loveliest of brunettes, with large soft brown eyes; gentle, amiable, and popular. Jeannie McNulty made no pretensions to beauty but, small dark and vivacious, she had her own little court. Ella Maxwell died young of what is now quickly diagnosed as appendicitis, but in that benighted era was beyond the comprehension and skill of any doctor; all any one of them

could do for the shrieking sufferer was to dose her with
laudanum and let her die.

Another belle was Nelly Gordon, who was the sport of a
malignant fate. Mr. Gordon was born in Yorkshire, England,
near the village of Haworth, the home of the famous Brontë
sisters. He was intimate with their brother Branwell, a dissipated young man, and, although he himself was not, he went
on an occasional spree with his friend. He went on one too
many and, when he recovered, found himself married to a
handsome barmaid, a friend of both the young men, whose
ambition it was to be a "great lady," and who had long
marked Gordon as her victim. He was horrified and humiliated. Never would he introduce her to his family, not even
to the servants in a remote country house. Like the rest of
the world, he had heard of California, and he made up his
mind to take the woman where nothing was known of her
antecedents. She raged and stormed and vowed vengeance,
but she was obliged to accompany her husband or return to
her old job of handing out drinks. Unfortunately for him,
she went. On the voyage he made the discovery that she was
a hard, albeit secret, drinker; previously she had been clever
enough to feign illness "when the fit came on her." He could
have thrown her overboard any dark night and often wished
he had not been so well brought up.

Gordon was young and buoyant; he determined to make
the best of his broken life. He took a considerable fortune
with him and soon became an active citizen in San Francisco.
As her spells became more frequent, due to her hatred of
the crude new country, it was not difficult to keep her in the
background.

It was Gordon who laid out South Park and imported the
rows of ugly brown houses that encircled it. By the time the
families of Gordon's new friends arrived, his wife had advanced from spells to steady drinking and lived in sullen
seclusion, hating everyone. She was supposed to be an invalid,

and the few who knew Gordon's unhappy secret kept it loyally. The butler he had brought from England took complete charge of her. Gordon fervently hoped she would drink herself to death and as speedily as possible.

His daughter Nelly, pretty, bright, charming, vivacious, grew up with the other girls and was beloved by all. There was always that horror in the background, and a secret fear locked away in her brain, but youth is volatile and she was happy and light-hearted when in the homes of her companions.

She was sixteen when Mr. Gordon sought an interview with his friend Mr. Faxon Dean Atherton, who knew his marital history, and told him that he had recently made a frightful discovery. In one of her tantrums, his wife had screamed that she had accomplished her vengeance: Nelly would one day be a drunkard like herself. She had mixed whiskey with her baby food, given her larger and larger doses as she grew older until her system demanded it even as it demanded bread and sweets, water and solid food. Sometimes a stronger craving seized her and she crept into her mother's room at night and they had a little spree together. One night she sprang suddenly to her feet, dashed the contents of her glass into her mother's face, vowed she would never touch the stuff again, and ran out of the room. "But she will," chuckled the woman. "She will. It's in her blood—two ways. Your darling Nelly will disgrace you yet—and break your heart in the bargain."

Mr. Gordon, hardly believing, had sought Nelly at once. She had confirmed her mother's story with a wild burst of grief and sworn she would conquer the horrible craving. She would! She would! It was only occasionally that she felt the desire. It would be more and more infrequent—she knew it! She gave her father her solemn word of honor she never would drink so much as a glass of wine again.

But Mr. Gordon was not so sure, and in his despair he had

sought the advice of his friend. What should he do to save his idolized daughter?

Mr. Atherton's response was immediate. His girls at that time were not yet grown and his family lived the year round at his country place, Valparaiso Park. Let Nelly visit them for a year and study with their governess; she would be happy and diverted there—the girls spent much of their time out of doors, playing croquet, walking in the woods, riding horseback—free from temptation. At the end of the year she would have outgrown the craving; then, Mr. Atherton advised, send her to a boarding-school in Boston to finish her education.

Mr. Gordon gratefully accepted the invitation, and so did Nelly. She was happy for a time and the demon slept. Then her mother managed to smuggle bottles of brandy into her laundry. Temptation finally overcame her and she left Valparaiso Park abruptly, announcing that she could not stand the separation from her father. She continued her tragic secret struggle and it was long before the truth leaked out. Mrs. McAllister gave her a coming-out party, and before midnight she was firmly established as one of the belles. There were parties every night; once more she was happily diverted.

One chance she had of salvation. An Englishman, whose name I have forgotten, visited San Francisco and fell in love with her and she with him. She told him the whole hideous story. He was horrified, but begged her to marry him immediately. He would take her to England, and happiness and the divorce from her old associations would surely effect a cure. But to this she would not consent. She was determined to conquer by her own will alone. He was to leave at once and return a year later. By that time she *knew* she would be cured. She had not felt the craving since the hour she had met him. He consented against his better judgment, but said that he would remain in New York, and return sooner if she sent for him. For nearly a year she was triumphant. Then he wrote her that he was obliged to go to Cuba where his brother was ill, but as soon as he had brought him back to New York and placed him in a hospital he would take the first boat or stage for San Francisco; not a day longer would he wait. But one thing and another detained him. His brother was seriously ill. Letters were lost. Months passed. Nelly, in a fit of despondency, believing he had forgotten her, succumbed. She wrote him a last letter forbidding him to return.

Mr. Gordon had a country place not far from Menlo Park, on an estate now the property of Stanford University. Here his wife had been installed as soon as the Englishman left. Thence Nelly retired after she dispatched her last letter.

Mr. Gordon died. The butler was left in charge of the household and he, too, drank. The dissipated or merely excitement-loving young men of the neighborhood paid frequent visits to that house and indulged in orgies that were the scandal of the aristocratic and eminently respectable faubourg. Nelly survived her father but a short time; she was determined to drink herself to death.

I made Nelly Gordon the heroine of my first novel, and read it over recently for atmosphere. But it gave me the horrors and I couldn't finish it. It has long been out of print. (Several copies found their way into the library of an English prison. The convicts, with a sudden recrudescence of virtue, made a bonfire of them in the prison yard.)

The Grain King

Isaac Friedlander was born in Oldenburg, Germany, in 1824, went to South Carolina with his family at the age of eleven, and grew up as ardent a Southerner as if the blood of a Thornton or a Crittenden ran in his veins. In 1849 he arrived in San Francisco, leaving his wife and baby girl to follow him later.

He played an active part in the development of the city;

later in that of the state itself where he owned immense ranches for the raising and export of grain.

Newcomers regarded him with awe; he was six feet seven and powerfully built. Even Gwin was forced to look up to him as they stood talking in the street, a pose little to the taste of the haughty Chiv, though he liked Friedlander himself.

When his family arrived, he established them in South Park, and other children were born there. Eventually he moved to a larger house in Bryant Street, one of the three streets within that cordon which, with Rincon Hill and South Park, separated the social mighty from the rank outsider. His eldest daughter married Augustus Bowie, one of the elect. His other daughters, Fanny and May, although handsome and popular, never married, but they entertained lavishly, for Mr. Friedlander was now one of the wealthiest men in the community, and his wife, like all Southerners, was an adept at the art of entertaining. His son Carey was almost as tall as himself, a brilliant young man and as popular as his sisters.

Mr. Friedlander was noted not only for his imposing height and noble countenance, but for his conversational felicity and, above all, for his fine manners, which served him well in that excitable city and upon one occasion caused him a good deal of amusement.

At a public dinner, sometime in the 1860's, he sat next to a young Englishman who had arrived in San Francisco a few days before. He liked the shy young man and entertained him with anecdotes of a time, now happily passed into history, when San Francisco was known as "the wickedest city on earth." The Englishman was entranced, not only by the Grain King's interesting conversation but by his massive dignity, his elegant vocabulary, and his polished manners. Suddenly he broke out with irrepressible naïveté, "I say—do you know—I never in the world would have taken you for a Jew,

Mr. Friedlander, and I know you must be from your name. It's—well—it's rather extraordinary, don't you know!"

"Young man," drawled Mr. Friedlander, "there are three kinds of Jews. There are Jews. There are damned Jews. And there are goddamned Jews. I am a Jew."

The Englishman stared, stuttered, "Ah—yes—quite—quite," and finally took it in.

Mr. Friedlander's fortune was seriously impaired by the terrible drought of 1877, and he died in the following year leaving but a fragment of his great wealth. But his family did not "drop out." One supreme virtue San Francisco society has always possessed: loyalty to its own. The Friedlanders moved into a smaller house and the girls received invitations to luncheons, dinners, parties, and balls as automatically as in the days of their splendor. Carey died, but "Fried" Bowie, eminent at the Bar, made another fortune and was devoted to his handsome aunts. He died unmarried and left them the greater part of his wealth.

The Red-Shirted Duke

Milton S. Latham, as I have told, married the beautiful Mollie McMullen and built what was then the most magnificent house in California as a proper setting for his young wife. It was elaborately furnished, and he had a chef, an English butler, a large staff of servants, a vintage cellar, and entertained on a grand scale. The Duke of Manchester was making a world tour in the early seventies and passed through California. He brought a letter to Mr. Latham, who left a card on him at once at the Palace Hotel, together with a note inviting him to dine and spend the following night at his country house and "meet a few friends."

The Duke telegraphed his acceptance, and invitations were sent out to the county gentry of Menlo Park, Fair Oaks, which included Valparaiso Park, and San Mateo. None was declined and Mrs. McAllister and Mrs. Barron came down on an afternoon train from San Francisco.

The Duke arrived by a late train and was escorted at once to his room. The company assembled in the drawing room, the women in Paris gowns and jewels, the men in their poor best. Not one had ever seen a duke, and they were agreeably fluttered.

The English butler, looking as if striken with palsy, threw open the door and announced in faltering tones:

"His Grace, the Duke of Manchester!"

And then the Duke strode in and the company, to say nothing of the host and hostess, nearly fainted. The Duke wore boots that reached his thighs, a pistol in his belt, and a red flannel shirt; no coat, not even a necktie.

The company behaved very well. Not a gasp escaped their lips, not a smile twitched their features. Mr. and Mrs. Latham went forward and greeted him cordially. It was the poor Duke who was as red as his shirt and utterly discomfited as he saw that company of ladies and gentlemen that would not have disgraced his ancestral halls. He stammered out his explanation to his suave and smiling hosts. All he knew of California he had gleaned from the pages of Bret Harte, and he had provided himself (in Chicago) with what he believed to be the proper western costume that all who entertained him might feel quite at their ease. As he had a slight cold, he had not left his room at the Palace until it was time to drive to the train. True, he had had misgivings when he saw the tasteful splendor of the house, but he had brought no other change and hoped against hope that all might be well.

The company had recovered from their stupor before he finished his embarrassed apologies, took the matter as a huge joke, and put him at his ease at once. I believe there was never a more successful dinner given in Menlo Park. The Duke invited them all to visit him in England, and went on his way delighted with Californians.

The Romantic Barredas

In 1879, San Francisco opened its arms to a family, once wealthy, now impoverished, but of immense prestige and incredibly romantic. And they made more fuss over them than they would have made over royalty itself.

Señor Frederico Barreda had been Peruvian Minister to Spain, France, England, and the United States. In Spain he had married an entrancing beauty, Doña Matilda Luisa Laveerrerie, who presented him with a son and five daughters with no loss of pulchritude. After his retirement he built a house on Madison Avenue, New York, and "Beaulieu" at Newport. Madame Barreda, as she was always called, was a reigning beauty, a queen of fashion, and the intimate friend of Mrs. Astor. All she knew of life was luxury, pleasure, and happiness. Of the abominable slums of New York she had never heard; the word poverty was not in her vocabulary. She had sixteen servants in her Madison Avenue house and several more in Beaulieu.

And then one day Wall Street had one of its periodical débâcles. Fortunes that for generations had been as secure as the rocky base of New York itself crashed and Mr. Barreda's with them. Whether he had indulged in speculation I do not know; it may be that he was badly advised and had invested unwisely the fortune he had transferred from Lima. But whatever the cause, that tidal wave of economic disaster swept him over its crest and he was a ruined man. Or almost. He sold his house in New York for its full value; Mr. and Mrs. Astor bought Beaulieu "for sentiment's sake."

And did the lovely butterfly weep and wail and lament her abrupt loss of luxury and consequence? Not Madame Barreda! For the first time she revealed to herself as well as to her astonished friends the sound practical core of the Spanish woman's character. Whatever her private regrets, neither her family nor the world knew of them. She sold her diamond tiara, breastplate, and necklaces, and took her young family to Paris where she could live comfortably on a small income and educate her children. She had made many friends there during her husband's incumbency, but she avoided all but a small circle.

Her eldest daughter died and she was plunged into grief for a time, but lost none of her courage nor her determination to make the best of all things. Mr. Barreda, who made several fortunate investments, traveled back and forth and, in 1879, announced his intention of settling in California. He had made one visit to San Francisco and decided that there was the place to make another fortune. Madame Barreda, being a dutiful wife, and also somewhat excited at the prospect of a change of scene, for she was tired of Paris, consented.

They traveled luxuriously across the Atlantic—but that trip across the American continent in the 1870's! Madame Barreda must have felt that all other ordeals paled before it. It took seven long days. Cinders flew in at the windows. The water was alkaline. The atmosphere reeked with smoke and the odor of food, for many carried lunch baskets. There was no restaurant car and passengers descended three times a day to assuage their hunger in eating houses where flies swarmed, tablecloths were spotted, the crockery none too clean, cups had no handles. Fried steak and potatoes swimming in grease were the staples. Mastication was necessarily slow, and often before it was accomplished the conductor appeared at the door and shouted, "All a-b-o-a-r-d. Step lively now!"

Madame Barreda and her daughters, Amalia and Rosa, endured in grim silence, but nothing could daunt the high spirits of Mattie, the eldest, nor of Christine, a little girl of six; they took the new experience as a great lark and no doubt bolstered the spirits of the others.

They arrived in San Francisco, tired, grimy, their hair stiff with dirt, but fortunately unheralded. Mr. Barreda rushed them to a hotel and its welcome bathtubs.

On his previous visit, Mr. Barreda had made the acquaintance of Frederick W. Macondray and called on him the day after his arrival. Macondray had married Elena Atherton, sister of the one-time belle, Alejandra, now Mrs. Rathbone. Born in Chile, Elena spoke Spanish as fluently as English. Her husband asked her to call on Madame Barreda, who might feel more at home in this strange new city if the first person she met greeted her in her own language. Mrs. Macondray called at once, taking her young daughter Nina with her as a companion for the little Christine. All were mutually enchanted.

Mrs. Macondray took the next train for Fair Oaks, the way station for a number of country places and preferred to the more bustling Menlo Park. She told her mother excitedly that now there was someone with whom she could talk Spanish and that Madame Barreda was "simply lovely."

Mrs. Atherton was five feet in height and two hundred pounds in girth. Although she kept open house, she rarely left Valparaiso Park until the winter, which she spent in San Francisco, but upon this occasion she made the effort for the enticing prospect of talking with a woman as full-bloodedly Spanish as herself. Within an hour after her arrival at the hotel the two women had become intimate friends, and she took the whole family back with her for a rest at Valparaiso Park.

Mr. Barreda quickly installed his family in a rented house, and all society rushed to do homage, incited by curiosity, sympathy, genuine interest, and not a little snobbery. They knew all about the Barredas' former magnificence, their tragic downfall, the great Mrs. Astor's practical devotion, the invincible courage of the once pampered beauty.

Madame Barreda charmed them all with her simple gracious manners, and, although her first beauty had faded and she had grown rather stout, her cameo-like features and the sweetness of her expression were unalterable. And such a family! Mr. Barreda, handsome and distinguished; Mattie, although plain, was gay, witty, and fascinating; Amalia, lovely with light chestnut hair, brown eyes and white skin; Rosa, an authentic dark Spanish beauty; and the little black-haired gray-eyed Christine as gay, lively, and carefree as her elder sister. To the boy, Frederico, the twin of Rosa, they paid little attention; adolescent boys are not likely to interest anyone but their parents.

All the rest of that family seemed to move in a visible aura; nothing so romantic had ever happened to San Francisco. When someone recalled that in the days of her glory Madame Barreda had borne so striking a resemblance to the Empress Eugénie that when she entered her box at the opera, blazing with jewels (including a high diamond tiara), the audience sometimes rose and remained standing until she was seated, San Francisco society felt more romantic than ever.

Mrs. McAllister never rushed anyone, but she, too, became an intimate and devoted friend of Madame Barreda. As for Mrs. Atherton and her new friend, they jabbered Spanish until their jawbones ached.

Mr. Barreda prospered for a time and bought a large house on Buchanan Street in the fashionable residential district, where they entertained modestly. Amalia "came out" and was hailed as a beauty; but, alas, she fell ill of rheumatic fever, and as no doctor knew anything of teeth infection, much less of the poison that might breed in throat and appendix, she died after a lingering and painful illness. Several years later Mr. Barreda's business venture, which had been slowly declining, expired, and he died shortly after.

Madame Barreda rented the house in Buchanan Street and moved into a small one in California Street. She had not forgotten her long experience in "managing," and once more accomplished wonders. She accepted no more invitations save to Valparaiso Park, although they were still showered upon her. Mrs. Atherton and Mrs. McAllister, who now also lived in the country, expressed their sympathy in a practical manner: they kept her amply supplied with hams, eggs, chickens, and fresh vegetables, which Madame Barreda accepted with dignity and some humor.

Society Marches On

In the nineties San Francisco society had two dictators: "Ned" Greenway, of Baltimore, and Mrs. Salisbury of the Thornton-Crittenden clan; the Southern imperial rule lasted until the end of the century.

Greenway held his cotillions in Native Son's Hall, Mrs. Salisbury her "Fortnightlys" in Lunt's Hall, a dancing academy in Polk Street. Neither place was very stylish, but no one would consider lending his house at regular intervals, and hotels at that time were not private enough to command the approval of the exclusive. They thawed out a decade later.

Mrs. Salisbury's affairs were mainly for the débutantes, who had been somewhat neglected hitherto. The girls adored her; she made each one feel as she entered that *she* was the favored and most welcome guest, also the prettiest and the most charmingly dressed. Not one was ever a wall flower. The young men stood in awe of her and if told to go and dance with the plainest girls they obeyed and performed their duty with grace if not with enthusiasm.

Mrs. Salisbury was a born leader. She was executive, amiable, firm, highly accomplished, stately, and handsome. She understood girls thoroughly—she had two of her own—and enjoyed seeing all her new flock gay and happy. Also carefully shepherded; no outsider, no new-rich ever obtained entrance to Lunt's Hall on shabby Polk Street.

Greenway, although "Mrs. Salisbury's girls" attended his cotillions, was more hospitable to those of a later vintage:

newcomers from other parts of the state or of the Union, or even those newly risen to wealth. Many a timid girl who longed for a "good time" but was balefully ignored by the ladies of the *ancien régime,* made her début at one of the "Greenways," and married into the "old set." Greenway knew their fathers, and was the agent for Mumms Extra Dry.

Young married women and a few of the elders were invited to subscribe to his cotillions, which, by the way, were more popular with the young men than were Mrs. Salisbury's, for his supper table was adorned with magnums of champagne; Mrs. Salisbury also served ample suppers but not wine.

Greenway, a plump amiable little man, was always genial and tactful and, after the cotillion was over, danced with the plainest of the débutantes; but once I saw him lose his temper. "What do you think!" he exclaimed. "That little brat," referring to one of the latest débutantes, "has refused to dance with —— because he is a married man! Says she won't waste her time! Trouble with her is she wasn't spanked often enough."

Few of the houses of that era were large enough for balls. The Haggins and Tevises built large and stately mansions on Nob Hill. Mrs. Haggin was a recluse, but Mrs. Tevis gave several elaborate balls during the season at which the chaperons made a jeweled dado against the walls and the young people danced until dawn. The Hobarts on Van Ness Avenue also gave parties and balls, and so did the Sidney Smiths and Mrs. Pierce, who, like Mrs. Salisbury, had two handsome daughters, and an ark in the new Western Addition.

And the Parrotts! They dwelt in a large and ugly house on Sutter Street and gave coming-out balls of utmost exclusiveness for each of their numerous daughters. They were an old banking family dating from the earliest fifties, and never forgot it.

They also had a fine estate in San Mateo, another fashionable faubourg "down the Peninsula." The house was now quite old, and the grounds bore some resemblance to an English park. Here they entertained with formal hospitality during the summer. But with all their worldly gifts they were somewhat deficient in humor. Gouverneur Morris—at a much later date—visited San Francisco during the summer and, bearing a letter to one of the Parrotts, was invited to Baywood for a week-end. The host took him on a long walk about the park, pointing out with pardonable pride its cultivated beauties. Finally, in a remote corner, they came upon a small but elegant family burying ground. The host waved his hand at the most imposing of the monuments. The guest dutifully read the inscription: "Here lies the first Parrott." Morris, being a perfect gentleman, swallowed hastily and controlled his features.

But to return to the social era of the seventies, eighties, and nineties. It was an era of incredible snobbishness, and, looking back, one sometimes gasps with wonder, for snobbery hardly exists in San Francisco today. As long as Mrs. McAllister reigned, society was actuated more by the instinct of self-protection than by what its descendants would call snootism, but as time went on and Mrs. McAllister took less interest in "the world," although still the titular queen, and other women of greater wealth and ambition entertained constantly and with increasing magnificence, snobbishness raised its ugly head and spread like a noxious weed. The familiar phrase "And *who* is *she?*" was accompanied by a lifting of the brows, a pointing of aristocratic noses, a downward curve of intolerant lips. The great fortunes made in the Nevada mines and other notable enterprises in the seventies swelled San Francisco to bursting with families animated by a natural desire to enjoy the privileges of patrician society. Some were indubitably "common," even vulgar, but others were quite as well educated, refined, and even traveled as any of the ancient aristocracy. Never mind. They were nobodies, upstarts. They didn't belong. Never should the tone of San Francisco society be minified by *persons* who had been born Heaven only knew where. Once a nobody always a nobody. What was mere wealth? Were not the old families wealthy enough? Swollen millions were vulgar. Newcomers from other parts of the state or nation were equally unfortunate unless they "brought letters."

When I was a young married woman, I once asked a friend several years older than myself if she would call upon the family of a friend I had made at boarding school. They had a nice house in San Francisco, were delightful people, and had already advanced a few steps within the sacred portals.

She raised her eyebrows. "I think not," she said coldly. "It is only a few years since they were living out in the Mission and doing their own work." And she did not. And a few years later her younger sister married the brother of my despised friend, who meanwhile had married a Southerner.

It is impossible even to guess how many poor rich girls, educated, accomplished, pretty, and charming, but still beyond the pale, were almost broken-hearted, and read with sadness or bitterness the society news in the daily papers, read of those lovely parties in ugly old mansions where a flaming dragon stood at the portals. And those girls within, no prettier, no wealthier, no "better" than they, were having such grand good times!

But their time came. Barriers went down slowly but steadily. Wealth, inborn social sense and tact, together with personality fortified by patience and persistence, are irresistible. Moreover, intelligent women within the cordon became bored with "the same old faces," "talking everlastingly about the same old things," and made excursions into other sets. Today San Francisco society may be "mixed" but it is far more interesting.

Burlingame

In 1895, the Burlingame Country Club was formed by Major Rathbone and Senator Frank Newlands (married to

Edith McAllister), who had founded the Chevy Chase Club just outside of Washington, D. C. These were the first and second country clubs in the United States. Burlingame, close by San Mateo and some twenty-five miles down the peninsula from San Francisco, had been named by Ralston in honor of Anson Burlingame when he passed through California on his way to his new post as United States Minister at Peking. It had been one of Ralston's many dreams to induce a number of San Franciscans to build country houses in that charming spot, and he even went so far as to import eucalyptus trees from Australia to serve as a windbreak; but his dream was to be converted into reality by others.

Rathbone was the first president of the Burlingame Club, and the original enrollment of twenty-five members included Charles Baldwin, Joseph Grant, Walter Hobart, Edward and Perry Eyre, William and Henry Babcock, Richard Talbot, Harry Simpkins, George Howard, George Pope, Edouard Baylard (a Frenchman who had married Lulu Howard), George Newhall, and others whose names I have forgotten.

Not all were descended from the Holy Few; the thaw had set in, and Major Rathbone was one of the first to give it impetus. Burlingame started as a polo and golf club. Several of its members drove four-in-hands and tandems with great éclat, notably Baldwin, Hobart, and Grant. It was cleverly "sold" as a desirable residential center and many houses were built at once and surrounded by fine gardens. As the years passed, slowly but inevitably the center of fashion shifted from San Francisco to Burlingame, where there came to be as great a concentration of wealth as in Tuxedo Park in the state of New York. Many gave up their city houses and lived there the year round, or spent but a month or two in winter at the city hotels. It was very gay, very hospitable, and the families, be their vintage old or new, were as informal among themselves as those of Rincon Hill, South Park, Harrison, Folsom, and Bryant Streets had been in an almost forgotten past.

The French Colony and Bohemia

There were two other clans in San Francisco—dating from the seventies—as exclusive in their way as the society that still spelled itself with seven capitals.

The dean of the French Colony was Raphael Weill, owner of a fashionable department store, a *bon vivant,* and a public-spirited citizen. The queen was Madame Gros, the most beautiful and perfectly gowned woman in San Francisco. Her son, Dr. Edmund Gros, finally moved to Paris and during World War I founded the American Hospital. Many of those cultivated men and women would have been welcomed in High Society as the enlightening years drifted by, but preferred their own. Several were among the founders of the famous Bohemian Club.

"Bohemia," more or less patterned upon the Latin Quarter of Paris, was composed of newspaper men, artists, sculptors, architects—and writers of fiction until they spread their wings and flew to New York, that Mecca of the intellectually ambitious.

They had a select circle of their own whose hub was the *Argonaut,* founded by Frank M. Pixley in 1877, the first weekly paper in modern San Francisco, a publication of high excellence, edited first by F. M. Somers and then for many years by Jerome A. Hart. Its literary standards were exacting and Bohemia accepted them; third-raters were severely excluded. The "Bohemians" met for lunch or dinner at the French, Italian, Spanish, Chinese restaurants and made them famous. The conversation was brilliant, they were gay and irresponsible in their leisure hours; when at work, the electrical fury of the climate possessed them. Many graduated from local eminence to national fame, and Ambrose Bierce, the first of the columnists, was so caustic, fearless, and original, his prose so distinguished, that he was invited to London and New York. He did make brief sojourns in both centers, but returned to San Francisco and the *Examiner,* the property of William Randolph Hearst and rival of the *Chronicle,* owned by M. H. DeYoung.

Bierce was a master of style, and, although he took liberties with the language and coined many words, such as "fastidiot," he never degraded it. Here is an extract from one of his philippics addressed to a wealthy citizen, whose name I have forgotten:

> *"You, whose gutter blood*
> *Bears in its dark dishonorable flood*
> *Enough of prison-birds' prolific germs*
> *To serve a whole eternity of terms. . . ."*

In 1872, the Bohemian Club was founded, and it retained its original character for several years. But as time went on wealth invaded it; many professional and business men joined, preferring its liveliness and informality to the exclusive Pacific-Union Club, too many of whose members had grown old and crotchety. (It used to be said that all the gossip in San Francisco originated in the P-U, whose members passed it on to the ladies.) In the early nineties the Bohemian Club bought a redwood grove in Sonoma County for its summer "jinks," and the rumors that drifted out of that sacrosanct preserve made the Club more famous and desirable than ever. They held a performance they called the Cremation of Care, and for two weeks thereafter banished all memories of the world without and devoted themselves to rest, relaxation, and pleasure. At first they slept in tents, but eventually many built bungalows, furnished them comfortably, and took a servant with them, although they dined at a community table. Thousands of visitors from all parts of the world have been entertained there and permitted to take part in their Low Jinks and High Jinks. But only men! Only once, as far as I know, have women set foot in that little forest.

The great feature of the outing was a play, written by one of the members and performed on a high platform with a backdrop of closely set redwood trees. Upon one occasion Joseph Redding wrote the play and it was received with such enthusiasm that he decided he would be happier still with the adulation of the sex that he so generously admired. The others demurred at first, but finally consented. I was one of the favored, my brother, William Horn, being a member. I was more impressed with the redwoods.

Before giving a brief account of the most spectacular host northern California has ever known, I will present the roster of names most prominent in the social history of San Francisco and "down the Peninsula" from the fifties until the present time. There have been few changes since the first decade of the new century save that during Prohibition the young people acquired copper-plated stomachs.

The members came in successive waves, but it may be as well to avoid chronology.

McAllister. Howard. Donahoe. Donahue. Friedlander. Mc-Mullen. Latham. Gwyn. Thornton. Crittenden. Salisbury. Parrott. Atherton. Macondray. Horn. McKinstry. Bowie. Otis. Barron. Baldwin. Haggin. Tevis. Castle. Pelham Ames. Lyman. Maillard. Page. Aahe. Tobin. Selby. Eyre. Babcock. Poett. Blanding. Dibblee. Sanderson (including Sibyl, who became the prima donna of her day in Paris). Casserley. Pierce. Talbot. Cushing. Beaver. Forbes. Boyd. Sloss. Reddington. Collier. Gerstle. Scott. Kittle. Tallant. Hayne. Low. Sidney Smith. Tubbs. Josselyn. Lillenthal. Beale. Roy Nickel. Wilson. Bourne. Phelan. Sharon. Colton. Hopkins. Peters (Charles Rollo, a great artist, and his son Rollo, the best of all Romeos within living memory). Martin. Harvey. Lapham. Brugière. Carolan. Fay (Maude Fay was a famous prima donna in Munich). Nutall. Alvord. Watkins. Lent. Spreckels. Descendants of James King of Wm. DeYoung. Goad. Hobart. Palmer. Brownell. Livermore. Newhall. Pope. Butterworth. Holliday. Philip King Brown, et al. Folger. Rathbone. Stewart Edward White. Livermore. Crocker. Hager. Sutro. Pringle. Schmedell. Page Brown—Ralston.

William C. Ralston

George W. Lyman and Julian Dana have written exhaustive and fascinating biographies of Ralston, so I shall confine myself mainly to his career as a host; and certainly he was the most spectacular host that California and, perhaps, the U. S. A., has ever known.

In the late sixties and early seventies all distinguished foreigners, and Americans from the other states, brought letters to the Bank of California or to Ralston personally. He entertained them at his country house at Belmont, some thirty miles down the peninsula. It was an immense white rambling structure situated in a wild and windy cañon, with a wide veranda enclosed in glass. One of the sights of those days was Ralston's four-in-hand coach or char-a-banc crowded with guests (generally breathless) dashing along the Old Mission Road. It might be daylight or black midnight. It was all one to Ralston; he never slackened his pace. He generally managed to arrive, however, just after dusk when the great house against the black walls of the cañon was ablaze with lights. There the hundred bedrooms were always ready, be the party small or large—the latter usually. The other guests followed at a more normal pace. Innumerable Chinese clad in white were at the service of the guests. At the head of the broad staircase was a room built like an opera box where it amused Ralston to sit with a few of his chosen friends and watch his company disporting itself below. Mrs. Ralston, a tall handsome black-haired woman, generally very bored, received at the head of the stair, Chinese servants behind her to escort the guests to their rooms.

When Anson Burlingame passed through California on his way to China, Ralston drove him down to Belmont at his usual furious pace. Shortly before dinner he escorted him to the library. There Mr. Burlingame found a large company gathered in his honor, but, waiving the formalities of introductions for the moment, Ralston told him to "take a front seat." All the guests were seated and faced one way. A few moments passed. All knew that some surprise was in store and that Ralston's originality could be relied upon. Suddenly the opposite wall gave a shiver, then rose slowly like the curtain of a theater, revealing a banqueting hall of magnificent proportions. The table, to seat sixty guests, was laden with gold and silver plate, glass from Bohemia, crystal and china from England, and every variety of fruit and flowers that were in season. As motionless as an army about to salute were the white-clad pig-tailed Chinese. Then Mrs. Ralston led Mr. Burlingame in to a repast that lasted for two hours. Afterward the guests went to the ballroom—where the highly polished laurel paneling, furniture, and piano shone like minted gold—and danced, with what energy was left in them, to the music of a private band.

On the day following their arrival at Belmont, Ralston generally took his guests for a more leisurely drive to see the countryside and call at the estates of his neighbors in San Mateo, Fair Oaks, and Menlo Park. Many of his guests were from Britain or the continent of Europe whom the other magnates were flattered to meet, particularly when they bore imposing titles. Upon one occasion, however, he took a congress of business men from the East on the rounds, and Mr. Atherton told me that after they left Valparaiso Park he found a business card on every chair. But Ralston was ever democratic.

At other times Ralston would take fifty or sixty guests to Yosemite Valley (many traveling thankfully in his private train), and one of his favorite stunts was to drive a party *through* one of the Big Trees nearby, and enjoy the astonishment at its phenomenal size of those so unfortunate as not to have been born in California.

He also made the Cliff House, out on the ocean's rim, famous with his parties, and sometimes he drove his guests to the top of Monte Diablo, or to Mount Hamilton's crest to look through the big telescope of Lick's Observatory. There was little the visitors did not know of northern California before they left.

All this grandeur and display lasted exactly ten years. Its climax was even more sensational, but, alas, there was no element of comedy in it.

Ralston's devouring ambition was to make San Francisco as great a city as New York and far greater than Boston or Chicago. He financed twelve tremendous business enterprises that enriched and enlarged the city, giving employment to thousands of laborers and white collar men and creating new millionaires. But he used the funds of the bank, after exhausting his own, taking no one into his confidence. Something occurred to rouse the suspicion of a rival bank and it abruptly called in its loans; other banks, alarmed, followed suit. On August 27, 1875, San Francisco rocked on its foundations. The Bank of California had failed.

More tragic news followed. Ralston had left the Bank and the cold implacable Board that had demanded his resignation, and gone over to North Beach where he was in the habit of taking a daily swim in the Bay. Several men saw him swim steadily for a few moments and then suddenly disappear. His body was recovered and an autopsy showed that he had died from a stroke.

Ralston was only fifty. There is no doubt that if he had lived he would have made another fortune and exercised his great civic imagination for the benefit of San Francisco. Perhaps he would have been more prudent.

Ralston's funeral rivaled that of James King of Wm. and of Broderick. People hung from every window and the roofs were black with silent figures. My grandfather, Stephen Franklin, walked alone behind the hearse, his head bowed and looking as if Earth itself were making its last journey. Behind him marched, four abreast, all the important men of the city and the employees of the bank. Then mounted militia, mounted "companies" of all kinds, and finally a long procession of carriages to move at snail's pace to Lone Mountain Cemetery on the western flank of the city. Preceding the hearse several bands played the Dead March.

PART FOUR

11. From the Earthquake Onward

A T fourteen minutes past five on the morning of April 18, 1906, San Franciscans were awakened by a roar that sounded as if the Pacific Ocean had stood on end and was heading through the Golden Gate. They sat up in their beds, wondering what that unearthly roar portended, and a second later a violent earthquake rocked the city. But the shock was brief, and with a shrug—for Californians have been brought up on earthquakes—they were preparing to lie down again when the real earthquake began. It leaped and plunged, it shook with a fury that threatened to dislodge every building from its foundations, plunged again from north to south, from east to west, downward and upward. Some of the good citizens were paralyzed with terror, women screamed and hid themselves under the bedclothes, but the majority of both sexes rose quickly and stood in doorways, whose framework was the strongest part of the walls.

Added to the increasing roar was the sound of falling plaster, of shattered windows and of crockery in the cupboards, of crashing chimneys, of collapsing masonry. Furniture led a merry dance. Pianos were smashed. Marble mantels fell clattering to the hearth. Dogs howled. Cats leaped through open windows. Then, just as all were beginning to wonder if the end of the world had come, the earth gave a sudden twist, and the worst earthquake in the historic period of northern California was over.

There were astonishingly few casualties. Except for the business district and one or two hotels, built for the most part of reinforced concrete and granite, it was a city of wooden houses.

Two minutes after the earth had subsided the streets of the various residential quarters were swarming with people in every variety of nocturnal costume, from red flannel to cambric and silk, from pajamas to nightshirts, although a number had paused long enough to throw on an overcoat or wrapper.

It is absolutely *de rigueur* in San Francisco to treat an earthquake as a joke (after it is over); otherwise you are no thoroughbred. "Quite a shake, wasn't it?" was heard—airily—on all sides. "That old fault must have made the slip of its life." "It certainly did its damnedest this time." "Hope the good old earth is tired out and will take a long rest."

But soon, on the hills, a voice was lifted, then another, and another. "What's that?" "What's that?" Columns of smoke were rising in the wide valley south of Market Street, crowded with the dwellings of the working class. "By Jove, they've lit fires, and every chimney cracked or down!" "Wonder will it spread?" "Not likely it will come this way. Market Street is too wide."

2

The wind was from the west and it swept the fire toward the waterfront where it caught the flimsy buildings of the Embarcadero, the wide street between the Bay and the city proper. The men from Oakland and Berkeley, where the earthquake had been equally severe, who came over at the usual hour to go to their business offices or stores, left the ferry building to be confronted by a wall of flame and smoke and were forced to turn back.

The wind veered and carried the flames into the business district. Granite and concrete might withstand the onslaught, but the heat broke the windows and the interiors were soon roaring furnaces; moreover, there was a number of wooden buildings at which the fire leaped with venom. The Occidental Hotel, the Lick House, the Russ House, were on Montgomery Street and crowded with guests. It was some time before these were convinced that the fire was beyond control and then they fled in whatever they could snatch to cover their night clothes. Several of the women wore opera cloaks, for Caruso had sung the night before. (One of the many stories of the earthquake-and-fire was that Caruso ran out of the Palace Hotel shouting, "Give me my old Vesuvius," and then lifted his voice again and ran a scale to make sure the shock had not impaired that golden organ.)

Presently all who lived on the hills and in the valleys on the eastern side of Van Ness Avenue, the wide street that divided the older part of the city from the Western Addition, were moving toward the Presidio, Fort Mason, or the sand hills near the ocean. General Funston, in command at the Presidio, had called out the troops to preserve order and prevent looting. On every lamp post was pasted a sign: "Looters will be shot."

Those far enough from the advancing flames had time to dress and fill a bag with necessities and what jewels they may have possessed. They walked slowly, for there were many children; fathers carried those too young to walk; others helped the old up the steep hills; there was little conversation and no more jokes.

As they passed some of the mansions in the Western Addition they saw that stoves had been set up on the lawns and ladies who had sat in bejeweled splendor in the Opera House the night before, were cooking a breakfast of sorts; the servants had fled to the sand hills.

South of Market Street another silent procession was trudging toward the sand dunes, many pushing baby carriages containing food and utensils as well as babies. Men drove carts along the flat surface of the valley, filled with household goods; others had paused only long enough to snatch a parrot or the cage of a twittering canary. Dogs trotted along beside the rich and the poor, hungry but trustful as ever that their masters would care for them.

Not long after the fires broke out loud blasts of dynamite mingled with the roar of the fire and the steady tramp of thousands of weary feet. The water mains had been broken by the earthquake. The Fire Chief had been killed in his bed by a chimney that fell through the roof. His assistant had ordered the dynamiting of certain buildings in an endeavor to arrest the fire before it reached Van Ness Avenue.

Mr. James D. Phelan, San Francisco's leading citizen, and possessing one of the few automobiles in the city, spent the best part of the three days of that raging fire carrying loads of dynamite wherever he was directed. It was during the first day that he had a singular experience. He was resting for a few moments on the lawn of his house out near the Mission, listening to the detonations, when he saw a piece of paper sailing before the wind. It fell at his feet and idly he picked it up. It was one of his canceled checks, and he knew that the Phelan Building, one of the finest office structures in the city, had been blown up. That bit of paper had sailed two miles and more to bring him the unwelcome news. But Mr. Phelan was ever philosophical; moreover, it was a minor disaster in the destruction of his beloved city. He shrugged, and went forth to pack his car with another load of dynamite.

3

An hour after the earthquake, Mr. J. Downey Harvey, another estimable citizen, tracked down the mayor and persuaded him to organize a Committee of Fifty for relief of the homeless. Mayor Schmitz was the tool of the notorious "Boss," Abe Ruef, one of the most unmitigated scoundrels in the history of San Francisco, who had made the city a byword for civic rottenness. A weak man and putty in the hands of any determined will, Schmitz obeyed Mr. Harvey and managed to assemble fifty men, afterward known as "The Citizen's Finance Committee." He met with no obstruction from Ruef who was in hiding and gloating over his opportunities; during the ensuing preoccupation of "eminent citizens," intent upon repairing their own damaged fortunes, the city would be completely delivered into his itching hands.

A horrified and sympathetic Congress voted a million and a half dollars for the relief of San Francisco, but were in a quandary. They knew the reputation of Messrs. Ruef and Schmitz. How could they assure themselves that this large sum of money would be used to ameliorate the unhappy lot of the refugees camping out in the sand dunes and forts and not vanish into the pockets of the Boss and his henchman?

When President Theodore Roosevelt heard that Mr. Phelan had been appointed chairman of the Citizen's Finance Committee, the problem was solved. He sent the money personally to Mr. Phelan and, furthermore, issued a proclamation directing the people of the United States to send all their contributions in the same manner. The contributions in due course amounted to several trainloads of supplies and ten million dollars.

Huts and tents were erected in what is now known as the Richmond District but at that time was a sandy waste redeemed only in the spring by little forests of purple and yellow lupins. The fire had been stopped at Van Ness Avenue, and the wealthy inhabitants of the Western Addition and those of districts less fortunate had sent all the blankets they could spare, but these by no means met the need, and nights under the stars with the fog rolling in and insufficient covering made the abundant stores that arrived by train as welcome as the food sent over from the East Bay cities and from the interior. Many, as soon as it was possible to get transportation to the ferries, crossed the Bay and put up at the hotels in Oakland, Berkeley, Piedmont, and Alameda.

All the contributions did not come from without the state of California, nor even from its undevastated cities. Raphael Weill, head of the French Colony, imported from the East a trainload of frocks, hats, coats, underclothing, even handkerchiefs, and saw to it personally that every woman in those refugee camps, of whatever degree (or morals) had a new outfit. Like a plump benevolent Santa Claus he walked among the temporary dwellings and made sure that old or young, good or bad, had their quota.

Strangers who may have visited San Francisco during the weeks following the fire and strolled along Van Ness Avenue would have been both puzzled and astonished. Instead of dour faces and listless feet, men, clad in khaki, were striding along or talking in groups, their faces eager and excited. Animated by the spirit of 1851 when the last of the old fires had destroyed San Francisco, all were fired with one purpose: to rebuild their city and as quickly as possible. Their faces were set toward the future. They forgot the millions that had spiraled upward in smoke; forgot the cherished private libraries, the priceless works of art—historic paintings and sculpture, tapestries, articles of vertù, the family silver, family portraits. All that was behind them, gone forever. They were pioneers, in at the rebirth of a city, and more interested and excited than ever before in their lives.

Elderly men who had "retired" looked thirty years younger. Middle-aged men were bursting with energy. Young men felt important, and determined to show their mettle, to play their part in carrying on one of the old traditions of San Francisco. Thousands helped the working men to clear away the still smoking débris.

And there were almost as many women as men on Van Ness Avenue, some from the camps, some from the great houses in the Western Addition, all looking as indifferent to the past and as eager for the future as they had ever been to see a new play or receive a trousseau from Paris. And they had at least one play!

A month after the earthquake-and-fire Sarah Bernhardt came to California and gave an afternoon performance of *Adrienne Lecouveur* in the open-air Greek Theatre, a present from William Randolph Hearst to the city of Berkeley. It held seven thousand spectators and every seat was filled. The tickets were three dollars, but nothing daunted the theater lovers of San Francisco and the smaller cities of the Bay area. She gave a magnificent performance to the accompaniment of a bird chorus in the trees that rose above the high walls of the amphitheater. The sky was blue, the weather undamnified by fog or wind. She told Ashton Stevens, dramatic critic of the San Francisco *Examiner,* that she had never felt so inspired in her life.

Lumber was brought from across the bay and the interior, and shacks were built where men could meet and lay their plans for the future; where the great quantities of food that rolled in with every train could be stored and distributed; where architects could draw their plans, to be put into effect as soon as the ground was cleared. Medical supplies and surgical instruments were among the abundant donations, and doctors, save when they received a hurry call to one of the camps, sat in their makeshift quarters all day and slept in them at night. Lawyers also opened offices for consultation, although they had a more restful time.

The Citizen's Finance Committee functioned admirably. They appointed the architects, appointed reliable men to see to the daily needs of the refugees, meet the trains and receive and store the donations and purchases—a thousand and one other details. There was no friction. All were eager to do their part. They greeted one another every morning as if they had just returned from a year's absence, instead of with the curt nod of other days. And so did everyone who met on

Van Ness Avenue. "Earthquake love," it was dubbed by that amiable cynic, Mr. James D. Phelan.

4

It would seem that San Francisco was destined to spasms of virtue followed by painful if not spectacular relapses. For twenty years or more after the fumigation of 1856, she was a respectable, prosperous, law-abiding city. Aside from the immense fortunes made in the Nevada mines and the Central Pacific Railroad—whose outward symbol was a group of huge and hideous mansions on Nob Hill (happily removed by the fire)—many men piled up wealth in the great corporations, as exporters and importers, stockbrokers, merchants, bankers, to say nothing of the professions. Vice was by no means extinguished, but was decently covered up. The women of commerce lived a retired life in their own quarter, gambling houses were run with discretion, and houses of assignation above French restaurants were less noisy than hotels.

The energetic and otherwise admirable citizens, absorbed in the pleasant occupations of making money and spending it, gave not a thought to the dangers that had beset the city in the past, and—San Francisco being what it was—might well befall it again. It was only by degrees that politics were appropriated by "bosses" and that graft assumed proportions that threatened disgrace if not disaster. The first notable boss was a blind man named Buckley, who, with his accomplices, the supervisors, inaugurated a system of wholesale bribery and corruption. When, in the early nineties, the respectable element did wake up and the Wallace Grand Jury was impaneled, the exposures were so shameful, the indignation was so universal, that Buckley fled for his life. The virtuous spasm over, San Francisco settled down comfortably again, persuaded that peace and decency would prevail thereafter. Mr. Phelan, who was later to organize the Citizen's Finance Com-

mittee, had been swept into the mayor's chair and all would
be well.

He at once appointed a committee of one hundred and
fifty trustworthy citizens to draft a charter that would en-
large the powers of the mayor, heretofore restricted. It provided a responsible city government, civil service reform,
home rule (independent of a corrupt Legislature) and declared for municipal government of those public utilities,
light, water, transportation, long preyed upon by the old
municipal council, which had the power to fix the rates.

Then he went to work with a vengeance. He disposed of
the boss system summarily, exposed the peculations of the
lighting monopoly, and saved the public $300,000 a year. He
diverted two millions from the greedy pockets of the supervisors by "blocking jobs," raised the standard of the wages
of the working class, and gave to San Francisco in public
gifts many times his salary as mayor. When the term of the
current supervisors expired, the public elected a board of
honest men.

Mr. Phelan had been known heretofore merely as a man
of great wealth, an able financier who had trebled the fortune left him by his father, an influential citizen of unblemished probity, a brilliant host, a generous patron of art and
charity. He had been universally liked and admired and had
few enemies.

But during his term of office he made many enemies, and
many were men of his own class. They resented his superiority, his executive ability and flair for politics, hitherto un-
revealed; too many of his reforms hit their own fortunes and
reputations.

During the last two years of his incumbency there were
serious labor troubles. The proletariat went on strike demanding higher wages and recognition of their unions. He
supported those who had just cause for complaint and broke
the backs of other strikes. More enemies.

Then it was that Abraham Ruef and his henchman Eugene Schmitz squirmed into power.

Ruef was the son of a well-to-do family, had graduated into the law from the University of California and established a lucrative practice. With his abilities, he might have become one of the most useful and respected citizens of San Francisco. But he was greedy and destructive. Above all he was ambitious for power, and the persistent demand of labor for recognition of their unions, the hostile attitude of capital, the growing unpopularity of Mr. Phelan, gave him his opportunity. He harangued the workers, promising them full union recognition and overflowing pails. He denounced capital with every adjective in his abundant vocabulary, and promised them a mayor who was "one of the people like themselves." Labor was delighted with him, and flattered at the interest of this able and well-known lawyer, who had "no ax to grind"—or so they thought.

Mr. Phelan's term expired. He was not re-elected. Eugene Schmitz, a fiddler, and president of the Musicians' Union, a big, bluff, hearty, and rather handsome man, was presented with the office by an overwhelming majority—composed not only of the proletariat but of capital, who wanted no more "reforms." There was no knowing how far the present incumbent might carry those reforms, and professional politicians could be bribed.

It was not until Mr. Phelan's board of honest supervisors came to the end of their term and he could install men of his own choosing that Ruef attained complete domination. But then he went to work with an energy worthy of a better cause. He fomented class hatred, grafted on vice, held up corporations and utilities and wealthy business men for huge sums before granting franchises or permits. Ruef, Schmitz, the board of supervisors waxed rich and arrogant with power.

And then he made his fatal mistake. With a lack of perspicacity inconceivable in so cunning a mind, he permitted an honest man to be elected to the office of district attorney. William A. Langdon, superintendent of schools, had a large following in labor circles, and Ruef assumed that he must be "all right."

But Langdon had no sooner taken the oath of office than he began a series of raids upon the notorious "French Restaurants" and the gambling houses, abolished certain disgraceful race tracks, and slot machines that flourished in every saloon and cigar stand. A terrific howl went up, and between dismay and wrath Ruef narrowly escaped a "seizure." Langdon pursued his way undisturbed by threats, or even by the remonstrances of his friends. Ruef might be boss, but he was the law.

He was valiantly supported by Fremont Older, editor of the *Bulletin,* and as militant for justice as James King of Wm. But Langdon was sadly in need of funds for legal investigations and prosecutions. Ironically enough, they were supplied—if somewhat obliquely—by Mr. Abraham Ruef.

5

One of the most notable and popular young men in the city was Rudolph Spreckels, son of the Hawaiian sugar magnate. At the age of nineteen he had quarreled with his father and left the paternal roof to make a fortune for himself. He had inherited the family talent and accumulated wealth rapidly, but for a time his only interests were business, his family—he had married the beautiful Nelly Joliffe—and the pleasures of society. Although a friend of Mr. Phelan, he had taken no part in his reforms, and, uninterested in politics, paid little attention to the slump in virtue that followed.

But one day Ruef, who still believed that every man had his price, approached him with a malodorous scheme for enriching himself further at the expense of the city. Spreckels realized for the first time that he had been living on the surface of an underworld of unspeakable rottenness, kicked Ruef out, and sought Mr. Phelan and Mr. Older, who completed his enlightenment. The spirit of the born crusader awakened within him. He vowed to wage war to the death against the "machine" and spend the last dollar of his fortune if necessary. In January, 1906, he came out publicly with an announcement of his intention to support Langdon, who proceeded with redoubled energy and all the money he needed.

Mr. Phelan helped Spreckels with advice and cash, but his personal unpopularity, born of his own attempts to clean up the city, prevented him from taking too prominent a part.

Ruef, still hopeful, made, through certain of his friends in the business world, a thorough investigation of the sources of Spreckels' wealth, convinced that no young man brought up in luxury could have accumulated it honestly.

He was disappointed.

Young Spreckels was hailed as a knight in shining armor, with a mailed fist, even by those who had vowed they had had enough of reform to last a lifetime; they had suffered far more at the hands of Ruef, Schmitz, and the board of supervisors.

Mr. Phelan, Mr. Spreckels, and Mr. Older secured the services of one of the ablest attorneys in the city, Francis J. Heney, and induced President Roosevelt to lend them the services of Detective Burns, at that time in the employ of the United States Government.

And then came the earthquake and fire in April. The "Graft Prosecution" was interrupted, and Ruef was jubilant. Schmitz went to Europe.

Attorney Heney and Detective Burns were engaged in Government work until June. As soon as they were available, Langdon announced that a general investigation would begin at once. As the governor's chair would soon be vacated and he was anxious to fill it, he appointed Heney assistant district attorney, empowering him to impanel the Grand Jury, and went off to stump the state.

By this time Ruef was thoroughly frightened, but he was as resourceful as his betters, although on somewhat different lines. T. H. Gallagher was president of the board of supervisors and acting mayor in the absence of Schmitz. He was ordered by the boss to remove Langdon from office on the ground of neglect of duty and appoint Abraham Ruef district attorney.

For a moment San Francisco—which should have been immune to shocks by this time—was stunned. But only for a moment. Such a roar of protest and indignation went up that Gallagher retired from the fray. The matter was quickly settled. Judge Sewell of the Superior Court held that the district attorney represented the people as a whole and the mayor had no jurisdiction over him. Once more Ruef was squelched.

Then began the troubles of the Grand Jury. The prosecution had assumed that it would be an easy matter to obtain affidavits from the distinguished victims who had been forced to pay tribute to Ruef and his creatures. But this illusion was brief. Every one of the heads of corporations, utilities, and what not who was questioned, swore that never had he been approached by the boss nor by any member of his gang, never paid a five-cent-piece of graft money.

They were the rich men of San Francisco and bore the reputation of being good citizens, as honest as they were able and prominent. But when Spreckels visited them personally and begged them to "come through" and save the city from disgrace and possibly ruin, they looked him calmly in the eye and replied that there had been an unfortunate misapprehension. Ruef, beyond a doubt, they said, had grafted on the French restaurants and other reprehensible establishments, and they devoutly hoped, as patriotic citizens, that he would spend the rest of his life in San Quentin, but even he had not dared to approach *them* with insulting propositions. They also urged their young friend to get out of the beastly mess before he made himself as unpopular as Mr. Phelan.

But Spreckels was neither fooled nor discouraged. He vowed he would "get them yet."

It looked as if the Grand Jury would not be able to gather evidence to convict the machine of anything but grafting on vice. But Heney and Burns suddenly changed their tactics. They offered immunity to the supervisors if they would give the evidence that would convict the "higher-ups," with whom they were now more disgusted than with the underworld scoundrels. The supervisors agreed. The Grand Jury was enabled to find indictments not only against Ruef and Schmitz, but against Mr. Patrick Calhoun, a popular and prosperous gentleman of ancient lineage and great social popularity, who was president of the United Railroads; of his manager Thornwald Mullaly; the finance committee of the San Francisco Gas and Electric Company; the agent of the Parkside Realty Company; the Home Telephone; the Pacific Telephone; the Prize Fight Trust.

But this was not enough. Gallagher had received his and the other supervisors' loot from the hands of Ruef; he had had no dealings with the bribed. He was unable to furnish either names or evidence as to the method by which the moneys had been paid by the "higher-ups." There was no alternative but to bargain with Ruef.

That gentleman had gone into hiding. He was living comfortably in a road house known as "The Trocodero" and situated in a wood some six miles from the center of the city. His good friends, the sheriff, the coroner, and the police, failed to discover him, but he was finally run to earth by an elisor appointed by the court.

Promised immunity, he incriminated Schmitz (who had returned from his jaunt in Europe), but his courage failed him when it came to "betraying" those rich and powerful men whom he had held up so lucratively in the past and hoped to "squeeze" again when all this worry and trouble was over; he was evidently a man of extraordinary optimism.

His answers were so evasive that immunity was canceled, and as he had incriminated himself in his testimony against Schmitz, he was placed on trial.

The trials, so abundantly financed by Rudolph Spreckels and Mr. Phelan, were held in Carpenter's Hall, a small building just beyond the burnt district, and before Judge Lawlor. They were enlivened by more than sensational testimony. The house of the chief witness against Ruef, T. H. Gallagher, was blown up by dynamite—fortunately when he was elsewhere. Fremont Older, whose thunderings in the *Bulletin* had never ceased, was kidnapped, but rescued before he could be put away for the duration of the trials. An attempt was made on the life of Mr. Heney. One day when he was on his feet and talking, a man named Haas sneaked up behind him in the crowded courtroom and fired, the bullet lodging in Heney's jaw.

There was wild excitement in Fulton Street, always crowded when a trial was in process, and the old shout of "Lynch him!" beat the air. But Haas was rushed to the jail in an automobile. That night he was murdered in his cell.

Heney was ill from shock for a time, but suffered no permanent disability save deafness in one ear. The prosecution in the Ruef case was continued by Hiram Johnson (the first step in a long and brilliant career), and by Matt I. Sullivan, another able and honest lawyer.

The astounded Ruef was convicted and sentenced to fourteen years in San Quentin prison.

Rudolph Spreckels was no longer the most popular young man in San Francisco save with the general public unaffected by the ugly exposures. His rich friends now hated as much as they feared him, and when Mr. Patrick Calhoun was brought to trial society exploded. Mr. Phelan, the Frank

Carolans, the William Denmans, the Fremont Olders, Mr. and Mrs. Heney, Miss Ethel Hager, and I were his only friends. Mrs. Spreckels, who had been one of the bright lights of Burlingame society, found herself ostracized, cut right and left by the wives of men who were in mortal terror of being exposed, tried, and sentenced as malefactors.

The trials dragged on and on. There was not sufficient evidence to convict Calhoun (the law, alas, has many loopholes) and the others brought before the court, although there was no doubt in anyone's mind of their guilt. But the Prosecution was not a failure. The outraged public elected Dr. Robeson Taylor, a highly esteemed citizen, as mayor; Schmitz had been tried and convicted but escaped on a technicality, his only punishment the loss of office. Hiram Johnson was elected governor of the state.

There was only one lapse. Dr. Taylor refused to build up a reputable machine and the next mayor was a reversion to type. He so disgusted the labor party which had elected him, however, that it put him out at the end of his term and helped to elect James Rolph, Jr., the first of a line of admirable mayors. San Francisco, all things being relative, has been, as far as politics are concerned, quite a decent city ever since the first incumbency of Mayor Rolph. It is by no means impeccable, but at least the words "boss" and "graft" are almost forgotten.

6

San Francisco was as speedily rebuilt as was humanly possible, and, although less picturesque than of old, the business district is massive and imposing, and the dwellings east of Van Ness Avenue, if not as large as those of the Western Addition, are modern and substantial. The greater part of the new structures, however, are hotels (Class A, B, and C), handsome apartment houses, glorified boarding houses, restaurants, and clubs. The once harmonious skyline has been destroyed by several skyscrapers perched on the hills, and the Coit Tower looks like a Lighthouse.

Beautiful "subdivisions" (polite variant of suburbs) cover the once barren sand hills that sent clouds of dust through the city whenever the wind blew from the west; they are thickly planted with trees, the architecture is excellent and varied, the houses gaily painted. They remind one of scenes in Grimm's Fairy Tales.

That district always known as "South of Market Street" is now devoted to business, its former inhabitants having settled themselves out in the Mission and the Potrero. The lower part of Dupont Street, once the wickedest street in the "wickedest city on earth," is now almost twice as wide and the core of the fashionable shopping district. China Town, just above, is not quite as glamorous as of old, but its shops, until Japan entered World War II and halted importations, were as tempting as ever with their magnificent brocades, jades, porcelains, crystals, teakwood furniture, and other Oriental offerings to an Occidental city always hospitable to variety. And there are no more Tong "wars." With the reformation of the police force the Chinese have found it well to keep the peace.

During Mayor Rolph's several administrations, San Francisco was further beautified by the new City Hall, the Public Library, the State of California Building, and the Exposition Auditorium (presented to the city by the Panama-Pacific Exposition), a stately group that forms what is known as the Civic Center. The Auditorium seats eight thousand and is used for popular concerts, political rallies, the annual policemen's ball, prize fights, flower shows, and circuses.

Later, Mr. M. H. DeYoung, owner of the San Francisco *Chronicle,* presented a fine museum to Golden Gate Park, and Mr. and Mrs. Adolf Spreckels erected and furnished the superb art gallery, known as the Palace of the Legion of Honor, which stands on a cliff overlooking the sea and the

Golden Gate. It is said to contain the largest collection of Rodins outside of France.

7

In 1915 San Francisco attracted the attention of the nation once more, and this time more respectably, with the Panama-Pacific Exposition, where thirty-one countries were represented despite the war raging in Europe. A group of exquisite and fairy-like buildings divided by courts was erected down on the Marina, a new district on "made ground" on the northern edge of the city and close to the Bay. The architect was that young genius Willis Polk (who had married Christine Barreda, incidentally), and he was ably assisted by a corps of twelve fellow architects. Everything that was modern in industry was exhibited, and the Palace of Fine Arts was hung with world-famous paintings that had never crossed an ocean before. Although not as large as the Exposition of 1939-40, it was more inspired, and at night such a scene of dazzling beauty with its deftly colored illuminations like scintillating jewels that it is talked of still. Thousands visited it from the United States, Canada, South and Central America, Mexico, and a few ventured across the Atlantic from Europe.

The hotels were crowded to the eaves, and the tourists who had expected to make the usual brief visit to a sublimation of the old "Fair," lingered on for weeks in a city that offered so many other attractions. They wandered through the shops in China Town, interested almost as much in the pretty Chinese girls in native costumes as in the tempting wares; welcome visitors, for they seldom left without "a souvenir"—sometimes a brocade dressing gown or a necklace of jade or crystal. They lunched or dined not only in the gaily decorated Chinese restaurants whose soft foods pleased or repelled them, but crowded those representing practically every nation under the sun: French, Mexican, Spanish, Swedish, Greek, German, Danish, Yiddish, Portuguese, Russian, Hungarian, and plain American. The delicate food of the French restaurants attracted the fastidious, the Spanish and Mexican those who enjoyed scorching their stomachs.

They took a day off to visit Little Italy, that city within a city, with its great church dedicated to Saint Peter and Saint Paul, and populated entirely by Italians. Sometimes they took a ride on the ferry boats that skimmed the waters of the Bay like great white swans, or took the little train to the top of Mount Tamalpais to spend the night at the Inn and hang out of the windows at four in the morning to gaze at a blood-red sun rising above an expanse of snow-white fog that had rolled down from the tule lands of the north, obliterating the Bay, its islands, and the cities surrounding it. On Fisherman's Wharf they watched the fleet of boats with their colored sails come home with the morning's catch, the Italian fishermen, sometimes laughing, sometimes cursing, almost as picturesque as their craft. They stood before the immense iron pots on the sidewalks where lobsters or crabs were boiling, and frequently went back to their hotels with a warm bundle.

They climbed to the top of Russian Hill and Telegraph Hill to view the red-and-gold sunset beyond the Golden Gate, the windows on the islands and in the cities across the Bay ablaze with reflected light, turned spyglasses on Alcatraz where sentinels paced the walls of its military prison.

Altogether they took away many pleasant memories of San Francisco besides the Exposition, and as for San Francisco it was so proud of itself that it nearly burst.

Mayor Angelo J. Rossi succeeded Mayor Rolph, and his incumbency was brilliantly high-lighted with the construction of the Golden Gate Bridge, the San Francisco-Oakland Bay Bridge, the Federal Building in the Civic Center, the

Opera House and the Veteran's Building close by, a large number of playgrounds and summer schoolgrounds for children, the Golden Gate International Exposition on Treasure Island to which Mussolini sent a number of the most historic paintings in the famous Italian galleries. (These paintings were later exhibited at the New York Exposition and there is an underground rumor that Mussolini ordered them to be stored away in vaults on Long Island!)

It was during Mayor Rossi's administration that the Art Commission was founded, a body of twelve men and women whose aim it was to further the cause of art and music, improve the appearance of the city by removing as many of the eye-sores as possible, and keep a sharp eye on any statues that might be erected to the illustrious departed; many of those in being resembling caricatures rather than sculptured portraits.

Joseph Dyer was appointed permanent secretary (and has filled the position admirably, often being called upon to keep the peace, for dissensions have been many and sometimes violent). Later he and Supervisor Emmett Hayden, a member of the Board, initiated the yearly series of "Municipal Concerts," which have been as brilliant and popular as was to be expected of a city always abundant in local talent, and no mean rival of the "San Francisco Symphony" and the Opera season.

8

San Francisco had another cause for pride, and this was the character and increasing achievements of James D. Phelan.

During Mr. Phelan's term of office as mayor, he had taken the first step toward presenting the city with an adequate water supply. As California is dry for seven months of the year and subject, moreover, to droughts, it is largely dependent upon irrigation even in the coast valleys. San Francisco, as well as the towns across the Bay, had been insufficiently supplied by private corporations. In 1901, Mr. Phelan conceived the idea of constructing a dam in Hetch Hetchy, a valley in the Sierras about a hundred and fifty miles from the Bay area. By the erection of a watershed, the storm waters fed by the abundant snowfalls could be compounded and conserved, yielding 400,000,000 gallons of water a day.

This ambitious scheme met with furious opposition not only from private corporations and the power interests, but from nature lovers, for Hetch Hetchy was in the Yosemite National Park. It was not until the administration of President Wilson and while Mr. Phelan was in Washington as Senator that Congress was won over and the bill was signed.

James D. Phelan left an indelible imprint on the annals of San Francisco, but he accomplished far less than he strove for. He was among the first to recognize the menace of Japan, and warned California and the United States in many public speeches, but few would listen to him. He was one of the two best Senators (the other being Hiram Johnson) that California ever sent to Washington, but he failed of re-election. He was a Democrat, and, although his outstanding worth was generally recognized and many Republicans had voted for him the first time, that party was unwilling to take a back seat any longer. It had dominated the state for many years and feared that if Mr. Phelan continued to inspire the citizens with admiration and gratitude the party would lose its luster, and too many voters—among them farmers and the working class—would rally to the Democratic banner under his leadership. When the campaign for the second term began a number of Republicans told Mr. Phelan frankly that they never expected to have a better senator—but the party came first.

He was the foremost citizen not only of San Francisco but of California, but, although he was eager to give all his time and energies to the well-being of the state, he could accomplish little. He would have made a great President, for he was a consummate politician and a born statesman. He had a brain of infinite wisdom, a cool and balanced judgment, courage, an eloquent and persuasive tongue, and a thorough knowledge of men. And among his many virtues patriotism was chief. But California threw away its great opportunity; party spirit was stronger than any desire to serve the nation as a whole. And perhaps he had been too good a mayor!

He was forced to be content with his records as mayor and senator, to be known as "The Father of Hetch Hetchy," and as the most famous host since the collapse of William C. Ralston.

After the earthquake, Mr. Phelan did not rebuild in San Francisco, but bought himself an estate of some eight hundred acres near Saratoga, sixty miles south of the city. There he built a Spanish villa, surrounding three sides of a court at the back, the terrace in front overlooking a valley planted from end to end with orchards which were an unbroken mass of white blossoms in the spring. The house stood on the lower slope of a mountain dense with oak trees, manzanitas—a slender tree with a bright red bark—and wild lilacs. Between the court and a high wall at the back was a large swimming pool. Mr. Phelan named this lovely estate Montalvo in honor of the old Spanish author who wrote the best seller of his day in which he depicted a terrestrial paradise bearing the mellifluous name, "California."

Mr. Phelan loved entertaining and was not only the most genial of hosts but a lavish one. There was champagne every night for dinner, he had a chef, and a rather too abundant board for ladies anxious to conform to the fashionable plank-like shape. Moreover, he was the ideal host. The house guests were left to their own devices, they could drive, walk, play tennis, swim, gossip, read in the library, play billiards; they were never bored by being "entertained." But dinner, however gay, was formal; men wore their dinner coats, women their most elegant gowns.

As with Ralston, all visitors who could procure a letter of introduction to Mr. Phelan presented it promptly and were entertained at Montalvo, driving down from San Francisco in cars provided by their host. One of those guests was Philip Guedalla, who was fortunate to arrive in the spring when all Santa Clara Valley was in blossom. Mr. Guedalla was enchanted; but possibly more so when, after luncheon, Mr. Phelan led the company through the living-room into the library, where, on the large center table, was a stack of the author's latest book, and he was invited to autograph a copy for each of his fellow guests. No one could pay more graceful tribute to genius (nor to lesser lights when he thought them worth while) than Mr. Phelan.

A scholar himself, Mr. Phelan would rather honor a distinguished author than a duke. There were several authors who had country places not far from Montalvo and he frequently entertained them: the poets Sara Bard Field and Erskine Scott Wood; novelists Ruth Comfort Mitchell, Charles and Kathleen Norris; and Stewart Edward White who was also an explorer of note. Charles Caldwell Dobie lived in San Francisco, but was a frequent and favorite guest.*

Mr. Phelan was a patron of all the arts, and not only bought the work of California artists who had arrived but sent many young men and women to Europe to study. Of all

---

* It may be as well to mention here the names of certain California writers who have won acclaim during the last ten or fifteen years: Julia Cooley Altrocchi; Royce Brier; Jean Burton; James M. Cain; William Martin Camp; Stanton Coblentz; Mildred Cram; Mary Collins; Julia Dana; Robert Easton; Katherine Wigmore Eyre; Frank Fenton; M. F. K. Fisher; Martin Flavin; Inglis Fletcher; Kathryn Forbes; Clifford Gessler; Carroll Hall; Hildegarde Hawthorne; Charlotte Jackson; Joseph Henry Jackson; Robinson Jeffers; Idwal Jones; Janet Lewis; Oscar Lewis; George D. Lyman; Mrs. Fremont Older; Donald Culross Peattie; Fern Rives; Lawrence Rising; William Saroyan; John Steinbeck; Dale Wilhelm; Kathleen Winsor.

the local celebrities Helen Wills was the one in whom he took the deepest interest: not only because she was beautiful and charming but because she had added so abundantly to the laurels of California—whom, we all suspected, he loved more than he had ever loved any human being. She was his guest of honor at many entertainments both in San Francisco and at Montalvo, and at his request Haig Patargen made a bust of her which now stands in the Palace of the Legion of Honor.

Phelan and Ralston were not unlike in appearance. Both were short, rather heavily built men with the same sandy coloring and short beards. But Mr. Phelan had a head of noble proportions that might have come down to him, via Ireland, from ancient Rome.

He never married, yet, despite disappointments and frustrations, he must have been a happy man. He died in 1930.

9

During the 1920's and 1930's after the worst of the depression was over, ambitious young men complained that San Francisco was so smug, so complacently satisfied with itself that there were none of the old opportunities for making fortunes, for getting ahead. Big business was booming in the East and "mass production" was a new but familiar term. But it received no encouragement from San Francisco to establish branch factories and other industrial offshoots either in the city or in the Bay area. The old bustle was gone, although the city was prosperous enough; many men counted their wealth in millions, and there were lesser fortunes. There was little poverty and the Community Chest took care of what there was.

Why should they spoil their beautiful city? they asked one another. No city on the face of the globe was so delightful to live in. With its cooling fogs and winds the climate was ideal;

there were no more than a dozen hot days during the entire summer. And it was a friendly city; nowhere did people enjoy themselves more socially, have such interesting clubs. If one "belonged" no one cared whether you were poor or rich; nowhere were men and women so loyal to their own. Nowhere on earth was there such a variety of good restaurants, of sumptuous hotels, of moving-picture houses, of lovely country within an hour's drive. Business was good enough; one never saw hordes of men rushing about with anxious set faces. The best plays, opera, lecturers visited San Francisco. They liked the familiar faces they saw every day in the streets; they wanted no hordes of riffraff from other states. It was a city of beautiful women and handsome men. What more could a man ask?

San Francisco recalled the lines of Bret Harte:

> *"Serene, indifferent to fate,*
> *Thou sittest beside the Golden Gate."*

It was altogether too serene to suit the ambitious youngsters, who envied and resented the increasing importance, population, and spectacular prosperity of Los Angeles. They would have packed up and gone south, but they, too, loved San Francisco and all its pleasures.

The southern city was once more the rival of the north, but unlike the Montereños of old, San Franciscans were indifferent, or, if they thought of her at all, it was to despise her incessant "boasting, boosting, promoting, as she flooded the East and Middle West with pamphlets dwelling upon the advantages it offered to dwellers in crowded old towns and cities." They shuddered with horror at the hordes who had doubled her population, shuddered at her plants and factories—branches of big business in the East; at mass production which would not only defile the landscape but bring thousands of working men, and they had worry enough with labor as it was, with its incessant strikes and demands—practically their only annoyance. No, San Francisco was the one perfect city in the U. S. A.

In 1940, the population of San Francisco was 624,536; of Los Angeles, 1,504,277. The population of the southern city's industrial area—which included the city—was 2,785,643. The population of the industrial area of which San Francisco was the queen city, and which embraced all the towns across the Bay and twenty miles down the peninsula, was 1,461,076— and this included Oakland, the second largest city of the north.

10

In December, 1941, San Francisco's era of smug complacency, with its alloy of youthful protest, came to an abrupt and revolutionary end. In 1944, her population had increased to nearly 800,000, that of her industrial area to over 2,000,-000. The Bay, even after the building of the Golden Gate Bridge, the Bay Bridge, and the retirement of the graceful, swan-like ferry boats, was beautiful to look at with its calm blue surface, its romantic islands and irregular hills beyond, colored so gaily in the spring. But its waters were rarely disturbed save by private yachts or the Italian and Portuguese fishing boats—motor-driven now—thudding to and from the sea. In 1942 and after, it was a dull heavy picture of troop ships, destroyers, tankers, airplane carriers, an occasional battleship in for repairs. High above was the constant low roar of aircraft, ever on the watch or off for South Pacific ports.

In San Francisco and over in Alameda the Bethlehem steel works multiplied their tempo. Other shipyards, eight or ten in number, rapidly surrounded the Bay, not only opposite San Francisco but far up on its northern arm; Vallejo's population increased from 10,000 to 50,000. Mare Island, the Navy Yard, heretofore turning out battleships at leisure, was "on the job" day and night; the arsenal at Benicia was livelier than it had ever been in its long and placid career. The three Kaiser yards at Richmond employed a hundred thousand. Marin shipyard ("Marinship") near Sausalito, facing the northern shore of San Francisco, was quickly converted from cargo vessels to tankers of sixteen thousand tons and turned out between three and four a month. All of these and other shipyards had built their own small "towns" for the workers and their families.

There was also a large shipyard in Stockton, and a magnesium plant in Los Altos, Santa Clara County. The Bay of San Francisco was no longer merely famous among tourists as a beauty spot. It was one of the greatest ports in the world.

San Francisco itself was transformed. The Japanese population had been swept out, and "Jap Town" became "Nigger Town"; thousands of Negroes were among the influx. Those of the hotels that were not appropriated by the Army or Navy were so crowded that no one could occupy a room for more than five days. Wages, always high in northern California, soared to fantastic heights. Large numbers of women strong enough to do a man's work deserted domestic service for the shipyards, and those that remained—as well as the Chinese too old to be drafted—demanded from $150 to $200 a month where before they had been content with $80 or less.

But, although every able-bodied man and woman was engaged in some kind of war work, San Francisco was comparatively calm. It prided itself upon not having succumbed to the jitters during those first days when it was within the probabilities that Japan would raid the coast cities after her sensational performance at Pearl Harbor. The blackouts and alerts it dismissed as "dress rehearsals." That long period of tranquillity had given it balance as well as smugness. Its pride in its superiority now ascended to a loftier plane. It had once more risen to the occasion. It was doing its damnedest for The Country. It was stuffing its strong boxes with war bonds, its men were exerting their physical strength to the utmost.

The women were equally active. The Red Cross absorbed the majority, but the Harbor Club, the Women's Voluntary Service, the United Service Organization, and countless other organizations provided war work for women eager to do it.

Many young women, brought up in comparative luxury, worked in shipyards as welders, draughtsmen, or what not. The Society pages of the newspapers were reduced almost to a column; they had few social activities to relate save weddings. Other girls left store jobs to drive street cars and taxis.

The city was crime-ridden, as was to be expected, for criminals from other states poured into San Francisco, their nostrils quivering at the prospect of easy money. No one cared to go out at night except in his own car. But if there was little entertaining in private houses, the night clubs, the cocktail bars, the gay restaurants with their superlative cooking—Italian, French, Chinese—flourished as never before. Unrewarded virtue is bad for morale, and the good citizens of San Francisco, to say nothing of the Army and Navy, took their rewards as they found them.

San Francisco was thoroughly alive.

Index

251

GOLDEN GATE
COUNTRY
RUSSIAN
RIVER
SACRAMENTO
FORT ROSS
BODEGA
BAY
SONOMA
VALLEJO
BENICIA
SAN RAPHAEL
CONTRA
ALCATRAZ
OAKLAND
GOLDEN GATE
PRESIDIO
SAN FRANCISCO
MISSION
DOLORES
SAN BRUNO
HILLS
SAN FRANCISCO BAY
SAN MATEO
PACIFIC
OCEAN
SANTA CLARA
SARATOGA
BAY OF
MONTEREY